the new digital scholar

exploring and enriching the research and
writing practices of NEXTGEN STUDENTS

Edited by
Randall McClure and James P. Purdy

ASIST Monograph Series

Published on behalf of the
American Society for Information Science and Technology by

Information Today, Inc.

Medford, New Jersey

First Printing, 2013

The New Digital Scholar: Exploring and Enriching the Research and Writing Practices of NextGen Students

Library of Congress Cataloging-in-Publication Data

The new digital scholar : exploring and enriching the research and writing practices of NextGen students / edited by Randall McClure and James P. Purdy.
    pages cm. -- (ASIS&T Monograph Series)
    Includes bibliographical references and index.
    ISBN 978-1-57387-475-5
    1. Report writing. 2. Research. 3. Generation Y. I. McClure, Randall, editor of compilation. II. Purdy, James P., 1978- editor of compilation. III. McClure, Randall, Min(d)ing the gap: research on the information behaviors of NextGen students.
    LB2369.N39 2013
    808.02--dc23

2012046801

President and CEO: Thomas H. Hogan, Sr.
Editor-in-Chief and Publisher: John B. Bryans
ASIST Monograph Series Editor: Samantha Hastings
VP Graphics and Production: M. Heide Dengler
Managing Editor: Amy M. Reeve
Editorial Assistant: Brandi Scardilli
Cover Designer: Lisa Conroy
Copyeditor: Dorothy Pike
Proofreader: Penelope Mathiesen
Indexer: Heather Hedden

www.infotoday.com

Contents

PART THREE: Pedagogical Solutions to Enrich the Research and Writing Practices of NextGen Students

Foreword

Alison J. Head and Michael B. Eisenberg

On college campuses everywhere, the same scene unfolds each term: In a classroom full of chattering, engaged students, an instructor utters five simple words: "Research paper due next week." Instantly, a pall falls over the room and laughter is replaced by a tense silence, and then a deep, collective sigh.

This situation may seem perplexing. Students are there to learn, explore, and discover, right? What better way than an in-depth research paper? Surely, students can't be worrying about finding resources and information to develop and write a research paper. The much-vaunted on-ramp to the information superhighway is just fingertips away, linking to rich resources like JSTOR, ABI/Inform, Wikipedia, Google, and the library catalog.

But one of the paradoxes of the digital age is that while finding information and answers may be easy, making sense and using all that information is not. This makes research assignments one of the most significant challenges college students face today.

For example, most NextGen students complain of being lost in a thicket of information. When we conducted a large-scale survey of undergraduates for *Project Information Literacy*, eight in 10 respondents reported feeling overwhelmed starting a research project and determining the nature and scope of what was expected (2010b). Nearly half of the students in our survey sample expressed nagging uncertainty about how to conclude and assess the quality of their research efforts. Whether they were researching something for a college course or for their personal lives, they struggled with the same frustrating open-endedness.

Almost every student surveyed used a safe and consistent strategy, which most developed on their own during their high school years. Many respondents reported relying on the same few tried and true resources—course readings, Google, library databases, instructors, and Wikipedia—for closing the aperture of the staggering amount of information available. This strategy, of course, underscores the gap between the plethora of web sources and rich information resources offered through campus libraries, and the limited toolbox of familiar sources and techniques that students actually rely on. This toolbox rarely includes consulting a librarian or, in many cases, even setting foot in the campus library.

We found that many students set out on their own as they try to fulfill prescriptive, mostly mechanical requirements detailed on a research assignment handout. Inside, they feel trepidation and angst, if not downright fear, of failing the assignment and, in some cases, the entire course. From one term to the next, few students fully comprehend what the research process asks of them and what is required for them to learn, grow, and succeed as critical thinkers during their college years and as lifelong learners.

This disconnect may be the secret shame of today's educational institutions. Many instructors admit they are time-crunched and flummoxed by still having to teach the same research and writing competencies to their students each semester. One professor we interviewed as part of our national study explained, "I have to make sure that I cover all parts of the assignment—a topic, and, well, finding articles that are related, and writing the paper, too. I take them to the library, I cover every part of the assignment in class—I have to do a lot—I assume nothing" (2010a, 9).

Such sentiments are the rule, not the exception. Many instructors are increasingly disheartened by the sense that they are losing pedagogical traction when it comes to teaching NextGen students how to conduct research and how to write. At the same time, many professors seem strangely out of touch with the reality of today's students' digital lives and how students find and use information and weigh its credibility, relevance, and thoroughness, while carrying out the ancient practice of inquiry.

Moreover, a sad truth is that students on all campuses undervalue librarians, even though these research professionals are experts in how to find information and evaluate its quality. Instead, in one of our student surveys, a large majority of the sample reported they don't even think about seeking help from a librarian; they only turn to instructors as their "research coaches."

Given this dismal picture, how is it possible to confront and address the critical issues with teaching the fundamental learning practices of research and writing? How can we understand NextGens' research and writing processes so we can make sustainable gains in the classroom, the library, and the workplace, and in students' lives after graduation?

Very little of substance has been published on how to instruct and educate students in research and writing in the digital age—until now.

In *The New Digital Scholar: Exploring and Enriching the Research and Writing Practices of NextGen Students*, Randall McClure and James P. Purdy have collected and contributed to a groundbreaking compilation of essays that tackles one of the most difficult pedagogical challenges of our time and offers clarity, solutions, and hope.

The New Digital Scholar takes readers through the NextGen research and writing process, explaining how to best engage today's students to improve these binary communication competencies. This collection of writings offers a score of new instructional practices, such as incorporating Web 2.0 technologies into research assignments, so students recognize their own strengths as primary researchers with the digital tools they know best. It also offers suggestions about how instructors and librarians can introduce programmatic solutions that are collaborative, fresh, and, most importantly, effective.

Purdy and McClure's premise in this major undertaking is spot on: Teaching NextGen students the fundamental competencies of research and writing should be *a shared responsibility across the academy*, rather than a marginalized learning outcome left to instructors of first-year expository writing and composition courses.

While many valuable works have focused on the practices, habits, and beliefs of a generation of students who have not known a world without the internet, Purdy and McClure's collection delivers something that is both original and urgently needed. *The New Digital Scholar* provides the essential ingredients to improve students' research by offering new (yes, *new*) ideas for teaching them how to be critical thinkers—a skill necessary for both academic and real world success.

The impressive contribution of *The New Digital Scholar* is that the scholars, information specialists, and researchers who have contributed to this unique collection are personally and professionally committed to advancing and sharpening how students research and write. As a result, the book has the potential to transform the way educators and librarians work with NextGen students, showing them how to reach these young scholars on their own turf.

Until now, few books have come close to filling this tall order. *The New Digital Scholar* makes a cogent and deeply thoughtful research contribution that, so far, has been neglected in the literature. It provides frameworks for rethinking old practices in addition to presenting a score of new instructional practices, accounts of collaborative teaching efforts between librarians and educators, and, perhaps, most important of all, inspiration for working with today's students. This collection has some of the finest research-writings about teaching NextGen students that have ever been collected in a single volume.

References

Head, Alison J., and Michael B. Eisenberg. 2010a. "Assigning Inquiry: How Handouts for Research Assignments Guide Today's College Students." *Project Information Literacy Progress Report*. Accessed September 7, 2012. www.projectinfolit.org/pdfs/ PIL_Handout_Study_finalvJuly_2010.pdf.

———. 2010b. "Truth Be Told: How College Students Evaluate and Use Information in the Digital Age." *Project Information Literacy Progress Report*. Accessed September 7, 2012. www.projectinfolit.org/pdfs/PIL_Fall2010_Survey_ FullReport1.pdf.

Acknowledgments

We are grateful to the contributors of this book for sharing their insights on students' research-writing and for approaching this project with patience and enthusiasm. We also thank Samantha Hastings, ASIST Monograph Series editor, for her guidance and encouragement in seeing this book through to publication. We likewise thank John B. Bryans and Amy M. Reeve for their enthusiasm for and commitment to this book. Ashley Kunsa and Matthew Heilman provided invaluable editorial assistance and proofreading for which we are deeply appreciative. This project came about from our work with students, and we're grateful for how they have inspired and taught us.

Randall thanks his co-editor Jim for his professionalism and diligence; his colleagues at Georgia Southern University and his friends at Grace Community Church for their unwavering support; his parents for their tireless commitment; and most importantly his wife, Christine, and his children—Connor, Aislinn, Rowen, and Flynn—for providing the joy that makes life worth living.

Jim wishes to thank his parents, James and Norma, and his sister, Amy, for their enduring love and support; his colleagues, past and present, for their feedback and friendship; Duquesne University for the sabbatical award to work on this project; Randall, for his ideas, initiative, and insight as co-editor; and his wife, Mary, for making his life whole.

Understanding the NextGen Researcher

Randall McClure and James P. Purdy

As a range of researchers—from anthropologists (e.g., Blum 2009) to writing studies professionals (e.g., National Writing Project, et al. 2010), from communication theorists (e.g., Hargittai, et al. 2010) to information scientists (e.g., Head and Eisenberg 2009, 2010)—have observed, NextGen students write more than perhaps any generation in history. NextGen students are those secondary and postsecondary students who are frequently writing on Twitter feeds and Facebook pages; sending texts and instant messages on their smartphones, tablets, and laptops; and contributing to wikis and community web-pages of all kinds. Both in and out of school, NextGen students are surrounded by and constantly composing text. We would add that they are researching more, too. NextGen students are routinely locked in to digital communication technologies that did not exist just a few years ago. From the web to the mobile phone, these technologies allow students to engage in the multiple activities of writing, reading, and researching simultaneously. This pervasive and amalgamated engagement makes the communication and information behaviors of NextGen students unique in many ways. Most notably, their immersion in the digital world causes them to see textual information differently. How they perceive, identify, use, and create information affects

1

not only their personal and social lives but also their academic ones. The rise of digital technologies has changed how NextGen students think of research and how they conceptualize research-writing.

Writing researchers have long considered and studied in depth the impact of computer use, multimedia, and the web on students as writers, yet comparably little work has been published on students as writer-researchers in the digital age. For example, most college-level first-year writing teachers are tasked with helping students become better researchers and better research-writers; still, this topic continues to have lower priority in the field of writing studies, as it is often seen as the province of others (namely, library and information scientists or high school teachers) or as a separate unit to be endured (and moved through quickly) in writing courses. Because digital technologies intertwine research and writing, this book takes as its premise that we—as professionals from a variety of fields—cannot ignore, marginalize, or leave to others the commitment to understand and help the new digital scholar.

In its four parts, this collection explores the facets of that commitment. The first two parts address how others have characterized students' research-writing behaviors and how students themselves conduct research and represent their research-writing practices. Part One reviews published discussions of NextGen students and their engagement with digital technologies for research-writing tasks, and Part Two shares research on students' actual practices, providing data to inform these discussions. The last two parts address ways to improve students' practices. Part Three provides a variety of pedagogical ideas, ways to respond in the classroom to what Parts One and Two reveal. The fourth and final part offers programmatic solutions and institutional approaches to preparing students to be successful research-writers. Taken together, these parts advance our understanding of the research behaviors of NextGen students and suggest ways to help them productively find textual information and compose with the information they find.

Authors in Part One, "NextGen Students and the Research-Writing 'Problem,'" provide background and multiple perspectives on the major forces that influence the research and writing decisions of the new digital scholar, including a comprehensive literature review of existing scholarship on student research practices and a detailed history of the research paper assignment. In Chapter 1, "Min(d)ing the Gap: Research on the Information Behaviors of NextGen Students," Randall McClure explores the impact of the web and other media on the information behaviors of students entering college writing classrooms. The goal of this opening chapter is two-fold: to offer readers a foundation for the chapters that follow and to suggest a framework for the ways in which writing teachers, librarians, and other information specialists can study the digital research behaviors and skills of NextGen students. McClure synthesizes findings from several reports on students' computer, media, and web use in order to situate the digital scholar inside the writing classroom. He writes of this project, "In order to engage students in the information behaviors appropriate to academic, professional, and social contexts, I contend we must understand what behaviors they have already internalized, the behaviors that shape their research processes."

In doing so, McClure distinguishes information behavior from information literacy. He defines information behavior as "not simply the skills desired of information users in or out of the writing classroom. Instead, information behavior is concerned with the complex processes and influences on the information seeker." McClure discusses information behavior's value for the study of students' research habits in the digital age and, more importantly, for the teaching of writing. Broadening the teaching of research skills into the larger domain of information behavior, McClure announces the "authors collected here argue that we must better understand the ways in which students work with information in the digital age if we are going to best leverage the web to fulfill [its educational] promise." In fact, McClure's call to action provides the bridge to the rest of the chapters in the book:

> Until we modify our curriculum and instructional practices
> in research-writing with a broader and deeper understand-
> ing of digital worlds, of the explosion in the amount and
> consumption of information they facilitate, and of the
> resulting information behaviors for our students, we will
> continue to reside in separate spaces. And if producing dig-
> ital scholars is our goal, then move to meet our students on
> the web in every way—writing, reading, *and* researching—
> we must.

This movement, of opening the traditional reading-writing binary to include research, is echoed throughout the rest of the opening chapters.

Bringing reading, writing, and researching closer together requires a historical framework upon which to build. Karen Kaiser Lee, in Chapter 2, "The Research Paper Project in the Undergraduate Writing Course," offers such a framework by reviewing important highlights of what we know about the history of the research paper assignment. In her comprehensive analysis of the major anthologies on research paper instruction published to date and their approaches to the topic, Lee notes that "there has been criticism of the research paper project almost as long as the project itself has existed." Lee goes on to detail the many critiques that have been leveled against the research paper since its ear-liest days in the college curriculum, and she describes in detail one of the more influential responses to the traditional research paper assign-ment, Ken Macrorie's I-Search Paper. Lee's research into the enduring criticisms and occasional responses leads her to conclude that writing professionals need "to consider what is meant by 'research'" in ways that "reflect the nature of research practices now heavily reliant on computers and computer networks."

In Chapter 3, "Professional Statements and Collaborations to Support the New Digital Scholar," John Eliason and Kelly O'Brien Jenks pick up on Lee's call for a new perspective on the new digital scholar. The authors, one a librarian and the other a writing program administrator, explore several pieces of current literature that explicitly connect "information literacy with writing instruction," particularly those works demonstrating collaborations between writing instructors and librarians. In doing so, Eliason and Jenks "identify professional statements that might inspire future collaborations" and "past collaborations that scholars have already successfully established and nurtured into scholarship." Viewing research as just as complex as the writing process, the authors echo both Lee and McClure in the call for a broader and deeper understanding of research, one that embraces information literacy and calls upon the expertise of both writing and library professionals.

In concluding the book's opening section, Brian Ballentine, in Chapter 4, "Fighting for Attention: Making Space for Deep Learning," contends that reading and researching online actually change the way our brains engage with text. Against this backdrop, Ballentine echoes the authors of other chapters in claiming that our strategies for teaching students to be researchers will require a productive overhaul in the years to come, that "going forward will require much of us." To frame this overhaul, Ballentine draws on the spirit of the hacker community and the tenets of Web 2.0, suggesting that the act of personalizing and customizing the research space to meet individual students' needs in part creates an intrinsic motivation for deeper engagement with both the tools and the materials of research. The deep engagement with information, with the research-writing process, is a concern of most all of us working in higher education in the digital age, and the next three sections of the book provide a collective response.

Part Two, "Explorations of What NextGen Students Do in the Undergraduate Writing Classroom," provides empirical evidence of the depth (or lack thereof) of student engagement. By offering data-driven research on students' research-writing practices in the digital age, chapters in this section take a close look at where students are now. Including reports and discussions—from a local case study to a national research project and points in between—these empirical studies of students' research habits, information behaviors, and writing with sources inform the discussion of the research-writing "problem" found in Part One.

Sandra Jamieson and Rebecca Moore Howard's Chapter 5, "Sentence-Mining: Uncovering the Amount of Reading and Reading Comprehension in College Writers' Researched Writing," begins the section by reporting on the Citation Project, a national study of how college students incorporate sources into their work via four source-use techniques: copying, patchwriting, paraphrasing, and summarizing. They discuss actual student writing products, papers produced in the first-year writing course at 16 different U.S. colleges. The chapter offers a detailed examination of student research papers, including the analysis of bibliographic entries, internal citations, and both uses and interpretations of source material. Jamieson and Howard's research reveals that students successfully paraphrased in only two-thirds of their attempts, summarized sources in fewer than half of the papers, and drew nearly 75 percent of their citations from no deeper than page 3 of their sources. According to Jamieson and Howard, these findings point to the "need to overhaul the teaching of researched writing in college classes." Rather than despair at these results, however, Jamieson and Howard see them as an opportunity to direct needed focus and change existing approaches to research-writing instruction at the college level.

Other contributors to this section offer studies providing data to support this "overhaul" of research instruction in writing classes as well as propose steps for enacting it. In Chapter 6, "Scholarliness as Other: How Students Explain Their Research-Writing Behaviors," James P. Purdy calls for directing attention to students' processes in and reflections on research-writing rather than focusing primarily on flawed or potentially plagiarized products, as he argues plagiarism-detection technology does. Drawing on data from student research questionnaires, research logs, reflections, and digital research skills assessments, Purdy provides insight into how students think about research, conceive of themselves as researchers, and produce research-based texts. He points to three underlying tensions in how students approach research-based writing: Students have a strong proclivity for Google but sometimes recognize its limitations for scholarly work; students value scholarly sources but cannot necessarily recognize them; and students characterize themselves as open, focused, and interested researchers but claim not to enjoy research or have a unique research process.

Based on these tensions, Purdy concludes that students view "scholarliness" as "other," something found outside the digital spaces they normally inhabit and something they trust is found by those resources others label as scholarly. He argues these results show that admonishing students to use only "scholarly" resources has led them to internalize a limiting scholarly/nonscholarly binary. Purdy suggests that this binary needs to be replaced to "help students recognize that different types of sources work in different contexts [and] that 'scholarliness' is less an abstract text or database label and more a recognition of use value for particular kinds of knowledge-making."

In Chapter 7, "Can I Google That? Research Strategies of Undergraduate Students," Mary Lourdes Silva responds to Purdy's call for studying the research-writing processes of students. Silva reports from her comprehensive observation of three students' research-writing processes and study of an experimental instructional design to improve these processes. She highlights students' prevalent use of the "hub and spoke method" (going back and forth between the search results page and a target page using the back button) prior to training and increased use of alternative strategies, such as "mining a reference" (learning the "genre features of a citation and the corresponding databases that store the source material"), after training.

To begin the "overhaul" of research instruction in college writing classes that Jamieson and Howard advocate, Silva recommends a multiliteracies instructional package to improve students' information literacy and research skills. In particular, she suggests students need assistance with generating discipline-specific keywords; understanding the limitations of databases and search engines, particularly Google; creating rigorous, contextual criteria for source evaluation; and exploiting the "mining a reference" strategy.

This assistance should come from both the writing and library communities, and, in Chapter 8, "Encountering Library Databases: NextGen Students' Strategies for Reconciling Personal Topics and Academic Scholarship," Ruth Mirtz offers the perspective of a librarian who has taught writing. Mirtz, a reference librarian at the University of Mississippi, presents findings from her study of 18 first-year college students' individual searches for scholarly articles. Mirtz adds screen capture videos and transcripts to Purdy's use of questionnaires, research logs, reflective essays, and skills assessments and Silva's use of observations, interviews, videos, and student self-reports. In courses for which she was instructor and researcher, Mirtz used "screen capture software to record and evaluate students' searches at several points: pre-instruction (before demonstrating the features of scholarly articles and using library databases), post-instruction, and in a follow-up session." From her study, she, like Silva, suggests that students' research strategies within online library databases often "box in" their topics. Mirtz further argues that "both luck and persistence" affect students' success in searching and that students' choice of topic "may have more influence than instruction in search methods" on how students conduct research and what they ultimately write about.

Mirtz's findings suggest the value of a shared approach to research-writing pedagogy, an approach discussed at other points in this book. Instruction in using databases and search engines to investigate topics and find resources in the library is more productive for students, argues Mirtz, when coupled with instruction in invention and topic brainstorming in the writing classroom. Mirtz affirms the librarian's role as part of a collaborative effort in nurturing the digital scholar this way: "If we study students' research processes, we can redefine the classic research paper problem to include a more rhetorical look at database searching as a significant influence on research and writing processes."

Taken together, the chapters in Part Two provide data on students' research-writing processes and products that illuminate both why and how students engage with research materials for writing tasks. All point to the need to revise current approaches to studying students as researchers and to teaching research in the writing course. Part Three, "Pedagogical Solutions to Enrich the Research and Writing Practices of NextGen Students," provides practical strategies for making some of these suggested changes in the writing classroom.

Part Three opens with Chapter 9, "Undergraduate Research as Collaborative Knowledge Work," in which Christa B. Teston and Brian J. McNely suggest writing teachers explicitly position students as collaborative knowledge makers for research tasks. They explain pedagogy in which writing teachers minimize the fear and anxiety so often associated with conducting research in the digital age. In their approach, Teston and McNely view research as collaborative constructions of knowledge—collaborations made possible through, and afforded by, the digital technologies available to students. Teston and McNely deliberately position students as knowledge workers in these collaborations but emphasize the need for a pedagogy that asks students "to *position themselves* as knowledge workers and to develop and investigate researchable questions that do not make transparent the technologies available to them, but instead place the people and practices surrounding these technologies as objects of study."

Rachel A. Milloy likewise calls for valuing students' research experiences. In Chapter 10, "Re-Envisioning Research: Alternative Approaches to Engaging NextGen Students," Milloy works from a premise familiar to writing teachers. "NextGen learners have digital literacies they use each day to achieve tasks they deem important," writes Milloy, yet they "are often less comfortable using their existing digital literacies for academic research purposes." In response, Milloy presents her own alternative pedagogy designed to aid students in critically analyzing multimodal sources inside digital spaces in ways that challenge the traditional research model of finding and evaluating alphabetic texts. Working from five common issues students face as researchers in the digital age (going to Google, limiting keyword searches, feeling overwhelmed, etc.), Milloy presents alternative research assignments that build upon students' existing skills and interests in digital environments. Of this approach, Milloy makes clear the writer-researcher relationship that composes the NextGen scholar:

> Writing instructors can revise research assignments to incorporate Web 2.0 technologies so that students realize they *do* know something about researching and that they *can* learn to improve their strategies. As compositionists and librarians continue to redefine what it means "to research" and to be a "researcher," teachers can incorporate assignments that help students approach the vast world of digital spaces; that move away from the formulaic practices students believe research papers should imitate; and that move toward a research paradigm valuing creativity, exploration, and rhetorical choices appropriate for a digital age.

Working with the information behaviors students already demonstrate and within the digital spaces students already inhabit is a theme in Milloy's chapter and throughout the chapters in this book.

David Bailey picks up this theme in Chapter 11, "Embracing a New World of Research." Somewhat more theoretical than other chapters in this book, Bailey applies the Fourth Paradigm of Science to the ways in which teachers and students can approach research in the digital information age. The Fourth Paradigm of Science represents a theoretical shift in how teachers and students view the relationship between researchers and information. Rather than forming initial hypotheses and engaging in long periods of research and experimentation, information is collected en masse, and the researcher pores through it in search of patterns in order to form assumptions. Bailey writes:

> Everywhere one looks, communication and data consumption tools receive astounding attention and popularity. In the classroom, students communicate with smartphones and laptops. Businesses scramble for marketing opportunities on platforms like YouTube and Twitter, while RSS feeds deliver posts from the latest blogs on every conceivable

subject to devices of all kinds. This activity provides writing instructors many opportunities to engage their students in a new communication climate, one anticipating the coming Fourth Paradigm.

This scientific model has practical applications for working with student researchers in the writing classroom, and Bailey explores and explains several of them, calling for teachers to design assignments where student researchers search for patterns in collections of textual data.

Neil P. Baird offers positioning students as ethnographic researchers in digital spaces as one way to show them why digital resources are important and, in turn, presents another approach to overhauling research instruction in the writing classroom. In Chapter 12, "NextGen Students and Undergraduate Ethnography: The Challenges of Studying Communities Born Digital," Baird asserts, "more needs to be known about the challenges undergraduate researchers face, especially when researching digital communities." To begin to uncover these challenges, Baird draws upon the work of undergraduate students engaged in ethnographic studies of two digital communities: World of Warcraft and Second Life. In doing so, Baird examines how undergraduate researchers experienced and responded to the ways in which the virtual environment is transforming qualitative research methods and, with them, researcher identities.

Baird reminds us that students can capitalize on their digital proficiencies to act as primary researchers and that digital technologies raise important methodological questions for researchers at all levels. In particular, he argues that "single and stable conceptions of identity, reinforced by traditional ethnographic methods, produce accounts that fail to present the complexity of experience found in communities born digital," emphasizing that just as undergraduate researchers must learn the complexity, fluidity, and multiplicity of identity in digital communities, researchers and teachers must learn the complexity, fluidity, and multiplicity of students' researcher identities.

In Part Four, "Programmatic Solutions to Enrich the Research and Writing Practices of NextGen Students," contributors extend the book's focus outward. Collectively, the authors look well beyond the writing classroom to the definition of research, to writing programs, and to library resources. They suggest changes on the macro level, from reshaping the relationship of writing programs and university libraries to revamping digital resources themselves.

Barry M. Maid and Barbara J. D'Angelo, in Chapter 13, "Teaching Researching in the Digital Age: An Information Literacy Perspective on the New Digital Scholar," start at the point of definition. They argue that it is hard to consider what "research" is since the term has come to mean almost anything: "Research is the ultimate gold standard for what academics do. Yet application of the word 'research' has become so broad as to be almost meaningless." Due to the ambiguous nature of the term, Maid and D'Angelo believe that the teaching of research will not change until writing teachers reframe their definition of research and stop viewing research and writing as separate processes. To help illustrate the close connection between research and writing, Maid and D'Angelo offer an intertwined process framed by information literacy and designed to help NextGen students "understand that for most of their lives they will be working with information and writing."

Thomas Peele, Melissa Keith, and Sara Seely take the suggestion to connect information literacy and writing made by Maid and D'Angelo, Mirtz, and others to the institutional level. They offer research on a programmatic model for overhauling the teaching of research, one that establishes a dedicated partnership between a writing program and university library. Chapter 14, "Teaching and Assessing Research Strategies in the Digital Age: Collaboration Is the Key," details the assessment of a collaborative effort at Boise State University between the first-year writing program and university library. The effort, titled PoWeR, or Project Writing and Research, aims to help students improve their research-writing skills by formally partnering sections of two courses: Introduction to College Writing, and Research and Library Research.

Peele, Keith, and Seely report that students' research-writing portfolios produced in the PoWeR program were "more likely to be rated
'proficient' or 'highly proficient' than the portfolios written in stand-
alone English 102 classes" and students in the PoWeR program could
more effectively articulate their research-writing strategies and were
more likely to see themselves as "expert researchers." In addition to
offering ways to establish such partnerships and to assess student writing from a shared perspective on research, Peele, Keith, and Seely point
to the potential value of moving research instruction beyond the
purview of isolated writing classes and instead draw on the expertise of
library and information science specialists.

In Chapter 15, "Understanding NextGen Students' Information
Search Habits: A Usability Perspective," Patrick Corbett, Yetu Yachim,
Andrea Ascuena, and Andrew Karem take a more rhetorical look at the
library side of the digital scholar. Whereas Mirtz examines student use
of library resources and Peele, Keith, and Seely assess a collaborative
model of research-writing instruction involving librarians, Corbett, et
al. study the design of library resources themselves. The authors agree
with Mirtz that the design of an academic library's digital interface
shapes students' research practices—even if more psychologically than
functionally.

Through analyzing the inclusion of multimodal and Google-like
features in the University of Louisville's digital card catalog "Minerva,"
Corbett, et al. pursue Purdy's call for interrogating and challenging the
scholarly/nonscholarly binary that structures much research instruction. Reporting on usability tests of three prototype multimodal help
interfaces with a small group of writing students, the authors note that
they "were surprised to find that [students] could already use Minerva
to find sources, but nearly all said they would instead use Google to
complete their academic research-writing projects." This "Google
Effect" informs their analysis of students' approaches to what the
authors call "LastGen" resources. The authors promote the value of
usability testing in better understanding and designing the library and
other resources NextGen students use and affirm that "[i]mplemented

at the programmatic level, usability testing stands to inform strategic questions about the information architecture and usage of research interfaces."

The final contribution to the book, Chapter 16, "Remixing Instruction in Information Literacy," ends where the book began, with an overt focus on NextGen students. In this chapter, Janice R. Walker and Kami Cox offer direct insight into how students themselves understand research. Blending the voices of an established teacher-researcher (Walker) with an undergraduate writing major (Cox), the authors report in their own words how students use digital resources for research-writing tasks. Walker and Cox offer examples to illustrate the points about student research behaviors and research-writing discussed by McClure, Lee, Jamieson and Howard, and Maid and D'Angelo, among others.

Based on their interviews, Walker and Cox suggest integrating the teaching (and learning) of essential information skills with the common reading-and-writing approaches, yet in ways that are more readily transferable for the digital information age. In this model, contend Walker and Cox, writing teachers must approach research instruction "*at the point of need* rather than decontextualized from the actual process of research." By looking at the present state of the digital scholar in the college experience, Walker and Cox offer a starting point for the future, one that places increased emphasis on the study of the research-writing behaviors of NextGen students.

As we continue to learn more about the behaviors of the new digital scholar, our hope is that this collection will assist those of us who teach these NextGen students in helping them contribute fruitfully to knowledge production in our increasingly digital world.

References

Blum, Susan D. 2009. *My Word! Plagiarism and College Culture*. Ithaca, NY: Cornell University Press.

Hargittai, Eszter, Lindsay Fullerton, Ericka Menchen-Trevino, and Kristin Yates Thomas. 2010. "Trust Online: Young Adults' Evaluation of Web Content." *International Journal of Communication* 4: 468–494.

Head, Alison J., and Michael B. Eisenberg. 2009. "Lessons Learned: How College Students Seek Information in the Digital Age." *Project Information Literacy Progress Report*. Accessed September 10, 2012. www.projectinfolit.org/pdfs/PIL_Fall2009_Year1Report_12_2009.pdf.

_____. 2010. "Truth Be Told: How College Students Evaluate and Use Information in the Digital Age." *Project Information Literacy Progress Report*. Accessed September 10, 2012. www.projectinfolit.org/ pdfs/PIL_Fall2010_Survey_FullReport1.pdf.

National Writing Project, Dànielle Nicole DeVoss, Elyse Eidman-Aadahl, and Troy Hicks. 2010. *Because Digital Writing Matters: Improving Student Writing in Online and Multimedia Environments*. San Francisco: John Wiley & Sons.

PART ONE

NextGen Students and the Research-Writing "Problem"

CHAPTER 1

Min(d)ing the Gap: Research on the Information Behaviors of NextGen Students

Randall McClure

> Information permeates our lives, professional and personal, whether that information comes to us as the intended result of a focused and targeted searching, incidentally as the by-product of other activities, or simply because it is inextricably intertwined with our day-to-day social interaction.
> —Gary Burnett and Sanda Erdelez (2010, 44)

The New Digital Scholar and Information Behavior

I assume you are reading this book because you are interested in helping students become better readers, writers, and researchers. Like the authors of other chapters in this book, I wish to focus attention on the sometimes daunting challenge we are faced with when students enter our college writing classrooms, the challenge to help them become academic researchers in the digital information age.[1] This challenge is intensified by the amount and variety of writing, reading, and researching activity students engage in on the web, and by the information behaviors students have developed as a result of such activity.

Before going further, some clarification is necessary. A good number of readers are likely more familiar with information literacy (IL) than information behavior. Thus, I start this chapter by identifying the difference between IL and information behavior and explain why focusing on information behavior is so important.

Most readers are likely familiar with the definition of IL provided by the American Library Association (1989): IL is "a set of abilities requiring individuals to recognize when information is needed and have the ability to locate, evaluate, and use effectively the needed information" (American Library Association). The Association of College and Research Libraries (2000) adds that IL is "increasingly important in the contemporary environment of rapid technological change and proliferating information resources. Because of the escalating complexity of this environment, individuals are faced with diverse, abundant information choices" (Association of College and Research Libraries). In short, IL is a set of skills needed to understand, find, and use information—skills critical to life in the digital age. Viewed this way, IL is a goal, a target, an end result.

Information behavior[2] not only explores these processes, but also questions them. On the surface, information behavior appears strikingly similar to IL. Information behavior, like IL, examines what information is in the first place, how people search for it, find it, and use it. Yet, information behavior focuses first on just that—behavior—and not simply the skills desired of information users in or out of the classroom. Instead, the study of information behavior is concerned with the complex processes and influences on the information seeker. Viewed this way, IL takes on an expanded set of considerations that I believe have yet to be adequately addressed in writing pedagogy. Librarian Natalie Binder (2010) explains that information behavior is about "the real experience of dealing with information, which is not [always] about pursuing the new, but managing what we've got. ... I don't seek information. It *happens* to me." Binder believes that we should be less interested in skills per se and more interested in finding patterns in information to help students move information into a "finer, more precise, more ordered form" (Binder 2010). (For a detailed discussion of searching for patterns in information, see Chapter 11.)

Along these lines, the approach to IL work in the college writing classroom needs to include a richer understanding of information behavior, of research on the research habits of NextGen students. In order to engage students in the information activities appropriate to academic, professional, and social contexts, I contend we must understand what behaviors they have already internalized, the behaviors that shape their research processes. Teaching the new digital scholar is not just focusing on a set of prepackaged skills; it is helping students recognize the intersection of needs, skills, and, most importantly, behaviors.

In this chapter, I explore the impact of the web and other media on the information behaviors of students that find their way into our college writing classrooms. My goal is twofold: to offer readers a foundation for the chapters to follow and to suggest a framework for future research on research, hopefully some of which will be inspired by the chapters in this book. First, I offer an expanded discussion of information behavior theory for those new to it. Second, I situate the digital scholar inside the college writing classroom, chiefly by paralleling the arguments in Scott Warnock's *Teaching Writing Online* (2009). Next, I expand on the notion of information behavior and its perceived value for research-writing. I then offer a synthesis of several recent reports from the United States, United Kingdom, and Australia on computer, media, and web use as well as information behavior. I conclude the chapter by responding to claims from critics of the notion of information behavior and its importance to teachers and librarians invested in transforming the college writing student into a digital scholar.

Good and Bad Behavior

Information behavior, what T. D. Wilson (2010) defines as "how people discover, access, use, store for future use, share, and disseminate information of all kinds" (34), provides the frame necessary to work with student researchers in the digital age. In fact, I contend that information behavior can do for IL instruction what rhetoric, gender studies, and WAC theory, among other theoretical approaches, did for writing instruction decades ago: enrich the study of writing with theories and perspectives from a variety of fields.

Unlike IL, which has been relegated to "skill set" status, information behavior is treated much the same way that writing researchers treat their subject: as a dynamic, evolving, and recursive process. Barbara Wildemuth and Donald Case (2010) explain information behavior research this way:

> As a person finds useful [or not useful] information and applies it to the current goal, the goal itself may shift (or not). The person's ideas about the problem change as he or she learns more. Other external events may occur that affect the importance of the problem to the information seeker. These and other possible changes [affect] information behaviors as they occur … [and call] for the use of different research methods. (24)

For these reasons, information behavior researchers rely on multiple methods to study the roles, locations, and tasks of information users, research that places users at the center of information and explores their relationship with it. Researchers Gary Burnett and Sanda Erdelez (2010) describe information behavior as such: "Information behavior emerges as a visible link that users cling to as they navigate through the landscape of new information worlds with overlapping and constantly intersecting contexts" (45). Much like writing researchers have expanded the range of their inquiry over the past 50 years to much more than the written product, information behavior research studies "have unquestionably expanded well beyond a focus limited to information seeking activities" (Burnett and Erdelez 2010, 47). It seems time *and timely* to expand the ways in which we study the research-writing processes of students.

Why Research Research?

In his testimony in front of the U.S. House of Representatives Subcommittee on Telecommunications and the Internet, Sir Timothy Berners-Lee (2007), often credited as the founder of the internet, commented on the future of the World Wide Web: "The web takes the openness" of earlier technologies—postal mail, telegraphs, telephones, even roads and railroads—and moves it "one step forward and enables a continually evolving set of new services that combine information at a global scale not [previously] possible" (Berners-Lee 2007, 3). Web-based technologies and services now combine information for a truly global audience. Moreover, NextGen users of these technologies and services are now recognized by the ways in which they have become immersed in them. "Since the advent of the World Wide Web in the early 1990s, the 'Digital Generation' has been at the epicenter of major tectonic shifts," writes Kathryn Montgomery (2009), professor of communication at American University. She continues, "Never has a generation been so defined in the public mind by its relationship to technology. ... As active creators of a new digital culture, these youth are developing their own web sites, diaries, and blogs; launching their own online enterprises; and forging a new set of cultural practices" (2). The cultural practices are significant, including the practices of information, particularly with the web as *the* information interface.

In her book *Generation Digital: Politics, Commerce, and Childhood in the Age of the Internet,* Montgomery (2009) provides what might be the most complete account of the rise of the internet and its impact on the lives of young people. Synthesizing the research, scholarship, and news reports since the first days of the web and cataloging these texts in an index close to 100 pages long, Montgomery claims that the internet's educational promise helped drive its rapid expansion into American life. The chapters in this book approach the study of the web from a similar perspective—that the web continues to shape education in profound ways, particularly the teaching and learning of research-writing. However, the authors collected here argue that we must better understand the ways in which NextGen students work with information in the digital age if we are going to best leverage the web to fulfill this promise.

The authors collected here recognize the role the web plays in the information landscape, particularly for students. Montgomery writes that "young people have not simply adopted the internet, they have *internalized* it" (2009, 8) and they are the "*defining users* of digital technologies" (107). If we agree that today's students are defined by a web they have internalized, then studying the web's impact on their writing *and* research behaviors seems critical. Just how critical? Just how much does the web define our students today? Recent reports have the percentage of teenagers spending time online at higher than 90 percent, with many teens online not just every day, but several times a day (Montgomery 2009, 138). Defined indeed.

Teaching Researching Online

Writing teachers, among others, must intensify their engagement with research-writing scholarship if they hope to accurately understand and appreciate the writing and information behaviors of NextGen students. Scott Warnock (2009) urges this engagement in the afterword to *Teaching Writing Online*:

> Think about it. Arguments rage about the quality of the e-writing our students regularly engage in during their online experiences on social networking sites like Facebook and MySpace, with text messaging, or in the blogosphere; yet to me it's plain that no matter how we define it, they write a lot more than my generation did. They are writing all the time, almost frantically using textual language to communicate with one another, and coming up with remarkably clever ways to communicate their message ... We, as writing

teachers, are highly empowered in this environment to help channel the natural writing that students are doing anyway into a class experience. (179–180)

Though Warnock is writing these ideas in support of what he labels a "progressive" approach to remaking writing classes for online delivery, his claims are just as relevant for restructuring the approach to helping students develop research and information skills for the digital age, working from information behaviors out (Warnock 2009, x).

Warnock emphasizes that students today write more than those from previous generations. I believe they also seek out more information and seek it out more often than earlier generations of researchers did. Think about how you conducted most of your research during your K–12 and your college years, and long, planned trips to the stacks in the library likely fill your memory. Now, think about how you seek out information today. If you are like me, then you still love the time you spend in the stacks. But you also conduct much of your research on the open web, and this type of research has brought out its own set of information behaviors, ones for which students often have tremendous aptitude.

Warnock reminds us of what we all know quite well: Students are writing all the time. Any teacher who has spent time working with students knows that students are always plugged in, and most of them are writing in multiple applications at any one time—their Facebook, email, Twitter, CMS, and IM windows popping with activity. Just as students are writing all the time, they are reading all the time—conducting informal research, if you will, through their favorite websites and blogs, tagged pages, and RSS feeds (though studies have shown that students do not view these activities as "research"[3]). In fact, the Pew Internet & American Life Project study of teens' internet use finds that

- 62 percent get their news and information on current events online;

- 31 percent get their health and medical information online;

- 37 percent participate in video chats;

- 27 percent record and upload video to the internet; and

- 13 percent stream video live to the internet for other people to watch. (Lenhart, et al. 2010, 26–28; Lenhart 2012, 1)

Students are certainly engaged in a wide variety of types of writing and researching both in and out of school, including composing research papers. A recent study by the Writing in Digital Environments (WIDE) Research Center at Michigan State University of more than 1,300 students enrolled in first-year composition courses at seven higher education institutions found that students believe the academic paper and the research paper are more valuable to them than 26 of the 30 genres of writing in the survey, including many digital writing forms (Grabill and Pigg, et al. 2010, 6).

Warnock acknowledges what most of us readily concede: Today's students are often incredibly clever with the writing and researching they do. Text messaging, as Warnock indicates, is often cited as an example of the decline in writing skills. Viewed another way, however, text messaging—a writing activity that 82 percent of students not only engage in, but also spend an hour and a half on average doing every day—is incredibly relevant for the teaching of writing and could be an opportunity to engage our students in new, exciting ways not only in the teaching of writing, but also the teaching of research skills (Clark and Dugdale 2008, 34; Rideout, Foehr, and Roberts 2010, 3). In fact, the WIDE study found that texting is the most popular and valuable genre to students (Grabill and Pigg, et al. 2010, 5–6). Still, many teachers choose to ban cell phones from the classroom. This technology is viewed as a potential disturbance, not the instructional resource it could be.

Warnock believes that writing teachers are naturally situated to help channel the web into research-writing pedagogy. While they may be familiar with the writing students do on today's socially constructed and organized web, many teachers have yet to acknowledge and adequately address in their curricula the information behaviors and research practices students have developed on it. My experience and research (2007, 2011a, 2011b) suggests that most approaches to teaching students to become better researchers ignore behavior and resist the familiar, instead opting for what Randy Garrison and Norman Vaughn (2008) call "holding onto past practices that are incongruent with the needs and demands of a knowledge society" (ix). The continuing prevalence of the one-shot library instruction session in first-year writing pedagogy is as incongruent as it is ineffective.

Theodore Roszak (1994) claimed nearly two decades ago that "we suffer from a glut of unrefined, undigested information flowing in from every medium around us" (in Warnock 2009, 162). Considering the web is the medium most common to our students—the place where they receive "a full third of words and more than half of bytes" of their information—then it only makes sense to work closely and intentionally with the web as *the* information source for student writers (Bohn and Short 2009, 8). The web—not only the closed and controlled space of the web-based academic library, but also the unrefined, uncontrollable yet familiar space of the open web—is *the* site to research their information behaviors. It is time to understand what student writers do in this space and to join them there.

Stepping Back to See the Big ~~Picture Monitor~~ Screen

I am not saying that those in and out of education are unaware of the dramatic changes in computer use and information behavior. Professional organizations including the National Council of Teachers of English (NCTE) and the International Reading Association (IRA) have considered the affective value of the web. In its statements on a "Definition of 21st Century Literacies" (2008a) and a "21st Century Curriculum and Assessment Framework" (2008b), NCTE identifies six literacies critical for 21st-century learners, including the ability to manage, analyze, and synthesize *multiple streams of simultaneous information* (emphasis added).

A third NCTE report based on a survey of more than 900 members confirms its position on the critical nature of students' ability to manage information. In the 2009 report "Writing Between the Lines—and

Everywhere Else," respondents indicate that "the ability to seek information and make critical judgments about the veracity of sources" and "the ability to read and interpret many different kinds of texts, both in print and online," which 95 percent and 94 percent of respondents cite, respectively, were the two most important 21st-century literacy skills (1). Whereas nearly all respondents identified the pressing digital information need, only two-thirds of them responded that they have made changes to their curricula in order to prepare students to be 21st-century literate. The chapters in this book form a collaborative response to the digital information need.

The massive amount of information available to and surrounding students on the web has the attention of not only professional organizations like NCTE and IRA, but also campus leaders and education reformers. Three well-known university presidents along with two respected professors of education debate in *Newsweek* the future of higher education. When the five contributors are asked about online learning, it is interesting to note that their responses do not focus on online courses or programs, but on the rapid expansion of the web and specifically the amount of information now available to and now challenging students. Elaine Tuttle Hansen, president of Bates College, comments that online learning is "one way colleges and universities have managed to begin … to address some of this explosion of knowledge" to which Diane Ravitch, professor of education at New York University and former assistant secretary of education, responds, "the explosion of knowledge may require more education and more time for education, not less" and will require what Robert Zemsky, professor of education at the University of Pennsylvania, labels stronger skills of critical inquiry (Rosenberg 2009, 33).

The respondents acknowledge the information explosion and the need for educators to react to this explosion, yet they concede, in the words of Lee Bollinger, president of Columbia University, that we do not fully "understand, however, how the web is going to reshape what we do" (Rosenberg 2009, 33). The web has led some educators to rethink how they see knowledge and information. But I do not think most educators have a rich understanding of the amount of information our students are exposed to and the behaviors they are using to try to manage it. More importantly, I believe that most have held on to teaching practices and curricula no longer relevant for the new digital scholar.

Fact, Fiction, or Fantasy

Think about the measurement 3.6 zettabytes. Think about 34 gigabytes. They sound like numbers out of a science fiction movie. However, the numbers are much more fact than fiction. Roger Bohn and James Short (2009), researchers from the University of California, San Diego (UCSD), have found that American households in 2008 combined to consume more than 3.6 zettabytes[4] of information (Bilton 2009). Even more interesting, Bohn and Short note that information consumption earlier predicted not to reach 1 zettabyte worldwide by 2010 was more than tripled by 2009, and this was in the U.S. alone (2009, 8). According to Nick Bilton (2009) from the *New York Times* website, this number is "roughly equivalent to the capacity of 5.1 million computer hard drives, or all the hard drives in Minnesota." The UCSD researchers put it like this: "If we printed 3.6 zettabytes of text in books, and stacked them as tightly as possible across the United States including Alaska, the pile would be 7 feet high" (Bohn and Short 2009, 13).

Specific to the focus on digital information characterizing this chapter and much of this book, Bohn and Short (2009) suggest in *How Much Information?* that this 3.6 zettabytes breaks down to 34 gigabytes and 100,500 words per person per day, an estimated 350 percent increase in information consumption over the last three decades. "This doesn't mean we read 100,000 words a day," notes Bohn, "it means that 100,000 words cross our eyes and ears in a single 24-hour period" (Bilton 2009). In fact, these 34 gigabytes and 100,000-plus words take us, according to the UCSD researchers, a combined 11.8 hours a day to consume when all of our multitasking behaviors are included (Bohn and Short 2009, 13).

The findings from UCSD are supported by a report published by the Kaiser Family Foundation. In *Generation M2: Media in the Lives of 8- to 18-Year-Olds*, Victoria Rideout, Ulla Foehr, and Donald Roberts (2010) studied more than 2,000 students nationwide and found that media use for tweens and teens has increased by 1 hour and 17 minutes since 2004 to a total of 7 hours and 38 minutes a day. When multitasking behaviors are accounted for individually, this number rises to 10 hours and 45 minutes a day, a more than 2-hour increase from just 6 years ago, and a number that does not include time spent texting, using the computer for school purposes, or even talking on a cell phone (Rideout, Foehr, and Roberts 2010, 11; Rubin 2010).

Whether the UCSD number of close to 12 hours a day or the Kaiser figure of nearly 11 hours is more accurate,[5] the numbers confirm what Bates College president Hansen believes—students today are being bombarded by a lot of information, and this information is consuming much of their waking time (Rosenberg 2009). Moreover, as the lines between media become even harder to distinguish and as the computer becomes even more the "epicenter of media multitasking" for our students, it only makes sense that the information from the web is *the* information standard (Rideout, Foehr, and Roberts 2010, 23–24). If the computer is the information epicenter for students, then we must appreciate and work with this in our curriculum design and classroom practice. As Bollinger suggested (Rosenberg 2009), we must reshape what we do, and I believe that includes reshaping college writing, the teaching of which still often relegates research to second-class status.

Consuming Mass Quantities

Before discussing in more detail the information behaviors associated with the web, I want to discuss information consumption in general and information production, particularly in terms of writing. As one would expect, information consumers, including our students, right now give TV most of their attention, at 45 percent of their information time, with computers coming second, at 27 percent. TV accounts for close to half of information *time*, but less than a third of total information *exposure*. In fact, more than half (55 percent) of information exposure comes through interactive technologies, specifically computers and video games, which account for a little over a quarter (27 percent) of total information time (Bohn and Short 2009, 8). As one would also expect, reading print texts continues to decline in both information time and exposure, coming in at under 10 percent in both categories. "Print media [use] has declined consistently," notes Bohn, "but if you add up the amount of time people spend surfing the web, they are actually reading more than ever" (Bilton 2009).

Not only are students reading more than ever, but also they are writing more than ever. Two reports on writing and technology, one in the U.K. and one in the U.S., appear to confirm this. The report "Writing, Technology and Teens" co-sponsored by the Pew Internet & American Life Project and the National Commission on Writing finds that teens engage in significant amounts of writing, both in and out of school, with half of the 700 teens in the study reporting that they write in school every day. Interestingly, most students report that much of the writing they do in high school is often very brief and not research-based (Lenhart, et al. 2008, 10). The more than 60 pages of findings in the Pew report lead the researchers to conclude the following: "Teenagers' lives are filled with writing. All teens write for school, and 93% of teens say they write for their own pleasure. Moreover, the vast majority of teens have eagerly embraced written communication with their peers" (i).

The Pew (Lenhart, et al. 2008) findings are supported by a report from the National Literacy Trust (NLT) in the U.K. (Clark and Dugdale 2008) in which more than 3,000 students aged 8 to 16 were surveyed about their writing behaviors, and it should come as no surprise that these students are prolific writers, especially when it comes to computers: 73 percent of respondents regularly composed instant messages, 63 percent contributed regularly on social networking sites,

56 percent maintained a social networking page, and 24 percent were blog owners, findings that lead the researchers to conclude that "young people increasingly use written communication over any other" (Clark and Dugdale 2008, 4, 34). Not only are teens consuming mass quantities of information, but also they are producing significant amounts of new content for the web. For example, findings in the Pew report "Social Media and Mobile Internet Use Among Teens and Young Adults" suggest that 21 percent of teens are remixing content on the web, "taking material they find online such as songs, text, or images and remixing it into their own artistic creations" (Lenhart, et al. 2010, 23).

Additional findings from the NLT study that 49 percent of students in the survey use a computer every day for fun and 18 percent use a computer every day for school confirm the heavy use of computers, use that has 93 percent of U.S. teens and tweens going online and, depending on the report you read, 63–70 percent of them going online every day (Lenhart, et al. 2010, 5–7; Clark and Dugdale 2008, 28–30; Rideout, Foehr, and Roberts 2010, 20). These findings reveal a possible gap or lag, however, in leveraging computer technology in schools in ways that reflect use outside of them. These findings are even more telling when one considers them in light of a national survey conducted by PBS Education (2009) of more than 1,200 K–12 teachers which found that 81 percent of schools have computers and internet access in their classroom (11). Further, they provide at least some measure of support for claims from those like Scott Warnock (2009) and the NLT researchers (Clark and Dugdale 2008), the latter of which write that "it is paramount ... the school curriculum reflects and utlises [*sic*] writing forms that young people enjoy and engage with" (8). Comments like these are becoming increasingly commonplace in publications on teaching writing; however, claims to engage students with alternative research-writing pedagogies are much harder to find.

Surf's Up

Understanding the behaviors associated with information is critical to shaping research-writing pedagogy, particularly given the variety of ways and places students are locating information for academic projects. Primary Research Group (PRG) reports in a survey of 450 undergraduates from across the U.S. the following mean percentages (+/-1 percent) in student responses concerning where most of the information comes from for their research papers:

- General search engines: 42 percent

- Wikis: 9 percent

- Online databases, ebooks, online journals: 24 percent

- Print publications: 16 percent

- Other sources: 8 percent (2009, 26–27)

It is likely no surprise to most readers that students go to Googlepedia[6]—search engines and wikis—for more than half of their information.[7] Looking more closely at student responses by age group, the changes in information behavior become more apparent. For example, students aged 19 and younger reported the highest usage of information from wikis and students 30 and older reported the lowest (Primary Research Group 2009, 26). PRG does find that close to a quarter of students (24 percent) use information from a combination of sources, yet 30 percent use information exclusively from Googlepedia (77). This is not to say that such information lacks value, but this data provides a clear indication that the web has dramatically affected information behavior in terms of the retrieval of information.

Other data in the PRG report shows students have tremendous confidence with their information-seeking and research-writing skills. For example, 93 percent of students respond they are confident or very confident in their abilities to conduct research and write a research paper; 90 percent are confident or very confident in their ability to prepare citations; and 86 percent are confident or very confident in their understanding of plagiarism (Primary Research Group 2009, 124–144). Based on these student attitudes, one could argue that we are successfully preparing our students to research and write. Many contributors to this book are regrettably less confident.

Until this book, considerably less research has existed on actual observations and studies of students' information behavior on the web. In one previous study worth noting, however, Eszter Hargittai, et al. (2010) surveyed 1,060 students enrolled in first-year writing courses about their online research practices, and the researchers compare what students say they do with what they actually do.[8] The researchers recorded the research sessions of 102 first-year writing students, capturing their verbal responses as well as their on-screen movements. Each student was asked to work through 12 scripted information-seeking tasks on the web. In doing so, Hargittai, et al. found that students put considerable trust in search engines to return fair and unbiased sources of information, equate name brands of search engines and other sites (SparkNotes, MapQuest, Microsoft, Wikipedia, AOL) with credibility, and often turn to people they trust (family, friends, teachers) in situations when they want to verify information from the web rather than consider the authorship or credentials of the sources they located (Hargittai, et al. 2010, 479–484). These results lead the researchers to conclude that "how users get to a web site is often as much a part of their evaluation of the destination site as any particular features of [or information on] the pages they visit" (486).

A discussion of the new digital scholar would be incomplete without mentioning what might be the most provocative report on the subject: a briefing paper published by University College London (UCL) titled "Information Behaviour of the Researcher of the Future." The UCL researchers—David Nicholas, Ian Rowlands, and Paul Huntington (2008)—identify several computer uses and information behaviors common to young people today, a group they label the "Google Generation":

- Lack of understanding of their information needs
- Preference for basic search engines like Google rather than article databases
- Use of natural language terms instead of subject terms or keywords

- Quick scanning and skimming of information sites
- Little or no evaluation of the quality of the information used
- Cutting and pasting information into their papers without providing the correct citations (12–31)

These behaviors are certainly familiar to readers, and they have been noted in the literature reviews and findings of several recent reports. For example, the "quick scanning of information sites," or power browsing, is an information behavior which many readers have likely observed by watching students conduct research on the web. In fact, research on power browsing indicates that most users "exhibit a great amount of trust" in search engine results, and as a result spend no more than 8 or 9 seconds on a webpage. Though users tend to spend only seconds on any given page, the behavior of power browsing now accounts for 14 percent of users' information hours (Bohn and Short 2009, 20; Hargittai, et al. 2010, 470).

Minding the Gap

Researchers are now theorizing "that the ever-accelerating pace of technological change may be minting a series of mini–generation gaps, with each group of children uniquely influenced by the tech tools available in their formative stages of development" (Stone 2010). In a 2010 interview with Brad Stone from the *New York Times* website, Lee Rainie, director of the Pew Research Center's Internet & American Life Project, responds to the "ever-accelerating pace of technological change" this way: "People two, three or four years apart are having completely different experiences with technology. College students scratch their heads at what their high school siblings are doing, and they scratch their heads at their younger siblings" (Stone 2010). *USA Today* writer Sharon Jayson (2010) sees this same trend in her reading of Larry Rosen's (2010) book *Rewired: Understanding the iGeneration and the Way They Learn*, where Rosen argues that a shift from the search engine generation has already occurred. Whereas NextGen students have not known life without computers, Rosen's iGeneration, according to Jayson, cannot remember a time without either the internet or the affordances of Web 2.0 technologies: "i"ndividualization, "i"nnovation, and "i"mmersion (Jayson 2010).

If we are, as Rainie seems to suggest, scratching our heads on account of the many technologies that NextGen students work with and the behaviors they have formed using the web in the process of finding and producing information, and we are, as Rosen (2010) believes, already bearing witness to a new "iGeneration" that sees these technologies differently and engages in different behaviors with them, then what does this mean for writing teachers down the road? Is it possible to catch up with or even just understand the information behaviors of the new digital scholar? As educators, we have to at least try.

One path to meeting students in the digital information age is through the close study of information behavior as it relates to all aspects of college writing. Information behavior researchers Burnett and Erdelez frame the future of their research this way:

> While the tools through which human users come into contact with information may change—and may raise many interesting questions about the degree to which specific technologies transform our understanding of the contexts of information use and about the degree to which technological innovation and change determine (or, more accurately, influence) information behavior—the particular relationship between such human users and information itself remains the focus of information behavior research. (2010, 46)

Information behavior theory provides writing specialists and others a wide lens to focus research on the new digital scholar, to understand and respond to students' research-writing practices in ways best suited to them.

Through the lens of information behavior and through other lenses offered throughout this book, one point becomes crystal clear: The digital world is shifting around us (Nichols 2009, 528). Even more to the point: For our NextGen students, it already has. As Rideout, Foehr, and Roberts write in *Generation M2*, "The story of media in young people's lives today is primarily a story of technology facilitating increased consumption" (2010, 2). Until we modify research-writing curricula and instructional practices with a broader and deeper understanding of digital worlds, of the explosion in the amount and consumption of information they facilitate, and of the resulting information behaviors for our students, we will continue to reside in separate spaces. And if producing digital scholars is our goal, then move to meet NextGen students on the web in every way—writing, reading, *and* researching—we must.

Endnotes

1. For more discussion on the challenges of the digital information divide, see Randall McClure (2011a).

2. For a history of information behavior research, see T. D. Wilson (2010).

3. For more discussion on what students do and do not view as research, see Lenhart, et al. (2010).

4. A zettabyte is equal to one billion terabytes, or 1,000,000,000,000,000,000,000 bytes.

5. It should be noted that a 2009 report from the Nielsen Company attempts to contradict the findings from other recent reports on NextGen students' information behaviors and media use. The anonymous authors of the report *How Teens Use Media* believe that "the image of 'typical teen' listening to an iPod, watching TV, texting and browsing the internet all at the same time … is grossly misrepresentative" (1–2). While the authors are not clear on their research methods, claiming "the data and insights in [the] report are compiled from a range of Nielsen resources" (16), the findings do present a much milder picture of NextGen students.

6. For an elaboration on the term "Googlepedia," see McClure (2011b).

7. For a review of recent studies that analyze source and citation use in research papers written by U.S. college students, see Cooke and Rosenthal (2011).

8. For a similar approach to comparing students' research practices with their understanding of them, see Chapter 6.

References

American Library Association. 1989. *Presidential Committee on Information Literacy: Final Report.* Chicago: ALA. Accessed September 12, 2012. www.ala.org/ala/mgrps/divs/acrl/publications/whitepapers/presidential.cfm.

Association of College and Research Libraries. 2000. *Information Literacy Competency Standards for Higher Education.* Accessed September 12, 2012. www.ala.org/ala/mgrps/divs/acrl/standards/informationliteracycompetency.cfm.

Berners-Lee, Sir Timothy. 2007. "Testimony of Sir Timothy Berners-Lee, CSAIL Decentralized Information Group, Massachusetts Institute of Technology before the United States House of Representatives Committee on Energy and Commerce Subcommittee on Telecommunications and the Internet Hearing on the 'Digital Future of the United States: Part I—The Future of the World Wide Web.'" Accessed September 12, 2012. dig.csail.mit.edu/2007/03/01-ushouse-future-of-the-web.html.

Bilton, Nick. 2009. "The American Diet: 34 Gigabytes a Day." NYTimes.com. Accessed September 12, 2012. bits.blogs.nytimes.com/2009/12/09/the-american-diet-34-gigabytes-a-day.

Binder, Natalie. 2010. "[Information needed]: Modeling Information Behavior." The Binder Blog: Talking Tech, Media, Information, and Policy. Accessed September 12, 2012. thebinderblog.com/2010/11/02/information-needed-modeling-information-behavior. [URL no longer available.]

Bohn, Roger E., and James E. Short. 2009. *How Much Information? 2009 Report on American Consumers.* UC, San Diego: Global Information Industry Center.

Burnett, Gary, and Sandra Erdelez. 2010. "Forecasting the Next 10 Years in Information Behavior Research: A Fish Bowl Dialogue." *Bulletin of the American Society for Information Science and Technology* 36 (3): 44–49.

Clark, Christina, and George Dugdale. 2008. "Young People's Writing: Attitudes, Behaviour, and the Role of Technology." *National Literacy Trust (UK).* Accessed September 12, 2012. www.literacytrust.org.uk/research/nlt_research/261_young_peoples_writing_attitudes_behaviour_and_the_role_of_technology.

Cooke, Rachel, and Danielle Rosenthal. 2011. "Students Use More Books After Library Instruction: An Analysis of Undergraduate Paper Citations." *College & Research Libraries* 72 (4): 332–344.

Garrison, D. Randy, and Norman D. Vaughn. 2008. *Blended Learning in Higher Education: Framework, Principles, and Guidelines.* San Francisco: Jossey-Bass.

Grabill, Jeff, and Stacey Pigg. 2010. "The Writing Lives of College Students." East Lansing, MI: Writing in Digital Environments Research Center. Accessed September 12, 2012. compositionawebb.pbworks.com/f/whitepaper.pdf.

Hargittai, Eszter, et al. 2010. "Trust Online: Young Adults' Evaluation of Web Content." *International Journal of Communication* 4: 468–494.

Jayson, Sharon. 2010. "Tech-Savvy 'iGeneration' Kids Multi-Task, Connect." USAToday.com. February 10. Accessed September 12, 2012. www.usatoday.com/news/health/2010-02-10-igeneration10_CV_N.htm.

Lenhart, Amanda. 2012. "Teens & Online Video." Pew Internet & American Life Project. Accessed November 7, 2012. www.pewinternet.org/~/media//Files/Reports/2012/PIP_Teens_and_online_video.pdf.

Lenhart, Amanda, et al. 2008. "Writing, Technology and Teens." Pew Internet & American Life Project. Accessed September 12, 2012. www.pewinternet.org/Reports/2008/Writing-Technology-and-Teens.aspx.

Lenhart, Amanda, et al. 2010. "Social Media and Mobile Internet Use Among Teens and Young Adults." Pew Internet & American Life Project. Accessed September 12, 2012. www.pewresearch.org/pubs/1484/social-media-mobile-internet-use-teens-millennials-fewer-blog.

McClure, Randall. 2007. "Digital Soapboxes: Understanding the Growing Presence of Advocacy and Commercial Sites on the Web." *Journal of Literacy and Technology* 8 (3): 2–22.

―――. 2011a. "The Digital Information Divide." In *Adaptation, Resistance, and Access to Instructional Technologies: Assessing Future Trends in Education*, edited by Steven D'Agustino, 1–18. Hershey, PA: IGI Global.

―――. 2011b. "Googlepedia: Turning Information Behaviors into Research Skills." In *Writing Spaces: Readings on Writing*, Volume 2, edited by Charles Lowe and Pavel Zemliansky, 221–241. West Lafayette, IN: Parlor Press.

Montgomery, Kathryn C. 2009. *Generation Digital: Politics, Commerce, and Childhood in the Age of the Internet*. Cambridge, MA: MIT Press.

National Council of Teachers of English. 2008a. "The NCTE Definition of 21st Century Literacies." NCTE.org. Accessed September 12, 2012. www.ncte.org/positions/statements/21stcentdefinition?PHPSESSID=a80d8d2827512d929d0b6a09f40e697c.

―――. 2008b. "21st Century Curriculum and Assessment Framework." NCTE.org. Accessed September 12, 2012. www.ncte.org/governance/21stcenturyframework.

―――. 2009. "Writing Between the Lines—and Everywhere Else." NCTE.org. Accessed September 12, 2012. www.ncte.org/library/NCTEFiles/Press/Writingbetween theLinesFinal.pdf.

Nicholas, David N., Ian Rowlands, and Paul Huntington. 2008. "Information Behaviour of the Researcher of the Future." *EDUCAUSE*. Accessed September 12, 2012. www.jisc.ac.uk/whatwedo/programmes/resourcediscovery/googlegen.aspx.

Nichols, James T. 2009. "The 3 Directions: Situated Information Literacy." *College & Research Libraries* 70 (6): 515–530.

Nielsen Company. 2009. *How Teens Use Media: A Nielsen Report on the Myths and Realities of Teen Media Trends*. Accessed September 12, 2012. blog.nielsen.com/nielsenwire/reports/nielsen_howteensusemedia_june09.pdf.

PBS Education, and Grunwald Associates, LLC. 2009. "Digitally Inclined: Teachers Increasingly Value Media and Technology." PBS.org. Accessed September 12, 2012. www.pbs.org/teachers/_files/pdf/annual-pbs-survey-report.pdf.

Primary Research Group. 2009. *The Survey of American College Students: Student Library Research Practices and Skills*. NY: Primary Research Group, Inc.

Rideout, Victoria J., Ulla G. Foehr, and Donald F. Roberts. 2010. *Generation M2: Media in the Lives of 8- to 18-Year-Olds*. Menlo Park, CA: Kaiser Family Foundation.

Rosen, Larry D. 2010. *Rewired: Understanding the iGeneration and the Way They Learn*. NY: Palgrave Macmillan.

Rosenberg, Debra. 2009. "What's College for Anyway? A Debate Over the Role of Higher Education." *Newsweek* October 26.

Roszak, Theodore. 1994. *The Cult of Information: A Neo-Luddite Treatise on High-Tech, Artificial Intelligence, and the True Art of Thinking*. Berkeley: University of California Press.

Rubin, Bonnie M. 2010. "Teen, Tween Media Use Rising." ChicagoTribune.com. January 20. Accessed September 12, 2012. articles.chicagotribune.com/2010-01-20/news/1001190509_1_mobile-devices-media-young-people.

Stone, Brad. 2010. "The Children of Cyberspace: Old Fogies by Their 20s. NYTimes.com. January 10. Accessed September 12, 2012. www.nytimes.com/2010/01/10/weekinreview/10stone.html.

Warnock, Scott. 2009. *Teaching Writing Online: How and Why*. Urbana, IL: NCTE.

Wildemuth, Barbara M., and Donald O. Case. 2010. "Early Information Behavior Research." *Bulletin of the American Society for Information Science and Technology* 36 (3): 24, 35–38.

Wilson, T. D. 2010. "Fifty Years of Information Behavior Research." *Bulletin of the American Society for Information Science and Technology* 36 (3): 27–34.

CHAPTER 2

The Research Paper Project in the Undergraduate Writing Course

Karen Kaiser Lee

Research paper. Library paper. Term report. Thesis paper. Investigative theme paper. Whatever the nomenclature, the research paper assignment has long been a feature in the undergraduate writing course. Joseph F. Tuso (1995) characterized this sort of paper as "the usual, formal, written study of 1,500 to 4,000 words with notes, bibliography, and the usual multiple smudges and typos" (33). While it would be difficult to find an academic who did not value research-writing skills or who did not think students need such skills, teachers across the undergraduate experience remain frustrated by student papers written in response to the typical research assignment. Timothy R. Donovan and Janet Carr (1991) write that "when the papers are turned in, professors often despair that so many are just a rehash, cut 'n paste jobs, virtually plagiarized" (212).

Where instructors feel despair, students feel fear. Textbooks and guidebooks often acknowledge the apprehension research paper assignments tend to inspire. At the beginning of its chapter on research, the textbook *Writing: A Manual for the Digital Age* (Blakesley and

Hoogeveen 2008) sympathizes that "many writers view research projects with fear and trembling. When you are asked to write a dozen pages or write and design an informative website about an unfamiliar topic, the research process can seem daunting, even overwhelming" (248). This anxiety caused by research paper assignments has been around since at least the 1960s. Ambrose N. Manning quotes a participant responding to Manning's 1961 survey of research paper assignments who observed that "students dread the assignment, certainly, and they are confused and frightened at first, but the consensus is, after the work has been done, that it is the most rewarding experience they have ever had" (78). Students are generally expected to "feel the fear and do it anyway." Manning (1961) notes that research papers serve a purpose because "the discipline required in producing a 'baby thesis' makes the whole thing worthwhile" (77).

There has been criticism of the research paper project almost as long as the project itself has existed, and instructors often wonder whether or not the research paper project even belongs in the first-year writing course. James Ford (1995) terms the placement of research instruction within this course an "historical accident" (1). Ideally, most writing specialists believe the responsibility for research instruction should be shared across academic departments. The Council of Writing Program Administrators (2008) "Outcomes Statement for First-Year Writing," for example, suggests that by the end of their first year, students should be able to "locate, evaluate, organize, and use research material collected from electronic sources, including scholarly library databases; other official databases; and informal electronic networks and internet sources" and that instructors in *other* disciplines should then teach students "how to engage in the electronic research and composing processes common in their field."

In this chapter, I review what is known about the history of the research paper assignment, along with the more familiar criticisms lodged against it. I then review how students themselves have critiqued the traditional research paper, mainly by the research methods they tend to employ in completing such assignments, along with past and current responses to the problem of research paper instruction. I conclude by suggesting that one revision of the research paper project—Ken Macrorie's I-Search paper—has been the most influential reform to date.

Origins of the Research Paper Assignment

In 1961, Manning cites the somewhat recent (20 to 30 years prior to his article) appearance of manuals to help students write research papers as evidence that the research paper assignment is a relatively new addition to freshman writing courses. However, David R. Russell's (2002) extensive work on writing in the disciplines digs deeper into the origins of the research paper, detailing how higher education in the U.S. during the late 19th century took as its model the German notion of research scholarship and the written work associated with it. The earlier, chiefly British emphasis on recitation and oral demonstrations gave way to the seminar, laboratory, and lecture. The newer course structures modeled on the German notion of research brought with them the genres of the research paper, the laboratory report, and reading notes, respectively. The orality of the earlier university model created a community which provided a place for student work, typically in the form of literary societies or rhetoricals. But the newer privileging of written academic communication meant that scholarly discourse took place primarily in academic publications, chiefly journals. Since these journals were considered the purview of faculty, student-written discourse needed a setting of its own.

This setting eventually became the classroom, with "the audience of the individual professor representing a disciplinary community" (Russell 2002, 80). The student was now cast in the role of apprentice; the expectation was that students would carry out their own individual research projects with a professor acting as a guide, with the students "producing critical, 'original' interpretations of documents and data using the methods, conventions, and assumptions of a specialized discipline—not the 'common knowledge' of a particular social class"

(Russell 2002, 80). Much of this sounds positive, intended to foster student work that created new knowledge, as faculty work was expected to, and with the bonus of potentially reducing the influence of social boundaries within the university. Yet as faculty were encouraged to spend more time researching, less time was available to assist students, and so, as Russell (2002) observes, "extended student writing was exiled to an academic limbo: forced to look in only one direction, toward the ideal of research, but effectively cut off from the activities of disciplinary research, which gave academic writing its aims, its methods, and its meaning" (99–100).

By the middle of the 20th century, the ossification of the research paper within undergraduate education was well underway. Manning (1961) gathered information on the origins of the research paper as part of his investigation into the state of the research paper at that time, the results of which led him to declare, "we might as well face it: the research paper in Freshman English is here to stay!" (73); 83 percent of the institutions he surveyed required research paper assignments in first-year writing. Of these schools, only 10 percent reported that they were planning to alter their methods of teaching the research paper. Although Manning did find some who were critical of the research paper, these negative opinions were much less frequent. Manning concluded that this high approval rating meant the research paper in first-year writing "is in no danger of being relegated to a lower place or taken out of the curriculum; indeed, it has more prestige than ever" (78).

Prestigious or not, the research paper has remained a fixture in the undergraduate writing course. Twenty years after Manning, James E. Ford and Dennis R. Perry (1982) conducted a similar survey and found that 84 percent of first-year writing programs had a research paper instruction component, and 56 percent of instructors in these programs devoted 29 percent of their teaching time to the research paper assignment. Ford and Perry (1982) found, much as Manning (1961) did, that some teachers disliked the research paper assignment, yet most respondents were pleased with the results of research instruction.

These early surveys show that once the research paper assignment gained a foothold in the first-year writing course, it remained there.

Critiques of the Research Paper Assignment

Interestingly, the negative comments about the research paper remain similar throughout the decades. While most responses to Manning's 1961 survey are positive, negative comments include that students "are prone to copy" and "they lack interest" (74). One respondent notes that his school has gone as far as to ban research paper assignments in first-year courses because they are "an open invitation to busy work" (77). Summarizing the litany of complaints over time about the traditional research paper could, at the very least, fill this entire chapter, so what follows is a selection of some representative critiques that illustrate key problems with the assignment.

Critics have noted that this assignment tends to either oversimplify the research process or confine it to a single, often laborious task. Stephen North (1980) characterizes the typical research assignment as artificial, in that the steps to produce a research paper are presented to students in such a rigid fashion that the natural progression of research itself is restricted. Richard L. Larson (1982) asserts research papers isolate research from the writing process and the generic research paper assignment decontextualizes the activity for students, leading them to believe that research "is a specialized activity that one engages in during a special course, or late in the semester or year, but that one does not ordinarily need to be concerned about and can indeed, for the most part, forget about" (814–815). Doug Brent (1992) observes that it is a "supreme oddity" that "research, the universal ether that interpenetrates all formal inquiry, becomes 'the research paper,' a separate genre that occupies a separate little section of the [writing] course" (102).

Research is a prized skill among academics, yet the task of teaching research skills usually falls to first-year writing programs often housed in English departments. Therefore, many critiques of the research paper assignment center around writing across the curriculum–related issues. North (1980) says that the research paper assignment lingers "as a gesture of good will from the English Department to the rest of the university or college—a gesture, it seems fair to add, of growing futility" (17). While not overtly critical of the research paper, Robert A. Schwegler and Linda K. Shamoon (1982) note that if instructors plan to treat research papers as part of an academic apprenticeship, they "need to make sure that the aim, structure, and style of the papers [instructors] assign conform to the kinds of papers that content-area instructors will expect from [their] students" (821). Larson (1982) asserts that English departments cannot make the claim that their instructors have the ability or preparation to teach research because the various programs and majors within the university have disparate notions of what research is and how research is conducted:

> Faculty in other fields may wish that we would relieve them of the responsibility of teaching their students to write about the research students do in those other fields, but I don't think that as teachers of English we can relieve them of that responsibility [...] most of us are trained in one discipline only and should be modest enough to admit it. (815)

However, Brian Sutton (1997) takes issue with this claim, writing that since the early 1980s, writing-in-the-disciplines scholars have learned a great deal about how academics in other fields research and publish, and this awareness can be harnessed to make the research paper assignment in the first-year writing course more effective, mainly by helping first-year students learn how to write "good generalized academic writing" (55).

In addition to concerns over the transferability of research-writing skills from first-year writing to courses in other disciplines, a common criticism of the research paper is that students tend to simply repeat what others have published before, instead of coming up with their own insights and conclusions. Donovan and Carr (1991) characterize typical research papers as "a rehash, cut 'n paste jobs, virtually plagiarized" (212). Acknowledging the research paper assignment is "one of the most important forms of academic writing," Brent (1992) finds that his students produce papers that "remained hollow imitations of research, collections of information gleaned from sources with little evaluation, synthesis, or original thought" (xiii). Shelley Aley (2004) calls them "regurgitation reports" (119), and she compares the process of writing them to inputting text directly from sources into Microsoft Word then using the AutoSummarize feature.[1] Indeed, Tuso (1995) writes that research papers ensure that students "will equally gain practice in using source material foolishly, in choosing what is useless, in confusing the ideas of others, and in misorganizing and misinterpreting information" (39).

Plagiarism is also frequently cited as a key reason to overhaul or eliminate the assignment. Russell (2002) describes how an entire industry devoted to selling term papers to students flourished as the assignment became more popular, an industry constructed largely on the "gap between student and instructor, a gap created in part because faculty ordinarily did not teach or supervise writing, did not require papers to be discussed in conference or revised" (88). Aley (2004) notes that fear of unwittingly committing plagiarism can keep students from conducting meaningful research and that "unless care is taken to involve students in finding their own point of view within the context of their sources, they will simply avoid using a rich tapestry of sources to stay out of trouble" (120).

These criticisms ultimately indicate that students are able to find information, but they are unable to draw conclusions from and analyze it. Instructors want students to make the switch from simply reporting information to writing documents that uncover new insights on the topic, as the assignment was intended to do at its inception in the mid-19th century. Marlene Scardamalia and Carl Bereiter (1987) describe two models of composing that illustrate this apparent dichotomy, "knowledge telling" and "knowledge transforming." They define knowledge transforming as a complex interaction that happens in the composing process between the writer's content space, or what he or she knows, and the rhetorical space where strategies and goals for successful communication reside. These two models are not exact binaries, since knowledge transforming writing must contain an element of knowledge telling. Rather, they demonstrate how knowledge enters the writing process and what happens to it as a result of that process (147). Their findings show that one reason students stumble over making the shift to knowledge transformation is that this difficult mental process cannot be easily taught; instead, "it is the composing process as a whole that has to develop" (165). They go on to explain why traditional research paper assignments, despite the problems identified with them, can still have a benefit that even critics approve of: These assignments allow students to practice knowledge telling, an important writing skill and a necessary step to knowledge transforming (165).

Critiques From Students

When compositionists investigate the working habits of students completing research papers, the results reveal students feeling unhappy with the assignment, struggling with the task, and using an assortment of research strategies that usually undercut the entire point of the project. Students see the research paper as a project that requires them to find information about a topic and then summarize that information for a reader (the instructor) who is an expert in that topic, an understanding quite different from what their instructors want them to learn.

Jennie Nelson conducted several investigations into the attitudes of students on research assignments that confirm much of what writing instructors believe, and students' responses raise questions on how their attitudes and research practices can be changed for the better. In one study, Nelson (1994) surveyed 238 randomly selected students enrolled in first-year writing courses. The results enabled her to identify four different student approaches to research-writing:

1. The "compile information" approach: Students perceive the primary goal as collecting and presenting information (75 percent of respondents used this method) (67).

2. The "premature thesis" approach: Students develop a controlling idea prior to conducting any research, bypassing any actual engagement with the topic (10 percent of respondents) (67).

3. The "linear research" approach: Students access information a single time and develop topics or theses based solely on what the information contained (10 percent of respondents) (67).

4. The "recursive research" approach: Students engage in preliminary research on the topic, make more than one visit to the library, produce a tentative viewpoint or thesis, conduct more research to refine this viewpoint, and then write their papers (5 percent of respondents) (67).

In a later essay, Nelson (2001) notes that this fourth method is how academics typically describe their own research process, and she writes that these results are troubling because "so few first-year college students seem to view the research-writing process in this open-ended and recursive way, perhaps because too few of them have had an opportunity to experience research this way" (10).

Nelson and John R. Hayes (1988) examine and compare how first-year and advanced students search for information. In their study, all participants were given an assignment prompt for a hypothetical research paper. They were then asked to carry out the research they needed in order to write a first draft on the topic, though they did not actually write the paper. Students were given 5 days to complete their research and keep a complete log of the research trail they followed. The findings in this study indicate that students tend to take one of two approaches: content-driven or issue-driven. Students using the content-driven approach collect and reproduce what others have written on the topic, but those using the issue-driven approach discover a different angle on the topic or a way to argue for a position on the topic. Content-driven students develop strategies that call for less time and effort, which translates into less effective research methods, according to Nelson and Hayes. They found that, whereas first-year students tend to choose a content-driven approach that focuses on the most efficient manner of fact-finding possible, advanced students favor an issue-driven approach, one that enables them to uncover a particular angle or approach to guide their search for information.

Building on this data, the two conducted an investigation (1988) that involved naturalistic observations of students while they wrote research papers in order to learn how students see themselves within the writing situation. Eight students were selected at random from various courses requiring a research paper. These students maintained process logs for the duration of the research paper assignment, and the logs included all work on the assignment, such as conducting library research, discussing, writing, and thinking. Students' logs document research strategies requiring little investment of time, energy, and thought. Comments in the logs reflect students' belief that the goal of research paper assignments is to put together and reproduce knowledge for a teacher who is already familiar with the data. One student provides a clear example of this as she writes in her research log that her research paper assignment is "dumb busy work" and "boring" because "it's coming from some book and all I'm doing is regurgitating information that the teacher already knows" (12).

Comments like this reflect the findings of Schwegler and Shamoon (1982), who interviewed students and instructors on the subject of research papers. Students told the authors they feel that research papers are assigned so students find out more information on the topic, understand how to use library resources, and demonstrate how much they know about something. They feel that research paper assignments are more focused on informing and less on analyzing. This attitude stands in marked contrast to how the instructors describe the act of research, which they characterize as a complex, open-ended, extended process. Whereas instructors describe research as a more fluid or tentative process, they also note that documenting and publishing research is typically done in a prescribed manner, based on the requirements of academic journals' editorial guidelines and the expectations of fellow academics (820).

These investigations demonstrate that students have, and have had for some time now, a much different understanding of why research papers are assigned, and this understanding tends to influence their work strategies for these assignments. Students think that these projects are a scavenger hunt to retrieve information the instructor is already familiar with; this perception is out of sync with why most writing instructors assign research projects and what they hope students will learn from them. These different perceptions can help instructors understand students' approaches to these assignments, as it is easy to assume that students cut corners simply because they are lazy. If instructors understand that students often think the assignment is focused on just the act of fact finding, however, and this perception in turn sours students' attitudes and reduces their efforts, then steps can be taken to correct aspects of the assignment that lead them to such a conclusion.

Responses From the Past

Though the traditional research paper assignment has existed in higher education for quite some time, it is only recently that it has received more than occasional scholarly attention. James E. Ford (1995) is noted for his efforts to bring academic attention to the topic; according to Ford, his collection of essays on research paper instruction, *Teaching the Research Paper*, is the first book devoted to the subject. Ford points out in the introduction that the first published bibliography on the topic (which he co-authored) did not appear until 1982. As the first compilation focused on the topic, *Teaching the Research Paper* covers quite a bit of territory and includes well-known works such as Larson's 1982 critique and Schwegler and Shamoon's 1982 study. Other chapters discuss the rhetorical context of the research paper; describe specific examples of assignment prompts; and delineate strategies on note-taking, interviewing, and citation.

Ford's anthology brings together a number of ideas about research paper instruction; however, no retooling of the traditional research paper assignment has been taken up or adapted as much as Ken Macrorie's (1984) I-Search approach. An I-Search paper is a process-centric assignment designed to challenge and engage students and to encourage a sense of inquiry within them; the name of the project indicates its contrast to typical research paper assignments, which Macrorie characterizes as "Re-Searches, in which the job is to search again what someone has already searched" (14). The term I-Search is also meant to emphasize that the writer is always present throughout the process; it is meant to remind writers to attempt to correct for any of their personal biases, though writers cannot entirely remove their presence from their texts.

Macrorie (1984) explains that I-Search projects are the stories of the writers' adventures in seeking out information they need to know. As such, students are to view topic selection as a chance to look into something of interest or importance to their lives "rather than a teacher's notion of what would be good for [them] to pursue" (62). The I-Search paper is usually written in four chronologically divided sections:

1. What the writer knows

2. Why the writer is writing the paper

3. The writer's search

4. What the writer has learned

Macrorie also advocates primary research as part of I-Searches, suggesting that students bypass the library in favor of conducting interviews and talking to people, noting that "if you speak with experts on your subject, you'll usually find that they are also experts on the 'literature of the field'" (89). While the I-Search assignment represents a breakaway from the traditional research paper in terms of research practices and topic selection, Macrorie does not feel that undergraduates should be expected to reach the level of professional or academic research work, noting that "deep familiarity with the tools and materials of the field is not likely to surface in student I-Searches. But at the same time, many papers will be more exciting to read than professional reports" (350).

Macrorie's I-Search paper is often cited in essays that call for making research assignments more engaging, and the I-Search has been adapted to different kinds of writing courses. Nancy J. Veglahn (1988) adapts the I-Search assignment for technical writing courses to provide students experience in conducting research, as she finds that subject textbooks lack explanations on information retrieval. Bernadette M. Glaze (1995) uses I-Search projects in a high school interdisciplinary, team-taught class in American literature and history. Tom Reigstad (1997) uses the I-Search in advanced undergraduate and graduate writing courses, noting that the less formal manner of the "subjective" I-Search project benefits writers who are more used to traditional research projects. Pavel Zemliansky (2001) offers a condensed description of an I-Search assignment created for first-year students to help them shift from personal narrative to writing from sources. Most recently, the textbook *Academic Research and Writing* (Bergmann 2010) describes the basics of an I-Search paper project and includes an example of one.

More Recent Responses

Other echoes of the I-Search can be heard in recent efforts to improve research instruction in writing courses. In "Building a Mystery," Robert Davis and Mark Shadle (2000) classify research paper assignments as either "modernist" or "alternative," whereby a modernist research paper is the familiar objective, informative, and thesis-based report, and an alternative research assignment asks students to create new knowledge. They advocate the use of more compelling, meaningful alternative assignments not only to combat students' fear and boredom with the traditional research paper, but also (and more importantly) to combat the modernist "illusory claims to detachment, objectivity, and pure reflection" (422). Alternative research projects they propose include the researched argument, the personal research paper (which they trace to Macrorie's I-Search), and the perhaps less familiar research essay, which they describe as a "hybrid, post-Montaignian, research enhanced form (or collection of forms)" (431). Another alternative they advocate is the multigenre/media/disciplinary/cultural research paper, or "multi-writing," where "students explore topics of interest or fascination and use a variety of sources to inform projects that combine multiple genres and, in some cases, different media, disciplines, and cultures" (431).

Rather than impose a label that might complicate understanding the intent of research assignments, Dan Melzer (2009) adopts Davis and Shadle's (2000) "modernist" and "alternative" categories to help describe the research assignments he encounters for his cross-disciplinary survey. Melzer found that 83 percent of the 2,100 assignments called for transactional, or "writing to inform," work—what would fall in Davis and Shadle's "modernist" category (245). Of these, 66 percent called for informative as opposed to persuasive writing. Melzer points out that these transactional assignments focus on definitions or recall of facts, so that students given these assignments are writing in a "teacher-as-examiner" context (246). But the findings of Melzer's study do not point to an abandonment of research projects. Melzer finds that a wide variety of genres exist under the umbrella term "research paper," many of them matching the forms described in "Building a Mystery."

Cara Leah Hood (2010), however, does see a shift away from the sort of traditional research paper project that she describes as "an informative/explanatory piece of writing, written in an objective voice, using library resources" (6). Hood intentionally builds on the earlier surveys conducted by Manning (1961) and Ford and Perry (1982), collecting data from 166 respondents from first-year writing courses at both public and private 4-year, co-educational, secular, liberal arts universities and colleges within the U.S. This is a smaller section of institutions than Manning surveys, a decision made by Hood to discern the state of the research paper in a narrow yet national sample.

Her findings indicate that only 6 percent of respondents assign "typical" research paper projects, while 94 percent describe their research assignments as differing in some way ("Discussion of Survey Results"). When identified by genre, the more popular alternatives are analysis, evaluation, or investigation of an issue; when identified by format, the researched argument is dominant. Hood speculates that the popularity of writing textbooks focused on argument may be one reason for the increasing popularity of this approach to the research paper assignment ("Arguments and Outcomes"). However, the argumentative research paper itself is not necessarily a new idea; Hood herself points out that Schwegler and Shamoon (1982) discuss the argumentative nature of the research paper as one possible answer to the problematic nature of the assignment ("Researched Argument Assignments"). Hood's 2010 survey is illuminating, but her finding that the traditional research paper is on the decline is very likely skewed due to the limited size of her study and her classification of argumentative research papers as nontraditional.

Like the I-Search that came before, the idea of multi-writing has spread to courses in departments outside English. Davis and Shadle (2000) contend it is migrating beyond their institutions onto other campuses and even into the K–12 milieu. One likely reason for the ready acceptance of these newer forms of research-writing is the growing awareness of activity theory and its implications for writing instruction. Russell (1995) defines activity theory as a concept that

> analyzes human behavior and consciousness in terms of *activity systems*: goal-directed, historically situated, cooperative human interactions, such as a child's attempt to reach an out-of-reach toy, a job interview, a "date," a social club, a classroom, a discipline, a profession, an institution, a political movement, and so on. The activity system is the basic unit of analysis for both cultures' and individuals' psychological and social processes. This unit is a functional system consisting of a subject (a person or persons) and object(ive) (an objective or goal or common task), and tools (including signs) that mediate the interaction. [...] In an

activity system, the object(ive) remains the same and the mediational means, the tools, may vary. (53)

Russell applies activity theory to first-year writing courses and explains that the subjects are both the students and the instructors, yet the object(ive) cannot be clearly delineated because "writing does not exist apart from its uses, for it is a tool for accomplishing object(ive)s beyond itself" (57). Thus, for Russell, trying to improve student writing with general writing skills instruction is "like trying to teach people to improve their ping-pong, jacks, volleyball, basketball, field hockey, and so on by attending a course in general ball using" (58). The solution to this, Russell argues, is to increase efforts in writing across the curriculum projects and to introduce students to rhetoric, possibly by offering liberal arts courses focused on writing in society.

Continuing the trend of consideration of alternative research assignments is Grobman and Kinkead's *Undergraduate Research in English Studies* (2010), a compendium of essays on the topic of research instruction like *Teaching the Research Paper* (Ford 1995) and *Research Writing Revisited* (Zemliansky and Bishop 2004), only with a stronger emphasis on students conducting original research, not just writing research papers. Like the findings of the surveys conducted by Hood (2010) and Melzer (2009), this publication reflects the shift toward alternative research practices and projects. Whereas earlier compositionists such as Macrorie felt that research projects might not be expected to thoroughly train students in research methodology, the essays in *Undergraduate Research in English Studies* stress that research "involves students as apprentices, collaborators, or independent scholars in critical investigations using fieldwork and discipline-specific methodologies under the sponsorship of faculty mentors" (Grobman and Kinkead 2010, ix). This sounds remarkably like the intent of the research paper assignment at its inception as documented by Russell (2002), when a student was expected to develop into "an investigator, a discoverer, a creator" (Ephraim Emerton quoted in Russell 2002, 83).

Recent alterations to traditional research instruction practices have also taken digital resources into account. James Strickland (2004) reconstructs the research paper as the web-based genre of the FAQ (Frequently Asked Questions), which he believes has "real world relevance and can be created after someone has researched a topic of interest, using library skills and information literacy" (25). Randall McClure (2011) suggests that instructors see the tendencies of students to rely upon Google and Wikipedia as "not research crutches but useful presearch tools" (224). He recommends working with students using an eight-step process to "remix" student internet research practices with more successful research strategies, ultimately showing students how to be more thoughtful and analytical with the information they find online while gaining more confidence using the digital resources of the university library.

More broadly, Paula S. McMillen and Eric Hill (2005) recommend that students be taught research practices through the metaphor of conversation, a metaphor that is useful on several levels. For them, the idea of a conversation is common and familiar, so it eases students into the newer territory of academic writing and work; "research as a conversation implies participation and engagement with others who are also interested in the same issues" (13). Both research-writing and conversation are meaning-making, interactive, and recursive activities situated in context. For students, learning to conduct research and report their findings is like learning a second language in that in both situations,

> they need to hone certain conversational skills (such as careful listening), to master some basic vocabulary, and to learn certain grammatical conventions (such as citation styles). Otherwise, their contributions will display the same deficits in nuanced understanding or communication that, for example, a second language speaker may display in a conversation with native speakers. (10)

The idea of research as a conversation is also easily understood across the disciplines, and it is helpful to have such a useful metaphor when discussing research with colleagues outside of writing and English departments. Indeed, the proliferation of alternative research projects in writing courses also reflects a larger movement in undergraduate education emphasizing more active participation in research for undergraduates throughout the curriculum. Among the recommendations made by the Boyer Commission on Educating Undergraduates in the Research University (1998) is to make research-based learning the norm rather than have undergraduates who attend research universities merely be passive receivers of information: "In a setting where inquiry is prized, every course in an undergraduate curriculum should provide an opportunity for a student to succeed through discovery-based methods." The report describes how this paradigm is equally valid in the humanities, "where students should have the opportunity to work in primary materials, perhaps linked to their professors' research projects" (17).

Conclusion

From its beginning, the research paper assignment developed in a cross-curricular fashion as the university system in the U.S. grafted the German (primarily written) mode of higher education onto the British (primarily oral) mode that dominated prior to the mid to late 1870s. Intended to be a form of the scholarly discourse of instructors for students, the research paper quickly became a codified form that could only mimic what it was intended to teach, especially as it manifested itself in first-year writing courses. Compositionists working on the subject, along with scholars in other fields, are advocating a return to the model of student as active, neophyte scholar, replacing the model of student as passive consumer of information.

While undergraduates currently have more opportunities to fully participate in meaningful research activities as advocated by the Boyer Commission Report (1998), they need a new skill set to be able to successfully do so. Compositionists have responded to this challenge, as can be seen by the essays included in this book. Research methods and practices have undergone a drastic change in recent years, and this presents a new challenge in the teaching of research skills. Instead of happening at libraries or archives, research is now just as often conducted in front of a computer with access to databases, ebooks, and online journals. Thanks to easier access, it seems that research should be an easier task for students now. As the Ethnographic Research in Illinois Academic Libraries (ERIAL) study (Asher, Duke, and Green 2010) identifies, however, it is not. The challenge lies in helping students understand citations and information organization systems, develop a more comprehensive search strategy beyond merely Googling a word or phrase, and find and then evaluate information sources of all kinds, as chapters in Part Two of this book show. We, therefore, need to consider what is meant by "research" in writing assignments that students encounter across the undergraduate experience and consider possibly replacing "research" with the term "digital information literacy" to reflect the nature of research practices now heavily reliant on computers and computer networks.

There is also a need to build upon the more recent surveys of Melzer (2009) and Hood (2010) by conducting a national survey of undergraduate courses that require a research paper assignment to ascertain what sort of assignments and requirements are now in place. In other words, we need a larger baseline of data on the subject along with specific information on how research assignments are articulated by instructors and responded to by students, something that builds on Foreword contributors' Alison J. Head and Michael B. Eisenberg's study of research handouts (2010). This research and analysis should be part of a cross-curricular dialogue that works to understand how different fields define and teach research skills to their students. The findings from such research should allow us to better evaluate the efficacy of research projects in first-year writing courses, especially in terms of what sort of knowledge transfer carries over for students when they begin conducting research work in their various disciplines.

As reforms to the research paper project continue, Scardamalia and Bereiter's (1987) description of knowledge telling and knowledge transforming should be kept in mind. Can first-year college students be expected to conduct original, knowledge-making research projects? Can knowledge transforming work be done in first-year writing courses, or should it be left to individual disciplines and classes beyond the first year of college work? These questions, among others, deserve answers if we are to fully appreciate and more importantly educate the new digital scholar.

Endnote

1. According to Microsoft.com, the AutoSummary Tools in Microsoft Office Word 2007 can highlight and assemble key points of a document. For example, a student could use Office Word 2007 to create an automatic summary of a number of long science articles or to quickly create an abstract for a finished history report. The student runs AutoSummarize and then edits the summary.

References

Aley, Shelley. 2004. "The Collage Connection: Using Hypertext to Teach Research Writing." In *Research Writing Revisited: A Sourcebook for Teachers*, edited by Pavel Zemliansky and Wendy Bishop, 117–126. Portsmouth, NH: Boynton/Cook.

Asher, Andrew, Lynda Duke, and David Green. 2010. "The ERIAL Project: Ethnographic Research in Illinois Academic Libraries." Accessed September 13, 2012. academiccommons.org/commons/essay/erial-project.

Bergmann, Linda S. 2010. *Academic Research and Writing*. Boston: Longman.

Blakesley, David, and Jeffrey L. Hoogeveen. 2008. *Writing: A Manual for the Digital Age*. Florence, KY: Cengage.

The Boyer Commission on Educating Undergraduates in the Research University. 1998. *Reinventing Undergraduate Education: A Blueprint for America's Research Universities*. Stony Brook: State University of New York.

Brent, Doug. 1992. *Reading as Rhetorical Invention: Knowledge, Persuasion, and the Teaching of Research-Based Writing*. Urbana, IL: National Council of Teachers of English.

Council of Writing Program Administrators. 2008. "WPA Outcomes Statement for First-Year Composition." Accessed September 13, 2012. www.wpacouncil.org/positions/outcomes.htm.

Davis, Robert, and Mark Shadle. 2000. "Building a Mystery: Alternative Research Writing and the Academic Act of Seeking." *College Composition and Communication* 51 (3): 417–446.

Donovan, Timothy R., and Janet Carr. 1991. "'Real World' Research: Writing Beyond the Curriculum." In *Teaching Advanced Composition: Why and How*, edited by Katherine H. Adams and John L. Adams, 211–222. Portsmouth, NH: Boynton/Cook.

Ford, James E., ed. 1995. *Teaching the Research Paper: From Theory to Practice, From Research to Writing.* Lanham, MD: Scarecrow Press.

Ford, James E., and Dennis R. Perry. 1982. "Research Paper Instruction in the Undergraduate Writing Program." *College English* 44 (8): 825–831.

Glaze, Bernadette M. 1995. "A Process-Oriented Research Assignment: I-Search Before Research." In *Teaching the Research Paper: From Theory to Practice, From Research to Writing*, edited by James E. Ford, 75–97. Lanham, MD: Scarecrow Press.

Grobman, Laurie, and Joyce Kinkead, eds. 2010. *Undergraduate Research in English Studies.* Urbana, IL: NCTE.

Head, Alison J., and Michael B. Eisenberg. 2010. "Assigning Inquiry: How Handouts for Research Assignments Guide Today's College Students." *Project Information Literacy Progress Report.* Accessed September 13, 2012. www.projectinfolit.org/pdfs/PIL_Handout_Study_finalvJuly_2010.pdf.

Hood, Cara Leah. 2010. "Ways of Research: The Status of the Traditional Research Paper Assignment in First-Year Writing/Composition Courses." *Composition Forum* (22). Accessed September 13, 2012. www.compositionforum.com/issue/22/ways-of-research.php.

Larson, Richard L. 1982. "The 'Research Paper' in the Writing Course: A Non-Form of Writing." *College English* 44 (8): 811–816.

Macrorie, Ken. 1984. *Searching Writing.* Upper Montclair, NJ: Boynton/Cook.

Manning, Ambrose N. 1961. "The Present Status of the Research Paper in Freshman English: A National Survey." *College Composition and Communication* 12 (2): 73–78.

McClure, Randall. 2011. "Googlepedia: Turning Information Behaviors into Research Skills." In *Writing Spaces: Readings on Writing*, Vol. 2, edited by Charles Lowe and Pavel Zemliansky, 221–241. Anderson, SC: Parlor Press.

McMillen, Paula S., and Eric Hill. 2005. "Why Teach 'Research as a Conversation' in Freshman Composition Courses? A Metaphor to Help Librarians and Composition Instructors Develop a Shared Model." *Research Strategies* 20: 3–22.

Melzer, Dan. 2009. "Writing Assignments Across the Curriculum: A National Study of College Writing." *College Composition and Communication* 61 (2): 240–261.

Microsoft Corporation. 2012. "AutoSummarize a Document in Microsoft Office Word 2007." Accessed September 13, 2012. www.microsoft.com/education/en-us/teachers/how-to/Pages/autosummarize-document.aspx.

Nelson, Jennie. 1994. "The Research Paper: 'A Rhetoric of Doing' or a 'Rhetoric of the Finished Word?'" *Composition Studies/Freshman English News* 2 (22): 65–75.

———. 2001. "The Scandalous Research Paper and Exorcising Ghosts." In *The Subject Is Research: Processes and Practices,* edited by Wendy Bishop and Pavel Zemliansky, 3–11. Portsmouth, NH: Boynton/Cook.

Nelson, Jennie, and John R. Hayes. 1988. *How the Writing Context Shapes College Students' Strategies for Writing from Sources.* Technical Report 16. Berkeley: National Center for the Study of Writing and Literacy at University of California, Berkeley, and Carnegie Mellon University.

North, Stephen. 1980. "Teaching Research Writing: Five Criteria." *Freshman English News* 9 (2): 17–19.

Reigstad, Tom. 1997. "I Search, You Search, We All Search for I-Search: Research Alternative Works for Advanced Writers, Too." *Composition Chronicle* 10 (7): 4–7.

Russell, David R. 1995. "Activity Theory and Its Implications for Writing Instruction." In *Reconceiving Writing, Rethinking Writing Instruction,* edited by Joseph Petraglia, 51–77. Mahwah, NJ: Laurence Erlbaum Associates.

———. 2002. *Writing in the Academic Disciplines: A Curricular History.* 2nd ed. Carbondale: Southern Illinois University Press.

Scardamalia, Marlene, and Carl Bereiter. 1987. "Knowledge Telling and Knowledge Transforming in Written Composition." In *Advances in Applied Psycholinguistics,* Vol. 1, edited by Sheldon Rosenberg, 142–175. Cambridge, UK: Cambridge University Press.

Schwegler, Robert A., and Linda K. Shamoon. 1982. "The Aims and Process of the Research Paper." *College English* 44 (8): 817–824.

Strickland, James. 2004. "Just the FAQs: An Alternative to Teaching the Research Paper." *The English Journal* 94 (1): 23–28.

Sutton, Brian. 1997. "Writing in the Disciplines, First-Year Composition, and the Research Paper." *Language and Learning Across the Disciplines* 2 (1): 46–57.

Tuso, Joseph F. 1995. "Apologia Pro Pedagogica Mea: Or, How I Kicked the Research Paper Habit and Learned to Teach Freshman English." In *Teaching the Research Paper: From Theory to Practice, From Research to Writing,* edited by James E. Ford, 33–41. Lanham, MD: Scarecrow Press.

Veglahn, Nancy J. 1988. "Searching: A Better Way to Teach Technical Writing." *College Composition and Communication* 39 (1): 85–87.

Zemliansky, Pavel. 2001. "Hint Sheet 5: The I-Search Assignment." In *The Subject Is Research: Processes and Practices*, edited by Wendy Bishop and Pavel Zemliansky, 254–255. Portsmouth, NH: Boynton/Cook.

Zemliansky, Pavel, and Wendy Bishop, eds. 2004. *Research Writing Revisited: A Sourcebook for Teachers*. Portsmouth, NH: Boynton/Cook.

CHAPTER 3

Professional Statements and Collaborations to Support the New Digital Scholar

John Eliason and Kelly O'Brien Jenks

What is at stake for students researching and writing in the digital age? One common but unsatisfactory answer might be "anything and everything." After all, many people concerned about information literacy (IL) will predicate their hope and despair on topics ranging from discreet technological competency to global citizenship. In our respective roles as director of composition and instruction coordinator librarian, we, too, experience the fluid and far-reaching effects of teaching and practicing IL. Our daily interactions reveal the diverse set of obstacles and opportunities embedded in students' information behaviors and their notions of writing in the digital age. Students struggle to repel digitally induced cognitive overload that can so easily arrest their development as effective researchers in and through digital spaces.

Confronting the host of challenges necessitates a habit of continuous active learning for both students and educators. To this end, we explore in this chapter recent literature that explicitly connects IL with writing instruction, giving particular attention to works that suggest avenues for establishing collaborations and to published selections that actually feature collaborations between librarians and writing teachers. Our aim in the process is to emphasize what we and many others consider a natural connection between and among these professionals.

Organizational Statements on Information Literacy

The authors whose work we introduce in this chapter present citation lists simultaneously daunting and exhilarating. They draw upon sources from many intellectual corners of academe, from publications directed toward educators in libraries, writing programs, writing centers, teaching and learning centers, and information technology programs. Several authors mention key documents and associations that can help colleagues build collaborative relationships within and across institutions. One of the most recent, the "Framework for Success in Postsecondary Writing" (hereafter the Framework), was published in January 2011 by three influential professional organizations in higher education: the Council of Writing Program Administrators (WPA), the National Council of Teachers of English (NCTE), and the National Writing Project (NWP).

Even though the Framework was not produced in direct cooperation with professional organizations connected to librarians or the field of library and information science, the document clarifies for writing teachers in U.S. high schools and colleges the importance of offering IL instruction as an essential aspect of the teaching of writing. The Framework, a product of cooperative inquiry involving 2- and 4-year college and high school writing teachers from across the country, addresses habits of mind "that are both intellectual and practical and that will support students' success in a variety of fields and disciplines" (Council of Writing Program Administrators, National Council of Teachers of English, and National Writing Project 2011). It also advises teachers on "experiences" they can implement to develop students' abilities "to analyze a situation or text and make thoughtful decisions based on that analysis, through writing, reading, and research" (Council of Writing Program Administrators 2011).

Including the topic of research in the Framework was no accident, as it was based, in part, on the WPA Outcomes Statement for First-Year Composition. In that earlier publication, the WPA authors state that, by the end of first-year college writing instruction, students should "[u]nderstand a writing assignment as a series of tasks, including finding, evaluating, analyzing, and synthesizing appropriate primary and secondary sources" (Council of Writing Program Administrators 2000). Many readers will recognize the similarities between this content and that within the Information Literacy Competency Standards for Higher Education, a well-known and highly influential publication of the American Library Association and its Association of College and Research Libraries (ACRL). In the IL-specific document, as well, educators are encouraged to assist students in becoming information-literate individuals who can, among other things, access, evaluate, and incorporate information (Association of College and Research Libraries 2000).

As the Framework gains acceptance, an increasing number of high school and college writing teachers will turn to it for ideas and guidance in their efforts to help students ready for and succeed in higher education. The habits of mind articulated in the Framework—namely curiosity, openness, engagement, creativity, persistence, responsibility, flexibility, and metacognition (Council of Writing Program Administrators, National Council of Teachers of English, and National Writing Project 2011)—all apply to students who research and write. Consequently, we anticipate dynamic opportunities for those academic and research librarians interested in forging collaborations with writing teachers and writing program administrators who use the Framework to inform their professional practices.

Additional opportunities exist for developing interconnections that could stimulate productive collaborations between librarians and their colleagues in writing programs. The Liberal Education and America's Promise (LEAP) campaign, spearheaded by the Association of American Colleges and Universities (AAC&U), articulates "The Essential Learning Outcomes" for liberal education and workforce development. One of the outcomes, "Intellectual and Practical Skills," could present writing teachers and librarians with particularly relevant content for fostering shared approaches. For example, the nested list following the "Intellectual and Practical Skills" outcome includes the following categories, most or all of which are important both to writing teachers and librarians: inquiry and analysis, critical and creative thinking, written and oral communication, quantitative literacy, IL, and teamwork and problem solving (Association of American Colleges and Universities 2005).

AAC&U's Valid Assessment of Learning in Undergraduate Education (VALUE) rubrics have also gained prominence in the scholarship of assessment in higher education. For example, in AAC&U's journal *Peer Review*, Megan Oakleaf discusses how the Institute of Museum and Library Services has granted over $400,000 to support an initiative called Rubric Assessment of Information Literacy Skills, or RAILS (2012, 18). The purpose of RAILS is "to investigate an analytic rubric approach to information literacy assessment in higher education" (Institute n.d.), and Oakleaf provides an overview of five distinct institutions that investigate student IL competency with the aid of AAC&U's rubrics. As evidenced in Oakleaf's article, the VALUE rubrics are not intended to be taken in their published form and then imposed upon institutions. Rather, AAC&U provides the rubrics as tools for helping higher education professionals build their own assessment documents and structures. Two of the rubrics in particular, "Written Communication" and "Information Literacy," afford writing and information specialists yet another opportunity for enhancing dialogue about their students' research and writing practices (Rhodes 2010).

Not surprisingly, significant overlap exists in the content of the VALUE rubrics. The "Written Communication" matrix, for example, includes a category for sources and evidence, and the "Information Literacy" rubric details, again, the need for individuals to demonstrate abilities not only to locate, access, and value information, but also to use it effectively. At the capstone level, this information must be applied "to fully achieve a specific purpose, with clarity and depth" and with a "full understanding of the ethical and legal restrictions" on the use of the ideas and information drawn from resources (Rhodes 2010, 37). These two specific rubrics alone could spark dialogue between writing faculty and librarians focused on IL, as could the other VALUE rubrics, especially the one for the other IL, integrative learning.

AAC&U defines integrative learning as "an understanding and a disposition that a student builds across the curriculum and cocurriculum" (Association of American Colleges and Universities 2010a, 2010b). This definition works in tandem with the overarching purposes for research and writing. Since writing teachers and librarians alike generally privilege having students build capacities to transfer learning within and across contexts, those educators understandably want student research to yield far more than mere information and knowledge of information needs. In addition, they seek an active setting for learning where students appreciate how the pinnacle of academic achievement, in many instances, is realized when students connect experiences from their research and their own ideas and make contributions to a scholarly enterprise. Most librarians and writing teachers hope students will conceive of research and writing not as a series of skills or rituals but as intellectual conversation born from the sorts of habits of mind and experiences articulated by the major professional organizations referenced in this chapter.

In "Definition of 21st Century Literacies," the National Council of Teachers of English (2008) reinforces this perspective regarding what many educators want from and for their students. Competencies deemed necessary for a literate person include several that directly concern research and writing, with emphases on building proficiency with technology tools, designing and sharing information, and working effectively and ethically with a range of resources including multimedia texts. Another key competency, "Build relationships with others to pose and solve problems collaboratively and cross-culturally," applies as much to writing instructors and librarians as to the students they serve.

NCTE offers additional documents to amplify the list of outcomes, such as "Writing between the Lines—and Everywhere Else." In this report, the organization cites an NCTE poll involving more than 900 educator-respondents, a majority of whom indicated that "the key to advancing 21st century literacies in academic settings is making time for teacher learning, planning, and collaboration across subject matter areas" (National Council of Teachers of English 2009). Respondents to the poll were asked to indicate the top abilities required for student success, and the answers affirm the importance of the shared work of writing teachers and librarians: "1. The ability to seek information and make critical judgments ... 2. The ability to read and interpret many different kinds of texts ... and 3. The ability to innovate and apply knowledge creatively" (National Council of Teachers of English 2009).

In another of the organization's reports, "Writing in the 21st Century," writing scholar and former NCTE president Kathleen Blake Yancey provides historical perceptions of writing as well as a contemporary argument that educators "join the future and support all forms of 21st century literacies, inside school and outside school" (2009). Yancey asserts what many of us are learning more each day—that with digital technology, especially interactive (Web 2.0) varieties, writers are "everywhere." With this knowledge, Yancey contends, educators have an opportunity to embrace a new reality, one that sees students composing in a wide range of media for multiple purposes and audiences, with an ever-growing menu of information resources to support student efforts and abilities to write well.

Research and Scholarship on Information Literacy

Indeed, the myriad challenges and breakneck pace of change in research and writing instruction makes collaboration between writing instructors and librarians desirable, profitable, and, in our opinion, essential. With this conviction in mind, we committed to working together on identifying not only professional statements from scholarly organizations, but also recent scholarship that reveals partnerships that were directly or indirectly designed to provide students with enhanced possibilities for success as digital scholars. Our goal: Find resources that we believed would help us respond to what we and many of our colleagues see in our daily work with student researchers in first-year writing courses.

For our selection process, we developed a purposefully flexible set of criteria. As noted previously, we sought examples of collaborations, especially those described in publications from 2005 to the present, and we wanted to present examples from a variety of scholarly sources in our disciplines. Within the collaborations described, we attempted to learn about motivations of the authors and to identify commentary on how they reconciled their results with their desires. Moving through the literature with this general set of criteria in mind led us to identify repeatedly the authors' assertion that students are best served when afforded the responsibility and challenge of owning their scholarship, of self-directing their learning for the sake of their own goals. The authors in the articles we present emulate that philosophical stance, and they provide their readers with evidence of an acute sensitivity to treat students as researchers and writers rather than as subjects of inoculation against undesirable research and writing practices.

Our goal in this process of seeking published examples of collaborations between librarians and teachers of writing was never to attempt a comprehensive account of the existing literature on that topic. Therefore, the examples that follow are just that—particular selections among a deep and rapidly growing literature on collaborations between librarians and teachers of writing. In fact, other authors in this book—specifically Rebecca Moore Howard—have already made available through the open web extensive bibliographies focused on IL and writing (Howard 2012). Additional resources offering a range of perspectives pertaining to such collaborations can be found on CompPile (Haswell and Blalock 2012) and on the archives webpage for the Georgia International Conference on Information Literacy (McBride 2004). By design, the literature presented here is not annotated; instead, we offer a brief summary of resources to reinforce our claim that they all, in their own way, deserve consideration in the body of literature that draws into dialogue the concerns of librarians and teachers of writing. Following this section, we close with a series of major themes identified in the literature, examples of our own local collaborations, and a call for future participation.

Selected Examples of Collaborations in Information Literacy and Writing

Artman, Frisicaro-Pawlowski, and Monge

In their 2010 essay, "Not Just One Shot: Extending the Dialogue About Information Literacy in Composition Classes," Margaret Artman, Erica Frisicaro-Pawlowski, and Robert Monge take issue with the long-standing practice where the collaboration between writing faculty and instructional librarians is limited to a one-shot workshop or library tour. For them such discrete experiences limit students' understanding of information resources and, more importantly, severely restrict students' abilities to experience meaningful engagement with the concept of IL writ large. The writers posit that "creating rich opportunities for undergraduate engagement in diverse, dynamic research projects that develop such literacies is absolutely essential" (2010, 93). They echo data collected from Foreword contributors Alison Head and Michael Eisenberg's Project Information Literacy and express concern that many students will write throughout college using "only a handful of resources at their disposal" (2010, 94). Artman, Frisicaro-Pawlowski, and Monge argue that writing faculty must challenge their assumptions and accept "a more comprehensive disciplinary understanding of the global, recursive relationships between information literacy and student writing." Doing so will assist faculty in avoiding "outmoded notions of what it means to be information literate, or what it means to compose in a digital age" (2010, 95).

Barratt, et al.

"How can we help students to use more and better sources in their research papers in order to improve the quality of their written compositions?" ask Caroline Cason Barratt, et al. (2009, 37). The difficulty of answering this question motivated the authors to develop a collaborative research project focused on analyzing citation patterns of student essays in first-year writing courses at the University of Georgia, Athens. The work is built upon earlier scholarship in citation analysis, though the authors (two librarians, two compositionists) pursued a larger data set and charted a path of inquiry that considered individual teachers, writers, library instruction, and assignments. In their 2009 article resulting from these efforts, "Collaboration Is Key: Librarians and Composition Instructors Analyze Student Research and Writing," Barratt, et al. note that their study presented the opportunity "to scrutinize and compare their own evaluations of and assumptions about student research" (37). Assisting them in data acquisition was <emma>, an open source electronic markup and management tool developed at the University of Georgia. Barratt, et al. comment that, at the time of their writing, <emma> was being used by colleagues in writing programs at 19 other institutions.

Birmingham, et al.

In the spring of 2008, Elizabeth Joy Birmingham, et al. published "First-Year Writing Teachers, Perceptions of Students' Information Literacy Competencies, and a Call for a Collaborative Approach." In this article the authors build upon other work suggesting that, on behalf of students, librarians and compositionists should establish more frequent and higher quality partnerships. Birmingham, et al.'s call is predicated on the claim that librarians and writing instructors "share a number of closely aligned challenges." These include students' anxiety about the processes they follow when researching and writing as well as the frustration they experience as digital researchers doing (uncritical) searches on the internet (2008, 7). Another key point addressed is the shared propensity for being blamed by colleagues in other departments for students' deficiencies in researching and writing. Even so, Birmingham, et al. offer evidence from the programs of academic conferences in both fields as a means of demonstrating that colleagues in the two areas do not have an extensive record of engaging in collaborative scholarship. In their research, Birmingham, et al. moved beyond general calls for such partnerships and asked writing teachers "about their perceptions of [IL] skills, the importance of these skills, and what the teachers do to introduce or reinforce these skills in their own classroom" (2008, 8). The "Future Research" section of their article includes recommendations for scholars to conduct more analysis of specific data from first-year writing courses and "to understand what it means to students' writing to have [students] be better, more imaginative and informed researchers" (2008, 18).

Bowles-Terry, Davis, and Holliday

In "'Writing Information Literacy' Revisited: Application of Theory to Practice in the Classroom," Melissa Bowles-Terry, Erin Davis, and Wendy Holliday follow up in 2010 on compositionist Rolf Norgaard's *Reference & User Services Quarterly* articles (Norgaard, et al. 2003 and 2004) in which he encourages librarians and writing faculty to strengthen their professional bonds for the sake of their respective fields and the students engaged in researching and writing. Bowles-Terry, Davis, and Holliday (2010) agree with Norgaard's claim that compositionists and librarians have much to offer one another, noting that if writing teachers have not adequately understood and theorized IL as it pertains to writing, "this is, in part, because of librarians' failure to articulate the contributions that our theoretical tradition can make to rhetoric and composition and, by extension, learning in general" (2010, 225). However, the authors point to another problem besides clear communication: "a gap between IL theory and practice." Specifically, they attribute a traditional focus on information sources and procedures to the influence of behaviorism; conversely, the authors present an emphasis on strategies as an outgrowth of constructivist pedagogy. In an effort to privilege constructivist approaches, they present a case study with the intention of demonstrating how sociocultural theories of IL "can inform and reform instructional practice at the intersection of composition and IL" (2010, 226).

Brady, et al.

In 2009, Laura Brady, et al. published "A Collaborative Approach to Information Literacy: First-Year Composition, Writing Center, and Library Partnerships at West Virginia University." The authors—members of their institution's writing center, library, and writing faculty—describe a team-based strategy for teaching research, reading, and writing as interconnected rather than discrete processes. Through this collaboration, they were each compelled "to re-examine professional and disciplinary boundaries" and to "foster new literacies" (2009, para. 1). One point of agreement enhancing their collaboration was their willingness to critique the definition of IL, which they do by discussing content from the American Library Association and a range of literature on IL. The authors point to IL collaborations represented in published works and, based on their own work, affirm the work of Norgaard and others who argue that effective research and writing instruction are inseparable, that the endeavor is, as Norgaard, Arp, and Woodard (2004) put it, "writing information literacy" (221). The authors explain their collaborative structure for providing IL workshops to faculty teaching writing and writing-intensive courses at West Virginia University. Discussion of student feedback on the IL assignments in the first-year writing course includes statistics from the end of the 2-year pilot program.

Jacobs and Jacobs

Heidi L. M. Jacobs and Dale Jacobs published "Transforming the One-Shot Library Session into Pedagogical Collaboration: Information Literacy and the English Composition Class" in 2009 as a means of reporting on their librarian-and-writing scholar collaboration focused on exploring research as a process. Citing the common tradition for educators and especially writing teachers to view writing as a process-oriented endeavor, the authors explored "what might a focus on research as a process contribute to the teaching of IL in English composition courses" and "what can be gained by a collaboration that not only puts into dialogue two practitioners in two different disciplines but also two bodies of scholarship and professional knowledge" (2009, 72). In their shared inquiry, Jacobs and Jacobs set about to answer these questions and to advance the presence and import of IL scholarship that includes the direct contribution of scholars and teachers of college writing. In the section of their essay dedicated to defining future collaborations and teaching strategies, Jacobs and Jacobs explain how they are striving to make additional, meaningful changes at the program level.

Nutefall and Mentzell Ryder

In their 2010 essay, "The Timing of the Research Question: First-Year Writing Faculty and Instruction Librarians' Differing Perspectives," Jennifer E. Nutefall and Phyllis Mentzell Ryder discuss the results of their collaborative exploratory study at George Washington University and the implications for library instruction for writing courses. The article provides a brief background on their collaboration and then moves into a review of literature pertaining to "those articles in the library and composition literature that address the development of the research question or thesis statement" (2010, 438). Subtopics within that section include information-seeking behavior, false focus, and high recall searches. Transitioning to the details of their exploratory study, the authors explain how faculty–librarian partnerships work and reinforce that participants "are encouraged to collaborate on all stages of the course including choosing course texts, devising effective research assignments, and planning and teaching information literacy sessions" (2010, 441). The article is drawn to a close with the assertion that "the ways in which faculty and librarians see their work and each other have important implications for how they conceptualize and present the research process to students" (2010, 448).

Major Themes Identified in the Literature

From our reading of the work published by the organizations and the authors cited in this chapter, we derived a list of recurring and otherwise significant themes related to collaborations between writing teachers and librarians. We believe this collection of major themes could help us and others to think more expansively about research as intellectual conversation. Our intention is also to provide possible ideas for future scholarship that might further explore professional statements and collaborations that could support the efforts of new digital scholars in colleges and universities.

Of the several main themes we identified, dialogue might be the most important. Multiple authors mention not just the importance of having dialogue with colleagues, but also the necessity of attending to issues of power. Regardless of the fact that both groups of colleagues are professionals, hierarchies can exist, and they can disrupt efforts to assist students.

When and with whom dialogue in collaborations occurs are other themes. For example, some authors describe longitudinal and ongoing partnerships, while other scholars note that the timing of the interactions could be worth revisiting. We noticed, too, that the dialogue in the studies we examined was often constitutive of a sort of learning community. Membership, in some instances, entailed one writing teacher and one librarian. Other occasions involved multiple people from not only writing programs and libraries but also writing centers and other departments and programs across institutions. These learning communities dedicated to research and writing practices of undergraduate students sometimes were quite diverse and included students, adjuncts, librarians, tutors, and full-time writing faculty and program administrators. This we found inspiring, especially when students were included, as it makes sense to us that efforts to assist students in becoming digital scholars would involve students in the dialogue about how that help should occur and in what forms.

Another theme from the literature is who provides research instruction. Here, too, dialogue matters. Some of the authors note that they have moved beyond one-shot approaches and see the teaching of research as consonant with and even inextricably a part of teaching writing. Many of the authors cite the work of Norgaard, Arp, and Woodard who advocate convincingly that traditional distinctions or separations have been at best unhelpful (2003). Librarians and compositionists authoring the essays we read were thorough in raising inquiries about frequency of collaborative teaching, the physical and digital spaces where such teaching occurred, and the process approaches guiding the timing and content of their feedback to students researching as academic writers.

In fact, process—and the idea that just as writing is a process, so is researching—figures importantly in nearly all of the articles we selected to present in this chapter. We share these authors' crosscurrents of support for challenging a rules-based or a strictly product-oriented approach to IL instruction. Student researchers and writers certainly require technical skills, and without question they must possess the rhetorical awareness to communicate to a range of audiences. However, we share the belief that such elements should not be pursued or developed in isolation or at the expense of adaptability and critical thinking and creativity and recursive practices. All of these capacities together constitute hallmarks of the sorts of sophisticated scholarship and effective communication skills that educators want their students to demonstrate.

In addition to expressing concerns about IL instruction, several authors note what they consider an imbalance in publications on IL between writing and library and information science. Again, this is a position we share, though in the last several years, thanks to journals and editors at publications such as *Composition Forum, Composition Studies, Kairos, The Writing Lab Newsletter, Computers and Composition, The Writing Instructor, Teaching English in the Two-Year College, Research in the Teaching of English,* and *WPA,* the writing scholars partnering with librarians have enjoyed more opportunities to place their intellectual work in their own discipline's publications.

The studies reported in the literature we selected raise other themes that concern partnerships between librarians and teachers of writing, including the sharing of technical knowledge required for research instruction in this era of digital scholarship, as well as the relative benefits of working in concert to mine data from the interactions between students and instructors. Data mining of assignments, too, qualifies as a major point of emphasis. In fact, like dialogue, assignment design is a cornerstone of much of the published work we read. Authors raise questions about professional development initiatives on assignment-making that would benefit both librarians and writing instructors (especially graduate teaching assistants).

Also frequently mentioned are collaborative assignment design and the roles of reflective practice. An imperative for assignment design, from our perspective, is the explicit focus on designing learning experiences that take seriously the notion of students as researchers who are actively engaged in exploring and acquiring new literacies, something contributors to Part Three of this book address. In writing studies, for example, students are increasingly required to produce multimodal compositions that entail creative design experiences that often take students into multiple media and a wide spectrum of sources and research methods and methodologies. Librarians and writing instructors must continue to develop and connect theories and practices that will support students in doing well in the diverse types and kinds of intellectual work they encounter.

A final theme from the literature worth special mention is the call for a more ardent habit of challenging the assumptions that many students (but also many librarians and writing teachers) carry with them regarding research and research-as-process. We see a clear need for additional scholarship that probes and refines the ways in which outcomes and definitions and partnerships align with programs in writing and library and information science.

Local and Regional Collaborations

This project—and an awareness of the major themes of scholarship we identified as part of it—have served as a welcome milestone in our own collaborative partnership as director of composition and instruction coordinator librarian. We have come a long way together.

In fact, our effort to collaborate began even before we met in person. In an email message in the summer of 2008, just two months before we began working together at the same institution, we shared our intention of drawing stronger connections between our respective professional areas. Within that first year, we joined several other writing and library colleagues in our geographic area for a meeting to discuss our various institutional partnerships. Ultimately, we struck upon the idea that we could—and should—expand the dialogue regarding IL and create a larger learning community for the purpose of sharing ideas, building resources, and networking.

The result of that dialogue was Inland InfoLit, a regional consortium dedicated to advancing students' IL. The first conference for this organization, "Information Literacy and the Teaching of Composition," served approximately 45 people; the next year, we developed a second, similar conference and the number of attendees nearly doubled. During this same period, Eliason helped found and was elected co-chair of the High Mountain Affiliate (HMA) of the Council of Writing Program Administrators (CWPA). In the autumn of 2011, Inland InfoLit and HMA collaborated on a bigger regional conference that again included a substantial emphasis on IL and the teaching of writing. Approximately 150 colleagues representing 19 institutions participated in the conference. These types of professional experiences have led to increased collaboration in and across institutions throughout our area, and we look forward to additional opportunities with colleagues far and near.

Conclusion: A Future of Collaborative Possibilities

Through the literature and our lived experiences with colleagues, we have come to appreciate that research and research instruction are process-oriented, inquiry-driven endeavors. Our work here attempts to identify professional statements that might inspire future collaborations and to introduce our readers to past collaborations that scholars have already successfully established and nurtured into scholarship.

The processes in the authors' projects we highlight have been diverse, the inquiry equally so. The partnerships give us hope—for ourselves and our students. We marvel at the complexity of IL and writing, and we bask in the collaborative possibilities for writing teachers and librarians to support student scholars as they encounter the spaces and places of the digital world.

References

Artman, Margaret, Erica Frisicaro-Pawlowski, and Robert Monge. 2010. "Not Just One Shot: Extending the Dialogue About Information Literacy in Composition Classes." *Composition Studies* 38 (2): 93–110.

Association of American Colleges and Universities. 2005. "Liberal Education and America's Promise (LEAP)." Accessed September 13, 2012. www.aacu.org/leap.

———. 2010a. "Information Literacy VALUE Rubric." Accessed September 13, 2012. www.aacu.org/value/rubrics.

———. 2010b. "Integrative Learning VALUE Rubric." Accessed September 13, 2012. www.aacu.org/value/rubrics.

Association of College and Research Libraries. 2000. "Information Literacy Competency Standards for Higher Education." Accessed September 13, 2012. www.ala.org/acrl/standards/informationliteracycompetency.

Barratt, Caroline Cason, Kristin Nielsen, Christy Desmet, and Ron Balthazor. 2009. "Collaboration Is Key: Librarians and Composition Instructors Analyze Student Research and Writing." *Portal: Libraries & the Academy* 9 (1): 37–56.

Birmingham, Elizabeth Joy, Luc Chinwongs, Molly Flaspohler, Carly Hearn, Danielle Kvanvig, and Ronda Portmann. 2008. "First-Year Writing Teachers, Perceptions of Students' Information Literacy Competencies, and a Call for a Collaborative Approach." *Communications in Information Literacy* 2 (1): 6–24.

Bowles-Terry, Melissa, Erin Davis, and Wendy Holliday. 2010. "'Writing Information Literacy' Revisited: Application of Theory to Practice in the Classroom." *Reference & User Services Quarterly* 49 (3): 225–230.

Brady, Laura, Nathalie Singh-Corcoran, Jo Ann Dadisman, and Kelly Diamond. 2009. "A Collaborative Approach to Information Literacy: First-Year Composition, Writing Center, and Library Partnerships at West Virginia University." *Composition Forum* (19). Accessed September 13, 2012. www.compositionforum.com/issue/19.

Council of Writing Program Administrators. 2000. "WPA Outcomes Statement for First-Year Composition." Accessed September 13, 2012. www.wpacouncil.org/positions/outcomes.html.

Council of Writing Program Administrators, National Council of Teachers of English, and National Writing Project. 2011. "Framework for Success in Postsecondary Writing." Accessed September 13, 2012. www.wpacouncil.org/framework.

Haswell, Rich, and Glenn Blalock. 2012. "CompPile." Accessed September 13, 2012. www.comppile.org/search/comppile_main_search.php.

Howard, Rebecca Moore. 2012. "Information." Accessed September 13, 2012. wrthoward.syr.edu/Bibs/Info.htm.

Institute of Museum and Library Services. n.d. "Rubric Assessment of Information Literacy Skills (RAILS)." Accessed September 13, 2012. www.railsontrack. info/about.aspx.

Jacobs, Heidi L. M., and Dale Jacobs. 2009. "Transforming the One-Shot Library Session into Pedagogical Collaboration: Information Literacy and the English Composition Class." *Reference & User Services Quarterly* 49 (1): 72–82.

McBride, Kelly. 2004. "Georgia Conference on Information Literacy." Accessed September 13, 2012. ceps.georgiasouthern.edu/conted/infolit.html.

National Council of Teachers of English. 2008. "The NCTE Definition of 21st Century Literacies." Accessed September 13, 2012. www.ncte.org/positions/statements/ 21stcentdefinition.

———. 2009. "Writing between the Lines—and Everywhere Else." Accessed September 13, 2012. www.ncte.org/library/NCTEFiles/Press/Writingbetweenthe LinesFinal.pdf.

Norgaard, Rolf, Lori Arp, and Beth S. Woodard. 2003. "Writing Information Literacy." *Reference & User Services Quarterly* 43 (2): 124–130.

———. 2004. "Writing Information Literacy in the Classroom." *Reference & User Services Quarterly* 43 (3): 220–226.

Nutefall, Jennifer, and Phyllis Mentzell Ryder. 2010. "The Timing of the Research Question: First-Year Writing Faculty and Instruction Librarians' Differing Perspectives." *Portal: Libraries & the Academy* 10 (4): 437–449.

Oakleaf, Megan. 2012. "Staying on Track With Rubric Assessment: Five Institutions Investigate Information Literacy Learning." *Peer Review* 13 (4)/14 (1): 18–21.

Rhodes, Terrel L., ed. 2010. *Assessing Outcomes and Improving Achievement: Tips and Tools for Using Rubrics.* Washington, DC: Association of American Colleges and Universities.

Yancey, Kathleen Blake. 2009. "Writing in the 21st Century: A Report from the National Council of Teachers of English." Accessed September 13, 2012. www.ncte.org/library/NCTEFiles/Press/Yancey_final.pdf.

CHAPTER 4

Fighting for Attention: Making Space for Deep Learning

Brian Ballentine

> Users are distracted, and as much as they want fast information to use, they're not very good at managing the information they want. In fact, the more they get, the worse they are at using it. This is especially true if information comes too quickly, as it often does, or it comes amidst a torrent of other information, flowing from different channels into the same brain.
>
> —Brian Still (2010, 32)

According to Nicholas Carr's (2010) much-debated book *The Shallows: What the Internet Is Doing to Our Brains*, "Dozens of studies by psychologists, neurobiologists, educators, and web designers point to the same conclusion: When we go online, we enter an environment that promotes cursory reading, hurried and distracted thinking, and superficial learning" (115–116). Not only do online spaces interrupt us constantly, the cognitive overload created as we switch rapidly from distraction to distraction physically alters our brains. Carr fears that we have created a generation of "skimmers" with stunted abilities for both learning and analysis (138). Similarly, in 2007, N. Katherine Hayles pointed to a generational shift in cognition that she differentiated as "hyper" and "deep" attention. According to Hayles, "with the shift, serious incompatibilities arise between the expectations of educators, who are trained in deep attention and saturated with assumptions about its inherent superiority, and the preferred cognitive modes of young people, who squirm in the procrustean beds outfitted by their elders" (188). Far from the meshing gears of a well-tuned transmission, the "shift" in cognitive modes offers a jarring and dizzying array of future (dis)advantages.

Among the many predictions for the future of online learning environments, perhaps one of the safest forecasts contains the claim that the web will continue to produce more opportunity for superficial engagement with digital information and a hyper-attentive cognitive style. The more difficult prognostication will be how we as educators may reclaim deep learning in digital environments. New research (Borst, Taatgen, and van Rijn 2011; Judd and Kennedy 2011; Just and Varma 2007; Klingberg 2009; Small, Moody, Siddarth, and Brookheimer 2009; Small and Vorgan 2008) suggests that the need to reclaim this depth is not a rushed assumption; we have a fight on our hands. And, it is a fight being taken up by many of the contributors to this book. Of course, we should continue to remind ourselves that not all of our students will or will even want to become research scholars attached to any one of many academic fields. And, despite Carr's many comfortable references to Socrates, Plato, Hawthorne, Elizabeth Eisenstein, Ong, and McLuhan, a call to reclaim deep learning from the shallows of the internet must not center on selfishly preserving only academic interests in researching, reading, and writing. The "crucial question," as Carr (2010) calls it, is "What can science tell us about the actual effects that internet use is having on the way our minds work?" (115).

This chapter begins with an overview of the new research presented by Carr and others that addresses this question. In short, research suggests that reading and researching online actually changes the way our brains engage with text. Within this backdrop, I contend that the coming years are going to be hard-fought for those involved in undergraduate research-writing, specifically in regard to sustaining the substantive research and writing practices we require of our students. This is not to say that our expectations for thorough and ethical research must change but that our strategies for teaching research methods require a productive overhaul.

Given the new data on the effects of the internet on our brains and how we learn, the second portion of this chapter reviews specific strategies for teaching digital research methods. To a certain extent, the discussion on how to overhaul teaching digital research methods in the undergraduate writing course has started to take shape in journals like *Computers and Composition, Kairos,* and *Computers and Composition Online,* and the chapters in this book also offer valuable advice for teachers. In addition to reviewing some of that advice, I will demonstrate how to customize the open source browser Firefox by installing the "add-on" Zotero in order to better facilitate the "conflation of researching and writing spaces" (Purdy 2010b, 50). Drawing on the spirit of the hacker community and the tenets of Web 2.0, I contend that the act of personalizing and customizing research space to meet individual needs in part creates an intrinsic motivation for deeper engagement with both the tools and the materials of the NextGen researcher.

As it has been discussed throughout the professional literature and popular media, the affordances of Web 2.0 bring with them specific anxieties related to research and writing that range from internet-induced plagiarism to the demise of the library and "traditional" library research. In response, this chapter concludes with a reality check regarding the pervasiveness of technology and our penchant for incorporating it into so many facets of our lives. We can't turn back, but going forward will require much of us. As educators we will be asked to answer questions like J. E. Clark's (2010) in her article "The Digital Imperative: Making the Case for a 21st Century Pedagogy": "How do we help students learn to critically engage digital information?"

(33). That is, as educators we will have to help our students (and according to some data, ourselves) strike a balance between skimming and deep critical engagement.

The message here is not one of despair. A successful future for student learning and researching in digital spaces will depend upon writing instructors, information scientists, academic librarians, and our continued collective ability to play key educational roles in the process. What "counts" as writing in networked environments, for example, continues to expand in ways that complicate the teaching of research and writing in the digital age. However, practitioners and scholars continue to provide evidence that writing studies is, or will become, more central to the future successes of everything from interface design (Selber 2004; Selfe and Selfe 1994) to writing code (Ballentine 2010). Going forward, we must accept that the web will continue to alter the field and our definitions of writing and researching.

Plasticity and Memory

Carr first won our attention with his book *The Big Switch* (2008a) and subsequently his article in *The Atlantic*, "Is Google Making Us Stupid?" (2008b), with most of that article's contents serving as a frame for his newer work, *The Shallows* (2010). His latest book could have turned easily toward a Luddite screed on the evils of technology, but Carr instead offers a more thoughtful history of memory-altering technologies beginning with maps and clocks and leading up to the current research in memory formation. Taking Carr's lead, this section expands on the recent research delving into the complexities of the mind/brain relationship and human memory.

Memory is biological. It exists in a physical and material state in our brains. With advancements in functional magnetic resonance imaging (fMRI) and digital imaging software, scientists in just the last several years have been able to unravel some of the brain's mysteries at the cellular level. Studies have shown evidence for some time of a "young brain's plasticity" or, in other words, "its ability to be malleable and ever-changing in response to stimulation and the environment" (Small and Vorgan 2008, 8).

What scientists are now discovering is that even though our brains lose some of that plasticity as we age, our brains are much more malleable at later ages than previously thought. Researchers from a 2005 article in the *Annual Review of Neuroscience* have argued, "The brain, as the source of human behavior, is by design molded by environmental changes and pressures, physiologic modifications, and experiences" (Pascual-Leone, Amedi, Fregni, and Merabet 2005, 378). This molding or "plasticity" is not an "occasional state" but a "normal ongoing state of the nervous system throughout the life span" (379). More to the point, according to Michael Merzenich, a retired neuroscientist from the University of California, San Francisco and the chief scientific officer of Posit Science, a company that develops "brain training" software, "the brain is massively plastic—if engaged in the right way" (Graham 2008, 27–28).

Whereas Merzenich (Graham 2008) may have a vested interest in the software his company sells, new research suggests that how we engage our brains does in fact have a significant impact on what regions of our brains are activated and, in turn, how well we remember information from that engagement. Carr's (2010) argument made much of a recently published study, "Your Brain on Google: Patterns of Cerebral Activation during Internet Searching" (Small, Moody, Siddarth, and Bookheimer 2009), that the researchers themselves describe as "the first study to directly explore brain functional responses while volunteers engage in an internet search task" (122).

The study had 24 participants, 12 of whom were identified as experienced internet users (the "Net Savvy group") and 12 of whom were considered internet novices (the "Net Naïve group") (Small, Moody, Siddarth, and Bookheimer 2009). As a control for the experiment, researchers required both groups to read plain text to simulate print-based reading. There were no significant differences between the groups' brain patterns here as the "text reading task activated brain regions controlling language, reading, memory, and visual abilities."

The first key finding of the study was that when given a series of internet search tasks, however, brain activity in experienced Google users "demonstrated significant increases in signal intensity in additional regions controlling decision making, complex reasoning, and vision" (116). When performing their internet search tasks, the Net Naïve group displayed brain patterns that looked much like the results from their plain text reading task. Their brains were accustomed or "wired" to accommodate or favor their reading habits.

The second and more remarkable finding from the study was the quickness with which the brain patterns of the once Net Naïve group would change. The lead researcher for the experiment, Gary Small, director of UCLA's Memory and Aging Research Center at the Semel Institute for Neuroscience and Human Behavior, speaks to this secondary result in his co-authored book, *iBrain* (2008), where he reveals that it took "just five days of practice" for the Net Naïve group members to exhibit "the exact same neural circuitry" as the Net Savvy group. In other words, the plasticity of their brains enabled the Net Naïve group to become "rewired" (Small and Vorgan 2008, 16).

The study by Small, Moody, Siddarth, and Bookheimer was eventually published in the *American Journal of Geriatric Psychiatry* in 2009, and among its objectives was the exploration of whether or not internet use was an activity that could "improve brain health and cognitive abilities" in older adults (116). In fact, the study participants were all "aged 55–78 years" (117). As such, the additional brain activity noted during the internet search tasks is considered largely a positive result, especially since the brain stimulation is different from that of reading. However, the researchers also offer caution regarding possible negative effects: "These findings also point to the sensitivity of brain neural circuits to common computer tasks such as searching online, and constant use of such technologies have the potential for negative brain and behavioral effects, including impaired attention and addiction" (124).

The obvious and potentially dangerous implication, which has no simple solution, is that NextGen students can't maintain their focus long enough to engage in any kind of deep learning while attempting to perform as digital researchers. Indeed, the behavioral effects brought about by student digital research practices prompts Randall McClure in Chapter 1 of this book to call for a complete overhaul of writing curricula at all levels of education.

Hyper vs. Deep

For Carr (2010), this pairing of shortened attention or focus and an addiction-like desire for the constant flow of new information from the internet is responsible for our shallow state of cognitive affairs. Carr writes that

> the extensive activity in the brains of [web] surfers also points to why deep reading and other acts of sustained concentration become so difficult online. The need to evaluate links and make related navigational choices, while also processing a multiplicity of fleeting sensory stimuli, requires constant mental coordination and decision making, distracting the brain from the work of interpreting text or other information. (122)

Equally problematic, we actually enjoy and even seek out the "multiplicity" the internet has to offer. According to neuroscientist Torkel Klingberg (2009), we "want more information, more impressions, and more complexity," even if we are just superficially skimming through the data being served up on our monitors (166). All the while, though, we are training our brains to favor this hyper-attentive behavior.

Hayles's (2007) preference for the slightly more euphemistic descriptor "hyper" as opposed to Carr's "shallow" forecasts her position that this cognitive style may have its uses. She questions, "Whether the synaptic reconfigurations associated with hyper attention are better or worse than those associated with deep attention cannot be answered in the abstract. The riposte is obvious: Better for what?" (194). She goes on to posit that any number of jobs from air traffic controllers, to currency traders, to fast-food cashiers may benefit from the hyper-attentive quality of being able to switch rapidly from task to task. Perhaps, she suggests, our brain's ability to do so can even be interpreted as progress. According to Hayles, it is not "far-fetched" to conclude that our hyper attention represents "the brain's cultural coevolution" that corresponds with our exposure to rapid-fire information streams (194).

Additional skepticism of technology's detrimental effects is not difficult to locate (see Clay Shirky's July 17 [2008a] and July 21, 2008 [2008b] responses to Carr). In a June 10, 2010 opinion piece in the *New York Times*, Harvard psychology professor Steven Pinker asserts that new digital technologies should be added to the long list of prior technological advancements that throughout history have incited similar fears of information overload and even societal/cultural deterioration. As for plasticity, Pinker quips, "Yes, every time we learn a fact or skill the wiring of the brain changes; it's not as if the information is stored in the pancreas. But the existence of neural plasticity does not mean the brain is a blob of clay pounded into shape by experience" (para. 5). That is, regardless of the experiences we have, our brain's overall capacity to process information does not change. Our cognitive chops, so to speak, remain.

Pinker acknowledges the abundance of information made available via the internet but views that abundance and access to it as a productive means for keeping pace with contemporary levels of research and knowledge production. In what appears to be a jab at Carr's (2010) argument, Pinker (2010) defends technology and its use: "Far from making us stupid, these technologies are the only things that will keep us smart" (para. 11). He does add, however, that keeping our hyper-attentive or shallow activities in check while we are online is our own responsibility:

> It's not as if habits of deep reflection, thorough research and rigorous reasoning ever came naturally to people. They must be acquired in special institutions, which we call universities, and maintained with constant upkeep, which we call analysis, criticism and debate. They are not granted by propping a heavy encyclopedia on your lap, nor are they taken

away by efficient access to information on the internet. (para. 10)

In one very important respect, it appears that Pinker and Carr are talking past each other. Pinker's claim that the brain's overall capacity to process information does not change with experience is not necessarily in conflict with Carr's concern that the rapid flow of information instills within us the learned behavior of treating all information we encounter with the same shallow cognitive style. We retain our ability to engage deeply, as Pinker suggests; however, we are no longer in the habit of doing so. Hyper attention becomes our default setting.

The real danger comes when "habits" of deep reflection fade with prolonged internet use, especially if the habit of shallow skimming is not balanced with deeper reading and reflection. Concluding the worst from the latest research in brain and cognitive science, Carr reports, "As the time we spend scanning web pages crowds out the time we spend reading books … the circuits that support those old intellectual habits and pursuits weaken and begin to break apart" (2010, 120). If so, NextGen students are in jeopardy of not being able to research, read, and write with the levels of attention and depth required for even basic academic research. The question that remains is what to do about it.

Carr has been criticized for, among other things, not offering concrete solutions to combat our shallowness. Shirky (2008b), for example, calls Carr's inability to "offer much of a suggestion for what to do next" as evidence of Carr's own "pseudo" Luddism (para. 14). For Pinker (2010), how to proceed is obvious: "The solution is not to bemoan technology but to develop strategies of self-control, as we do with every other temptation in life. Turn off e-mail or Twitter when you work, put away your Blackberry at dinner time, ask your spouse to call you to bed at a designated hour" (para. 9). He makes it fantastically simple.

So, the question then becomes whether or not our current predicament in the classroom is anything unique or if we are merely attempting to fight off the latest invasive media species? Given the research exposing technological habits as addictive at a neurological level, educators are staring down a much tougher fight than they have faced previously. In a recent *PBS NewsHour* report, "Is Technology Wiring Teens to Have Better Brains?" (January 5, 2011), science correspondent Miles O'Brien interviews teenagers as they multitask their way through homework alongside Facebook updates and chatting as well as multiple instant messaging and video streams. When he attempts to interview his own daughter Connery, O'Brien can't even complete his question before his daughter looks away from him to check a new text message. When O'Brien calls her out on her behavior and she responds, "Sorry, it was just a reflex," he corrects her and says, "That's an addiction" (para. 39 and 40). Fortunately, the addictive qualities of new media helping induce our hyper, or depending on one's perspective, shallow attention have also spurred critical reflection and scholarship on pedagogical approaches to research and writing in digital spaces that can help us strategize for the future.

Deep Learning in a Hyper Space

Writing studies professionals have offered many assignments exploring the new modes of writing the internet enables. Blogs, webpages, wikis, Second Life avatars, Facebook profiles, and massively multiplayer online role-playing games (MMORPGs) have all been incorporated into the writing classroom and often with positive results. For example, Rebekah Shultz Colby and Richard Colby (2008) detail their experiences using emergent pedagogy to teach a writing course where students spent the semester playing the MMORPG World of Warcraft (WoW). Students posted to blogs and participated in forums that supported the WoW gaming community. The class did not operate around a fixed (print) object of inquiry, but rather treated the classroom as a malleable game space where student writing projects form dynamically from issues within their WoW community.

Likewise, the case studies presented in this book are proof that educators are invested in pedagogical improvements, specifically strategies for teaching research methods in digital environments. These assignments embrace the notion that a digital "text" takes many and multiple forms. That multiplicity is commonly ascribed to the affordances of Web 2.0, among which include its ability to sever content from form. The curricular possibilities Web 2.0 brings have not gone unnoticed by compositionists. Special issues of *Computers and Composition* (Day, McClure, and Palmquist 2010) and *Computers and Composition Online* (Day, McClure, and Palmquist 2009) have celebrated and critiqued the role of Web 2.0 in the writing classroom. Yet, as scientific studies raise more alarms over hyper attentive behavior online, the explorations begun in those special issues and in this book must continue. As I will discuss, taking a cue from Tim O'Reilly (2005) and the open source community presents a unique opportunity to assist educators in building deep learning activities into their curriculum by effectively combining student research and writing (1).

O'Reilly's principles of Web 2.0 have a great deal to teach us about our own teaching of research and writing. His criteria include establishing an architecture of participation, controlling (and sharing) one's own work, understanding the power of collective intelligence, and encouraging remixable formats and their distribution (2005, 1). Web 2.0, as O'Reilly defines it, owes much of its philosophical approach to the authorship and ownership of content to the open source development community and the "hacker ethic" (Himanen 2001). A specific facet of this ethic includes "the powerful sense that it is not merely inefficient but downright stupid, almost criminal, for people to solve the same problem twice" (Weber 2004, 138). As a result, the community's view on the repetition of work promotes access and a publicity of that work. Leaving work open deliberately fosters an environment of participatory problem solving and information sharing that has helped spawn an array of operating systems and applications that rival the best (and most expensive) proprietary software.

In sum, the hacker ethic can best be described as "the dedication to an activity that is intrinsically interesting, inspiring, and joyous" (Himanen 2001, 6). The good news is we have access to some very intelligent beginnings both in this book and elsewhere. Customizing online tools, publishing and sharing information with peers, and remixing work are all steps toward deeper engagement with student research and writing. I next take a closer look at a specific instance of using Web 2.0 technology to promote those levels of engagement in the writing classroom and offer a brief examination of the citation management application Zotero.

Web 2.0, Zotero, and the Changing Face of Research Spaces

Capitalizing on technologies that use the web as their platform and several of O'Reilly's Web 2.0 criteria, James P. Purdy (2010b) in "The Changing Space of Research: Web 2.0 and the Integration of Research and Writing Environments" demonstrates how to productively merge research and writing spaces. His article begins with the claim that traditional writing instruction is "antiquated" in the era of Web 2.0 and that our standard methods of teaching have NextGen students "march through linear processes that compartmentalize research and writing" (48). The rigid and tiered stages of research first and writing second deprive the entire process of becoming richly iterative and recursive. That is, in the midst of our many concerns regarding information overflow brought on by new internet-based technologies, we are missing out on an amazing learning opportunity.

Purdy (2010b) supports his claim by modeling functionality found in JSTOR, ARTstor, Delicious, and Wikipedia. These four technologies exhibit many Web 2.0 qualities and are representative of technologies labeled typically as either "academic" or "nonacademic." The "academic" resources, JSTOR and ARTstor, now have features that enable users to "compile and save personalized collections of archival holdings generated from customized searches" and "annotate and write notes about groups of images and access these notes and artifacts from any networked computer location" respectively (50). Purdy selected the social bookmarking site Delicious for its ability to publicly tag, save, and share online sources. And, although he acknowledges the many critiques of the "nonacademic" Wikipedia, Purdy argues convincingly for the encyclopedia's interface as a model for integrating research and writing. Each article invites readers to discuss, edit, and review past edits to the content; for an extended discussion on Wikipedia in the classroom, see Purdy's "Wikipedia Is Good for You!?" (2010a).

To Purdy's (2010b) coverage of JSTOR, ARTstor, Delicious, and Wikipedia, I would add the Firefox browser extension or "add-on" Zotero. Add-ons are separate applications that are developed to extend a variety of functionality to Firefox and are made possible due to the browser's open source code (Ballentine 2009). Combined, the four technologies discussed by Purdy enable students to collect, annotate, and share their writing and research publicly, customize their writing and research spaces, and access their work from any networked computer or browser-enabled device. Developed by George Mason University's Center for History and New Media, Zotero manages to incorporate much of this functionality in one application:

> Zotero includes the best parts of older reference manager software (like EndNote)—the ability to store author, title, and publication fields and to export that information as formatted references—and the best parts of modern software and web applications (like iTunes and del.icio.us), such as the ability to interact, tag, and search in advanced ways. (Center for History and New Media n.d., para. 1)

While Zotero's original mission was to be a customizable citation manager that worked within a web browser, its current list of features is much more extensive. Users can easily capture citation data from just about any website, whether it is the *New York Times*, Flickr, YouTube, or an article found on JSTOR. Zotero has plug-ins to sync with

Microsoft Word and OpenOffice and even a plug-in for the popular blogging site WordPress, so blog entries can be cited efficiently and appropriately. Full versions of article PDFs can also be saved via Zotero. Users can even sync multiple computers to their account on a Zotero server and then share search configurations and notes with colleagues and friends.

All of Zotero's rich features, its ongoing development at George Mason, and even its legal predicament (Thomson Reuters filed a $10 million lawsuit against George Mason claiming that Zotero violates their intellectual property) all move the application beyond being defined as a mere tool to a position among technologies that make it an object ripe for analysis (Purdy 2010b, 48). Indeed, many of the technical and legal limitations inherent to out-of-the-box proprietary software have restricted such analysis. The ability to customize, and thus personalize an application like Zotero, invites students under the hood of the application. There, what they will be working on, what we all have the opportunity to work on, are what media scholar Shirky (2008b) refers to as the "structures" necessary for supporting new modes of writing and research:

> My argument instead is that technologies that make writing abundant always require new social structures to accompany them. … It's not as if books and periodicals as we know them began to flow from Gutenberg's studio in the 1450s. Among the things that needed to be invented after books got cheap were the separation of fiction from non-fiction; the discovery of new talent; the index; numbered versions of the same work; and so on through a host of inventions large and small. (para. 8 and 9)

The affordances of Web 2.0 are powerful and can aid in inspiring deeper connections between students and their work. Those connections can be even stronger if we seize the opportunity to help shape the emerging structures Shirky references.

Plagiarism, Digital Libraries, and Digital Searches

This chapter would be incomplete without noting that Web 2.0 affordances along with new methods of searching, acquiring, and sharing work and even just the internet itself have incited fears in and out of the academy, mainly a fresh anxiety over plagiarism. More succinctly, "Plagiarism is *hot*" (Adler-Kassner, Anson, and Howard 2008, 231). Or, at least, it is hot again due to student access to an abundance of online materials. Rebecca Moore Howard's "Understanding 'Internet Plagiarism'" (2007) attempts to rein in some of the "sense of impending doom" brought by speculation that the "Internet is causing an increase in plagiarism" (3–4). With her cool approach, Howard (a contributor to this book as well) wants to shift us from setting out to snare "cheaters" and asks us instead to question "the very terms of textuality" (8). Building on existing theories of intertextuality and the work of scholars like Cheryl Geisler, et al. (2001), James Porter (1986), and Mark Rose (1993), Howard reminds us that ultimately "all writers are always collaborating with text" (9).

In Chapter 6 of this book, Purdy suggests that the academic community question its understanding of plagiarism and the role of plagiarism detection services. His chapter suggests we need to find new techniques for using plagiarism detection services not as threatening traps but as teaching tools. Recasting the role of such tools in the research and writing process may help educators change the culture of their classrooms by spotlighting intertextuality and collaboration. Today's technology-driven collaborations are faster and easier, but if we want NextGen students to do more than just "limit the depth of their search to whatever is returned by the webcrawler on the first screen or two," it may mean that we start using and teaching tools with which we may leverage the web (Baron 2009, 220). Among the good news in the fight for deep attention in digital environments is that tools like Zotero are free, open source applications; the challenge is becoming comfortable enough with these applications so that they may be migrated successfully into the classroom.

For example, I used my library's eJournal site to locate the issue of *Computers and Composition* that contained Howard's (2007) article on internet plagiarism. With a single click, I used Zotero to import the citation information as well as a full PDF of the article. I added the article to a "collection," or folder, in Zotero that I had started to support the research and writing of this chapter. As I read Howard's article on screen, I pasted quotes that were relevant to the project into Zotero's "notes" panel. The notes panel looks and behaves just like a word processor, and I use this feature in part as a composing space to capture ideas about the article I am reading. I can then update or sync this collection with my Zotero account in order for the new information in this collection to be available to me from any device with an internet connection. Were I collaborating with other authors, I could set my collection and my notes to be shared with others. In this instance, more access to more information does not appear to "shallow" my research but instead gives me, the researcher and writer, a better sense of the relationships between the materials I am working with and my overall argument regarding deep learning online.

For many of our students and for many of us, research begins in a web browser. University libraries provide electronic access to numerous scholarly journals, and an internet connection means access to offerings from Google, including Google Scholar and the Google Book project. Ironically, visits to the library may have little to do with the handling of books or print journals but instead be a quest for computer access. Carr (2010) states bluntly, "Today's library is very different. Internet access is rapidly becoming its most popular service" (97). The problem, of course, is what students often choose to do with their connectivity. If their research processes proceed roughly parallel to the Zotero scenario just described, then most educators would probably feel comfortable with the future of research online or at least its potential.

Unfortunately, students do not regulate the torrents of information available onscreen, even at the library, to include just their research findings. When a trip to the library to conduct research online mingles heavily with Facebook time and instant messaging, students can leave with an "illusion of competence" (Glenn 2010, para. 3). Reflecting on her own multitasking experiences, Sherry Turkle, director for MIT's Initiative on Technology and Self, alludes to this "illusion" in an interview:

> [I]f all I do is my e-mail, my calendar and my searches … I feel great; I feel like a master of the universe. And then it's the end of the day, I've been busy all day, and I haven't thought about anything hard, and I have been consumed by the technologies that were there and that had the power to nourish me. (Rushkoff February 2, 2010, "There's a quote you gave me at one point from Shakespeare" section, para. 2)

Turkle notes her susceptibility to the effects of the same frenetic multitasking that gives students the sense that they have learned and accomplished much more than they truly have. In worst case scenarios, the library and its digital connectivity become a space of not just fictitious accomplishments but illusions of rigor.

The Future of Deep Learning: Research and Writing Within New Structures

Given the findings on the brain presented in this chapter along with those on NextGen students' research skills and information behaviors offered throughout this book, our need to fight for deeper learning online may be as dire as Carr (2008b) claims. And, it may be time to acknowledge that the research habits of the new digital scholar must be proactively counterbalanced with a curriculum that deliberately seeks to foster deep research, writing, and learning. In his second response to Carr, Shirky (2008b) acknowledges:

> We have a challenge before us in figuring out how to keep the distractions of the net at bay, now that new material is no longer hard to discover or access. Perhaps Carr is right

that this time we will fail. Perhaps a medium that radically expands our ability to create and share written material will end up being bad for humanity. But that would be a first, in the three thousand years between the Phoenician alphabet and now. (para. 10)

Even the slightest hint at capitulation from a staunch technology advocate like Shirky comes as a surprise. Still, his comparisons between the internet and past paradigm-shifting technologies like the alphabet and even the printing press are, according to some new media scholars, mismatched.

In Douglas Rushkoff's (2010) *Program or Be Programmed: Ten Commands for a Digital Age*, he stops just short of designating each new digital technology *sui generis*. He explains:

Computers and networks are more than mere tools: they are like living things, themselves. Unlike a rake, a pen, or even a jackhammer, a digital technology is programmed. This means it comes with instructions not just for its use, but also for itself. And as such technologies come to characterize the future of the way we live and work, the people programming them take on an increasingly important role in shaping our world and how it works. (8)

Granted, engineers like Henry Petroski would probably object to Rushkoff's too-easy elision of extant "mere tools," as the pencil is the subject of one of Petroski's more famous books (1990). Rushkoff's claims for digital technology and programming do offer, however, an important warning: If we don't participate now, then returning to digital technologies as objects to analyze may not be possible. That is, Petroski's analysis of the pencil salvaged lead, wood, and rubber "technology" from its own ubiquity (Petroski 1990, 6). Rushkoff seems to suggest that when we reach this same point with our digital technologies and we have not been participating meaningfully in their development, we may never be able to understand these new tools on a critical level. It is not completely accurate to claim that when we customize research and writing spaces within Firefox and install extensions like Zotero that we are indeed "programming," yet such customization does represent a deeper level of critical awareness and engagement. We are on a very meaningful level taking control of our research workspace.

According to Rushkoff (2010), neglecting to participate, to "program," will only help to place fault on ourselves. Several basic strategies can be employed in our classrooms to help our students and ourselves initiate Rushkoff's participation:

1. Have candid conversations with our students about hyper and deep cognitive styles and the supposed "shallowing" effects of internet-based technologies. This is not a wholesale subscription to Carr's theory, but instead an opportunity to involve students in an ongoing debate in which their research and writing habits are being discussed. Assign a chapter from Carr's (2010) book, Hayles's (2007) article, or a piece by Shirky (2008a, 2008b) or Rushkoff (2010); regardless of the exact work, the reading should provide students a point of entry into the discussion.

2. Explore and teach new technology "structures" that Shirky (2008a, 2008b) claims are necessary in order to fill voids accompanying new modes of writing. Have students critique these structures not just as "mere tools," but as Purdy (2010b) suggests, as "objects of analysis" (48).

3. Use the integration of new research and writing technologies as an opportunity to refocus on a course's learning objectives. As Karen Kaiser Lee also discusses in Chapter 2 of this book, our writing courses that ask students to invent, develop, and support arguments with responsible research often struggle to "disabuse students of their misperceptions that research simply entails finding and repeating what someone else has written" (Purdy 2010b, 55). With this in mind, we need to help NextGen students explore how well the integration of

these technologies does or does not aid them in developing and expressing their own arguments.

4. Recognize that the teaching and integration of such technologies will not be unilaterally successful. Therefore, we should promote student customization of the research-writing space.

As NextGen students make these spaces their own, they should also (ideally) become aware that no matter how powerful the technology, none of them possesses the science-fiction-like superpowers that relieve us from the duty of thinking.

References

Adler-Kassner, Linda, Chris Anson, and Rebecca Moore Howard. 2008. "Framing Plagiarism." In *Originality, Imitation, and Plagiarism: Teaching Writing in the Digital Age*, edited by Caroline Eisner and Martha Vicinus, 231–246. Ann Arbor: University of Michigan Press.

Ballentine, Brian D. 2009. "Hacker Ethics & Firefox Extensions: Writing & Teaching the 'Grey' Areas of Web 2.0." *Computers and Composition Online*. Accessed September 13, 2012. www.bgsu.edu/cconline/Ballentine.

——. 2010. "On the Tradition of Anticipating User Need: Methods and Warnings on Writing Development Narratives for New Software." *Technical Communication* 57 (1): 26–43.

Baron, Dennis. 2009. *A Better Pencil*. New York: Oxford University Press.

Borst, Jelmer P., Niels A. Taatgen, and Hedderik van Rijn. 2011. "The Problem State: A Cognitive Bottleneck in Multitasking." *Journal of Experimental Psychology: Learning, Memory, and Cognition* 36 (2): 363–382.

Carr, Nicholas. 2008a. *The Big Switch: Rewiring the World, From Edison to Google*. New York: W. W. Norton.

——. 2008b. "Is Google Making Us Stupid?" *The Atlantic* July/August. Accessed September 13, 2012. www.theatlantic.com/magazine/archive/2008/07/is-google-making-us-stupid/6868.

——. 2010. *The Shallows: What the Internet Is Doing to Our Brains*. New York: W. W. Norton.

Center for History and New Media. n.d. "Zotero." Accessed September 13, 2012. chnm.gmu.edu/zotero.

Clark, J. Elizabeth. 2010. "The Digital Imperative: Making the Case for a 21st Century Pedagogy." *Computers and Composition* 27 (1): 27–35.

Colby, Rebekah Shultz, and Richard Colby. 2008. "A Pedagogy of Play: Integrating Computer Games into the Writing Classroom." *Computers and Composition* 25 (3): 300–312.

Day, Michael, Randall McClure, and Mike Palmquist. 2009. "Composition in a Freeware Age: Assessing the Impact and Value of the Web 2.0 Movement in the Teaching of Writing." *Computers and Composition Online.* Accessed September 13, 2012. www.bgsu.edu/cconline/Ed_Welcome_Fall_09/compinfreewareintroduction. htm.

———. 2010. "Composition 2.0." *Computers and Composition* 27 (1): 1–74.

Geisler, Cheryl, Charles Bazerman, Stephen Doheny-Farina, Laura Gurak, Christina Haas, et al. 2001. "IText: Future Directions for Research on the Relationship Between Information Technology and Writing." *Journal of Business and Technical Communication* 15 (3): 269–308.

Glenn, David. 2010. "Divided Attention." *The Chronicle of Higher Education,* February 28. Accessed September 13, 2012. www.chronicle.com/article/Scholars-Turn-Their-Attention/63746.

Graham, Lawton. 2008. "Is It Worth Going to the Mind Gym? *New Scientist* 197 (2638): 26–29.

Hayles, N. Katherine. 2007. "Hyper and Deep Attention: The Generational Divide in Cognitive Modes." *Profession*: 187–199.

Himanen, Pekka. 2001. *The Hacker Ethic and the Spirit of the Information Age.* New York: Random House.

Howard, Rebecca Moore. 2007. "Understanding 'Internet Plagiarism.'" *Computers and Composition* 24: 3–15.

Judd, Terry, and Gregor Kennedy. 2011. "Measurement and Evidence of Computer-Based Task Switching and Multitasking by 'Net Generation' Students." *Computers & Education* 56: 625–631.

Just, Marcel A., and Sashank Varma. 2007. "The Organization of Thinking: What Functional Brain Imaging Reveals About the Neuroarchitecture of Complex Cognition." *Cognitive, Affective, and Behavioral Neuroscience* 7: 153–191.

Klingberg, Torkel. 2009. *The Overflowing Brain.* New York: Oxford University Press.

O'Brien, Miles. Jan. 5, 2011. "Is Technology Wiring Teens to Have Better Brains?" *PBS NewsHour.* Accessed September 13, 2012. www.pbs.org/newshour/bb/science/ jan-june11/digitalbrain_01-05.html.

O'Reilly, Tim. Sept. 30, 2005. "What Is Web 2.0? Design Patterns and Business Models for the Next Generation of Software." O'Reilly.com. Accessed September 13, 2012. www.oreilly.com/pub/a/oreilly/tim/news/2005/09/30/what-is-web-20.html.

Pascual-Leone, Alvaro, Amir Amedi, Felipe Fregni, and Lotfi Merabet. 2005. "The Plastic Human Brain Cortex." *Annual Review of Neuroscience* 28: 377–401.

Petroski, Henry. 1990. *The Pencil: A History of Design and Circumstance.* New York: Knopf.

Pinker, Steven. 2010. "Mind Over Mass Media." *New York Times,* June 10. Accessed September 13, 2012. www.nytimes.com/2010/06/11/opinion/11Pinker.html ?_r=1.

Porter, James E. 1986. "Intertextuality and the Discourse Community." *Rhetoric Review* 5 (1): 34–47.

Purdy, James P. 2010a. "Wikipedia Is Good for You!?" In *Writing Spaces: Readings on Writings,* edited by Charles Lowe and Pavel Zemliansky, 205–224. Anderson, SC: Parlor Press.

———. 2010b. "The Changing Space of Research: Web 2.0 and the Integration of Research and Writing Environments." *Computers and Composition* 27 (1): 48–58.

Rose, Mark. 1993. *Authors and Owners: The Invention of Copyright.* Cambridge, MA: Harvard University Press.

Rushkoff, Douglas. 2010. *Program or Be Programmed: Ten Commands for a Digital Age.* New York: OR Books.

Rushkoff, Douglas (Interviewer) and Sherry Turkle (Interviewee). 2010. *Digital_Nation: Life on the Virtual Frontier,* February 2 [Interview transcript]. Accessed September 13, 2012. www.pbs.org/wgbh/pages/frontline/digitalnation/ interviews/turkle.html.

Selber, Stuart A. 2004. *Multiliteracies for Digital Age.* Carbondale, IL: Southern Illinois University Press.

Selfe, Cynthia L., and Richard J. Selfe Jr. 1994. "The Politics of the Interface: Power and Its Exercise in Electronic Contact Zones." *College Composition and Communication* 45 (4): 480–504.

Shirky, Clay. 2008a. "Why Abundance Is Good: A Reply to Nick Carr." Encyclopedia Britannica Blog, July 17. Accessed September 13, 2012. www.britannica.com/ blogs/2008/07/why-abundance-is-good-a-reply-to-nick-carr.

———. 2008b. "Why Abundance Should Breed Optimism: A Second Reply to Nick Carr." Encyclopedia Britannica Blog, July 21. Accessed September 13, 2012. www.britannica.com/blogs/2008/07/why-abundance-should-breed-optimism-a-second-reply-to-nick-carr.

Small, Gary, and Gigi Vorgan. 2008. *iBrain: Surviving the Technological Alteration of the Modern Mind.* New York: HarperCollins.

Small, Gary, Teena Moody, Prabha Siddarth, and Susan Brookheimer. 2009. "Your Brain on Google: Patterns of Cerebral Activation During Internet Searching." *American Journal of Geriatric Psychiatry* 17 (2): 116–126.

Still, Brian. 2010. "Usability for a Ubiquitous Computing World." *Intercom* (July/August): 31–33.

Weber, Steven. 2004. *The Success of Open Source*. Cambridge, MA: Harvard University Press.

Zotero. "Get Involved with Zotero." n.d. Accessed September 13, 2012. www.zotero.org/getinvolved.

Explorations of What NextGen Students Do in the Undergraduate Writing Classroom

Sentence-Mining: Uncovering the Amount of Reading and Reading Comprehension in College Writers' Researched Writing

Sandra Jamieson and Rebecca Moore Howard[1]

The *Writer's Guide and Index to English*, a college writers' handbook in wide circulation at the middle of the last century, articulates an ideal for students' work from sources that endures today:

> A student—or anyone else—is not *composing* when he is merely copying. He should read and digest the material, get it into his own words (except for brief, important quotations that are shown to be quotations). He should be able to *talk* about the subject before he *writes* about it. Then he should refer to any sources he has used. This is not only courtesy but a sign of good workmanship, part of the morality of writing. (Perrin 1959, 636; emphasis in original)

This brief statement buried deep in an antiquated writers' handbook is remarkable for several reasons, not least of which is its crisp, accessible presentation of a complex truism of academic writing. The idea that writers must be able to "*talk* about the subject" is at the heart of the notion of writing as "conversation" that is repeated in scholarly articles, outcomes statements, and the language of current pedagogy. While prewriting activities use writing as a means of discovery, that process of discovery is embraced by many as a way to enable students to be able to "talk about" their topic before they begin to construct arguments and papers. Few of us would feel the need to *say* this today, but studies of students' researched papers suggest that we should.

Perrin's (1959, 636) statement is remarkable because of its association of "get[ting] it into his own words" with understanding—"digesting"—the source. The passage excludes copying from the realm of composing. When one copies, says the *Writer's Guide*, one is not composing. One is merely copying. Note that when he speaks of "copying," Perrin is not talking about unattributed copying, but *all* copying, including attributed quotation. When one copies, he says, one is not talking about the subject, but merely transcribing others' talk. This claim is complicated. Some academic disciplines value the transcription of others' talk, calling for quotation of significant text rather than paraphrase. Others reject quotation, calling for a synthesis of ideas and findings rather than an emphasis on specific words. Yet across this difference is a shared desire for students to *understand* their sources. If students are quoting or paraphrasing one or two sentences at a time, they are not "digesting" the ideas in the source and using those ideas to compose papers and reports of their own. They are, in Perrin's terminology, copying.

The field of college writing instruction values and teaches the skills of paraphrase and summary—the "digesting" of texts considered by Perrin to be integral to composing from sources. Faculty outside of writing studies also value these writing skills in discipline-specific and general student writing. Conducting cross-disciplinary research on the ways college instructors experience intellectual property and represent it to their students, Lise Buranen and Denise Stephenson describe a chemistry instructor who encourages his students to paraphrase rather than quote, in part to increase their understanding of the source text (2008, 73). The belief that the act of paraphrasing or summarizing helps writers understand their sources is articulated in faculty development work and guides to research, and it is frequently asserted in writing studies scholarship and textbooks. It seems to be a disciplinary or even academic given; nowhere have we seen a compositionist challenge this tenet. We have ourselves promoted the value of summary and paraphrase in our teaching, our work as writing program administrators, and, beginning as early as 1992, our scholarship (Howard 1992).

Our experiences as teachers and administrators of college writing lead us to fear that Perrin's (1959) last principle—that copying is not composing—is being obscured by our current culture of plagiarism hysteria. In their rush to discourage plagiarism, college instructors across the disciplines may be so concerned about students' successful enactment of the mechanical process of *acknowledging* copying that the rhetorical and intellectual dimensions of cross-textual work fade into the background. And when those instructors assess student writing, the result may be that students are rewarded for successful citation out of proportion to the rhetorical and intellectual quality of their texts. Instructors may not always be noticing whether or how much students are, in Perrin's formulation, copying from sources instead of composing from them.

In order to change this dynamic, we first need to know how much students actually use paraphrase and summary in their writing from sources. We also need to know how much they patchwrite, which the Citation Project and others define as working too closely with the language and syntax of the source when they attempt to paraphrase.[2] If we are to explore student *understanding* of texts, we need to see what they do with their sources. Working from multi-institutional research known as the Citation Project, this chapter provides data that begin to answer that question.

Background

A study of student source use by Rebecca Moore Howard, Tricia Serviss, and Tanya K. Rodrigue (2010) found that students worked with sources at the sentence level instead of representing the larger ideas in the source through summary. Expanding on Diane Pecorari's study (2003) of the ways nonnative speakers of English incorporate sources, they explored the extent to which college students' researched writing incorporated four source-use techniques: copying, patchwriting, paraphrasing, and summarizing. Their study found no summary in the 18 researched papers analyzed. It also found that within those papers, it "is consistently the sentences, not the sources, that are being written from" (Howard, Serviss, and Rodrigue 2010, 189). This research, based at one institution, prompted us to ask more questions and design a multi-institutional quantitative study of student papers produced in the first-year writing course or course sequence at 16 U.S. colleges and universities. Those institutions were chosen to represent the entire geography of the country and its most common types of institutions.

As with the single-institution study, the multi-institutional analysis found that the most common form of citation was direct quotation (45.84 percent of all of the citations in the 174 papers in this study), followed by paraphrase (31.87 percent) and patchwriting (16.01 percent). Only 6.28 percent were summary—even if we define that term generously. In other words, 93.72 percent of the citations were created by students working with their sources at the sentence level and not demonstrating that they had "digested" what they read. But these data were not, in fact, our most compelling findings. In addition to not summarizing their sources, our data suggest that many of the students whose papers we analyzed may not even have read beyond the first few pages of the source.

Our research is based on some essential principles. The first is that as scholars and administrators we need to base our claims about what students do on solid data. The contemporary obsession with plagiarism is possible because those who report and repeat it are working from experience, anecdote, and over-generalized claims about student integrity. For example, it seems logical to assume that the expansion of the internet would increase student plagiarism, especially if one is pre-disposed to believe that students will cheat if given the opportunity. Yet we do not have data about the extent of plagiarism before the internet, so we have nothing to compare with post-internet plagiarism. All we know is that the internet makes it easier to catch plagiarists. Without meaningful data, anecdote and beliefs about students will continue to dominate the conversation. Similarly, although writing teachers spend considerable time teaching summary and paraphrase, and alone or with librarians emphasize information literacy and source retrieval, we could not evaluate our success until we had local and multi-institutional data to tell us how our students used that information.

The second principle of the Citation Project is that to be meaning-ful, data needs to come from a wide variety of institutions. Those insti-tutions need to be different in kind and geographical location. While data from single institutions are invaluable for assessment and as pilot research to allow the formulation of more nuanced questions and more efficient data processing, they cannot be used to make broad general-izations about what students do or do not do. In order to be able to speak meaningfully about the trends in student writing in the United States, we undertook to compile a data-based portrait of how students in writing courses work with their sources. That portrait is drawn from the work of 174 students at 16 colleges and universities from a wide geographical distribution in the U.S. Participating institutions are located in 12 states (Alabama, Colorado, Georgia, Idaho, Indiana, Kansas, Massachusetts, New Hampshire, New Jersey, New York, Texas, and Washington) and include community colleges, Ivy League institu-tions, liberal arts colleges, religious colleges, private colleges and uni-versities, and state colleges and universities. The goal of the Citation Project is to collect and share multi-institutional data that will inform the work of scholars, teachers, and administrators, and the design and assessment of pedagogies and policies.

The Citation Project also works on the principle that researchers in the field of writing studies must adopt or adapt methods of quantitative analysis already established in other fields if they seek to develop an overall understanding of what students do when they write.[3] Since Chris Anson's call for data-based research in writing in his keynote address at the Council of Writing Program Administrators conference in 2006, the field has seen an increase in this kind of research, and we were also motivated by that speech (published in expanded form in 2008). It is still somewhat unusual to attend sessions at conferences where scholars are presenting data generated by SPSS (Statistical Package for the Social Sciences; the leading computer program for social science-based statistical analysis), but this trend is increasing and we are no exception. Our research uses citation context analysis, a set of research methods established in the fields of applied linguistics and information studies, and adapts it to the field of writing studies.[4] We also employ qualitative and rhetorical methods with which our field is more familiar. Using qualitative data to present an overall picture and generate questions and using quantitative data to explore those questions[5] allows deep and nuanced understanding. And as the qualitative analysis generates more questions, the cycle repeats.

Methods
Source and Paper Coding
Phase I of our research focused on the researched writing produced in standard first-year writing courses. We invited participating institutions to send us at least 50 researched papers of seven or more pages written in at least four sections of first-year writing taught by at least three different instructors. Those papers were randomized; then we rejected any that were too short or whose sources we could not find. We gathered papers from three institutions in Spring 2008 and the remaining 13 in Fall 2009 and Spring 2010, reporting our findings from those first three institutions in a number of presentations while we collected and analyzed the remaining papers. This was a very

labor-intensive process that included a team of 25 compositionists, both faculty and graduate students, working alone and in pairs.[6]

Our database includes 50 pages of student writing—between 1,000 and 1,150 lines of prose—from each institution. So between them, the 16 participating institutions gave us 800 pages of student research, a total of 17,600 lines of prose. In most cases, those 50 pages came from pages two through six of each of 10 papers. By beginning on the second page, we were able to focus on the source use in the body of the paper where the students were most frequently engaging with researched material. The coded pages in each set of papers from each campus included an average of 119 citations to 58 sources, which combined to give us an overall total of 1,911 citations to 930 sources. We found those sources,[7] coded them by type, and then coded the ways they were used in the student papers. In the interest of space, the specific methods we use to code papers and sources are described only briefly here; however, they are available in much more detail on our website (www.citationproject.net), where our training materials and handouts may also be found.[8] Because the citations we studied came from only 10 to 12 papers per institution, our findings for each institution are of limited use when taken alone; however, our project was to look for patterns across institutions. If we found those patterns and if the data from each institution fit the general pattern, the data would be useful locally and also as a way to trace overall trends.

Our data concerning sources selected and used will be published elsewhere as part of our analysis of the information literacy practices of the students in our study. (All publications are listed at www.citation project.net.) This chapter focuses on the ways students incorporated information from their sources into their papers. The descriptions we used for each of these types of source uses were described for paper-coders in Table 5.1.

While it is easy to define what we mean by "copied" and "quotation," the other three terms are not so straightforward. In 1992, Howard defined patchwriting as "[c]opying from a source text and then deleting some words, altering grammatical structures, or plugging

Table 5.1   Types of Source Use, From "Instructions for Paper Coders"

Passage copied exactly, but not marked as quotation	Exact copying with a citation but no quotation marks or indentation to signal that this is quoted material. (May include minor errors in transcription.)
Passage copied exactly, marked as quotation	Exact copying with a citation and quotation marks or indentation to signal that this is quoted material. (May include minor errors in transcription and errors in citation as long as the copied material is identified as such.)
Passage patchwritten	Restating a phrase, clause, or one or more sentences while staying close to the language or syntax of the source.
Passage paraphrased	Restating a phrase, clause, or one or two sentences while using no more than 20 percent of the language of the source.* Paraphrase does not necessarily involve significant reduction in length.
Passage summarized	Restating and compressing the main points of an entire text or at least three or more consecutive sentences in the text, reducing the summarized passage by at least 50 percent and using 20 percent or less of the language from that passage.*

*NOTE: This 20 percent does not include accurate synonyms, articles, prepositions, proper names, technical terms, or other keywords. This 20 percent does include words whose morphology is changed (a change in verb tense, for example).

in one-for-one synonym-substitutes" (233); however, this definition implies an intentionality that we have not always found to be the case. For this research, we set out to define the term as neutrally as possible. We felt compelled, however reluctantly, to quantify paraphrase and summary. We did not find ourselves counting words very frequently, though. Passages that were patchwritten generally used significantly more than 20 percent of the source material (more than 50 percent most of the time).

In contrast, because our definition of summary requires a reduction by 50 percent of the material in at least three consecutive sentences, passages of summary generally include significantly less than 20 percent of the language of the source. Brown and Day (1983) report on six "rules" that writers follow when summarizing: Two involve deletion of material from the source text; two involve generalizing from specifics in the source text; and two require invention of sentences that capture the gist of one or more paragraphs (4). Although they were not part of our coding guidelines, these rules did seem to be at play in text coded as summary.

In most cases, patchwriting can be identified with as much ease as can summary once one has read the original source. Table 5.2 shows an example from a student paper in the study, which demonstrates this. In each text, words copied directly from the source are underlined with a single line and word substitutions are indicated with wavy underline. Marginal notation indicates how we coded the source use.

The student paper from which these extracts were taken includes three citations to material from five paragraphs of a webpage produced by NORML, an organization that describes itself as "working to reform marijuana laws" (www.norml.org). The section of the NORML website accessed by the student includes a link to a downloadable PDF of a 57-page report, which is summarized on the pages the student cites; however, the citations clearly reference this website rather than the article. The student works sentence-by-sentence through each of the paragraphs on what prints out as the second page of the three-page source. Two of the three citations to this source are included in Table

Table 5.2 Sample From Source Text and Student Paper

	Student text (page 6 of paper)	Source text (page 2 of source)
(1) Paraphrase	Evidence of a jump in interest can be seen in a jump from **258 journal articles** that were **published** in **1996** on the subject of **cannabis**, to **over 2,100 studies** that were published in **scientific** journals in **2008** (Recent Research on Medicinal Marijuana).	A keyword search using the terms "cannabis, 1996" (the year California voters became the first of 14 states to allow for the drug's medical use under state law) reveals just **258** scientific **journal articles published** on the subject during that year. Perform this same search for the year **2008,** and one will find **over 2,100 published** scientific **studies**.
(2) Patchwriting	Most importantly, **investigators are** now **studying the anti-cancer properties of** cannabinoids. There is an increasing amount **of preclinical and clinical data** that conclude **that cannabinoids** stop **the spread**ing **of specific cancer cells** through **programmed cell death** and the prevention of the forming of **new blood vessels** (Recent Research on Medicinal Marijuana).	**Investigators are** also **studying the anti-cancer activities of** cannabis, as a growing body **of preclinical and clinical data** concludes **that cannabinoids** can reduce **the spread of specific cancer cells** via apoptosis (**programmed cell death**) and by the inhibition of angiogenesis (**the formation of new blood vessels**).

STUDENT CITATION:
"Recent Research on Medical Marijuana." NORML. April 1, 2009. www.norml.org/index.cfm?Group_ID=7002.

5.2. The third is another example of patchwriting on the same page of the student paper.

The material in the first block of student text in Table 5.2 meets our definition of paraphrase ("Restating a phrase, clause, or one or two sentences while using *no more than 20 percent of the language of the source*"). Although this sentence follows the order of the two sentences in the source text and includes some of the same words, the information is reproduced in one sentence that uses original language. The words that are reproduced are mostly single words and many are specific terms, such as "journal article" and "scientific."

The second extract in Table 5.2 is taken from the next paragraph of the student paper. If we compare the first extract with the second, which we code as patchwriting, we can see the difference between these two ways of incorporating source material. In this second passage of student text, 26 of the 41 words in the source sentence have been reproduced exactly, and another seven have been replaced by synonyms or closely related terms ("cannabis" is replaced by "cannabinoids," and "growing body" with "increasing amount," for example). While some words and phrases have been omitted, the student text follows the same order as the source text and does not add anything original to the sentence or the presentation of the information. This fits our definition of patchwriting: "Restating a phrase, clause, or one or more sentences while staying close to the language or syntax of the source." In addition to repeating words and phrases, the student sentence follows the overall shape of the passage from the source.

Even if the sample of patchwriting in Table 5.2 had been rewritten into a successful paraphrase, it would still be working from just one sentence of the source. We would not, though, be able to see that if we did not read the source material and then track how the student used it.

Inter-Coder Reliability

Coders were placed randomly into pairs so no two coders worked together on all of the papers from a single institution (and at least one of the two coders was from an institution other than the one whose papers were being coded). Data from their coding was entered into a spreadsheet for each paper, and then coders convened to review their coding and recode as needed, until consensus was reached. Then the information was added to the source-coding information in the SPSS database.[9]

Where it occurred, variation tended to come from a form of halo effect: Coders sometimes "gave the benefit of the doubt" to otherwise well-written papers and coded passages as paraphrase rather than patchwriting, or summary rather than paraphrase.[10] We found ourselves wanting the students to do well—a very different experience than we have when we set out to "catch plagiarism." Once we became aware of this tendency, we adjusted for it and the process of calibration corrected any potential miscoding by requiring coders to "report the evidence, not a rating" as recommended by those who have studied the effect (Thorndike 1920, 29). The lead researchers blind-coded sources and papers to further ensure inter- and intra-coder reliability and very rarely disagreed with a classification in the final, calibrated data.

Findings
The Papers

The majority of the papers in our database are traditional first-year writing research papers with an argumentative thesis in the introduction and sources used to construct and support that thesis. In their study of handouts for research assignments collected from 28 colleges and universities, Alison Head and Michael Eisenberg (2010) found that "although the topics vary, the assignments consistently demand inquiry, argument, and evidence" (2) with 83 percent requiring students to "write a paper that provides supportive evidence from outside sources" (7).

We did not ask institutions to provide the assignments to which the papers we coded responded, but based on our analysis of the papers, we hypothesize that if we had done so, our findings would be similar to Head and Eisenberg's. Only 54 percent of the assignments in Head and Eisenberg's sample left the students to select their own topic, but their sample came from faculty and courses from across the curriculum (6). Given the range of topics in the papers submitted from each of the 16 institutions, we believe that the majority of students in our sample selected their own topics.

The Data

Our first research question was focused on Perrin's (1959) claim that a writer "should read and digest the material, [and] get it into his own words (except for brief, important quotations that are shown to be quotations)" (636). How frequently is it the case that students "get it into [their] own words?" How many times do they choose to paraphrase or summarize their sources as they develop a researched paper, and how often does the paraphrase fall short and become patchwriting instead? Our research did not ask whether students made wise decisions, or why they made the choices they did. We simply coded and counted incidences of each. The data in Table 5.3 show the frequency of each kind of citation among the 1,911 citations we coded.

Reading the table row by row, one quickly sees that when these 174 students cited exact copying, they usually marked it as quotation, either with block indenting or with quotation marks. Only 4.34 percent of the 1,911 citations were to direct copying not marked as quotation, whereas 41.50 percent of the citations were to direct copying marked as quotation. Regardless of whether the omission of quotation marks was accidental, what we see is that 45.84 percent of the students simply

Table 5.3   Analysis of Source Use in 1,911 Student Citations[11]

Predominant use of source material within the citation		Frequency	Percent	Valid Percent	Cumulative Percent
Valid	Copy without quotation marks	83	4.34	4.34	4.34
	Copy with quotation marks	793	41.50	41.50	45.84
	Patchwriting	306	16.01	16.01	61.85
	Paraphrasing	609	31.87	31.87	93.72
	Summary	120	6.28	6.28	**100.0**
	Total	**1,911**	**100.0**	**100.0**	

transcribed the words of others. A further 31.87 percent of all of the citations were paraphrased, and 16.01 percent were patchwritten. Adding these to the percentage of citations that were to quoted material, we see that 93.72 percent of the 1,911 citations were written from isolated sentences in the source texts. Only 6.28 percent of the citations were to three or more sentences that the student writer had summarized.

The data in Table 5.3 present overall patterns of source use within the 1,911 citations; however, these numbers do not tell us how many individual papers included each type of source use—which was our second research question. We answered this question by analyzing individual papers, and that analysis reveals a slightly different pattern. The data in Table 5.4 show how many of the 174 papers included at least one example of each type of source use in the sample coded.

We only coded five pages in each paper, so there may have been other types of source use in parts of each paper that we did not code. This means we cannot say categorically that something did *not* occur *in the paper*—only that it did or did not occur in the sample we coded. With that caveat, we see a distinct contrast between the frequency of each type of source use in the 1,911 citations and the frequency within each paper.

Table 5.4   Analysis of Source Use in Each of the 174 Student Papers

		Frequency			Percent		
Type of Source Use Occurring at Least Once in the Paper		Occurs at least once in pages 2–6	Does not occur in pages 2–6	Frequency Total	Occurs at least once in pages 2–6	Does not occur in pages 2–6	Percentage Total
Valid	Copying not marked as quotation	33	141	174	19.0	81.0	100
	Copying marked as quotation	159	15	174	91.4	8.6	100
	Patchwriting	91	83	174	52.3	47.7	100
	Paraphrasing	135	39	174	77.6	22.4	100
	Summarizing	71	103	174	40.8	59.2	100

Table 5.3 reveals a total of 120 incidences of summary in the 1,911 citations; however, Table 5.4 shows that only 71 of the papers (40.8 percent) included *any* incidences of summary. Further analysis of those papers reveals that of the 103 that included no summary, 18 included no paraphrase either, although seven of them included patchwriting— failed paraphrase. The remaining 11 papers depended exclusively on copying in the pages we coded. Although only 11 papers contained no source use other than quotation, the vast majority, 159 of the 174 papers (91.4 percent), included at least one quotation. The majority of papers also included at least one incidence of paraphrase (77.6 percent), but a little over half (52.3 percent) included patchwriting. Of the students who patchwrote, the majority also paraphrased at least once.

If 40.8 percent of the papers include at least one summary and 77.6 percent include at least one paraphrase, we might conclude that the students in our sample are engaging with the material, after all. However, other data complicate this interpretation. Our third question asked where in the source students found the material they cited (see Table 5.5).

Table 5.5   Page in Source From Which the Cited Material Is Drawn

Page in source from which material is cited	Frequency	Percent	Valid Percent	Cumulative Percent
Valid Page 1 of the source	885	46.31	46.31	46.31
Page 2 of the source	443	23.18	23.18	69.49
Page 3 of the source	151	7.90	7.90	77.39
Page 4 of the source	100	5.23	5.23	82.62
Page 5 of the source	73	3.82	3.82	86.44
Page 6 of the source	48	2.52	2.52	88.96
Page 7 of the source	31	1.62	1.62	90.58
Page 8 of the source and beyond	180	9.42	9.42	**100.00**
Total	**1,911**	**100**	**100**	

The majority, 46.31 percent of the students' 1,911 citations, come from page 1 of the source. Adding in page 2 takes this percentage up to 69.49 percent, and a full 82.62 percent of all of the citations came from one of the first four pages of the source cited—regardless of the length of the source. Only 9.42 percent of the citations refer to material from page 8 or beyond in the source. Taking this finding into account casts doubt on how engaged the student writers were with the sources they were citing.

Discussion

Misused Source Material: Incorrectly
Quoted or Patchwritten Passages

Of the 1,911 citations we studied (Table 5.3), only 4.34 percent were to material that was cited and copied but not marked as quotation; however, when we look at the 174 papers themselves (Table 5.4) we see that this phenomenon is quite widespread. A total of 19.0 percent of all of the papers include at least one incidence of direct copying that was cited but not marked as quotation. Similarly, Table 5.3 reveals that within the 1,911 citations, 16.01 percent were patchwritten from the source; however, as we see in Table 5.4, a total of 52.3 percent of the 174 papers included at least one incidence of cited patchwriting within the pages we coded. In all, over half of the papers (56 percent), a total of 98 of the 174 papers, included at least one instance of either incorrectly marked quotation or patchwritten prose, and 26 (15 percent) of them included both. These two ways of incorporating source information are designated at best as misuse of sources, and at many institutions they are classified as plagiarism.[12]

This phase of the Citation Project research works only with decontextualized textual artifacts, so we cannot yet report on student intentions. Our hypothesis, though, is that when writers cite patchwritten material, they are attempting to produce paraphrase. Similarly, we suspect that most student writers who cite a source but omit quotation marks are not intending to deceive. Regardless of intentions, the fact that over half of the students reproduced the ideas of the source in a copied or patchwritten passage that they cited but did not mark as quotation should give us pause. It suggests that policies defining these forms of source use as plagiarism may need to be revised or at least revisited; the textual evidence suggests that the students were not writing well from their sources, but not that they were attempting to claim authorship of passages they did not themselves compose. The difference between unsuccessful writing from sources and academic dishonesty is an important one.

Data-Mined Source Material:
Quoted and Paraphrased Passages

When we focus on academic integrity as the gold standard for assessing students' use of sources, we spend less time asking what is happening in student papers that use sources correctly. The cumulative percent column of Table 5.3 raises a different issue, one that we consider more significant than *mis*use of sources. Within the 1,911 citations, 45.84 percent are to passages that incorporate source material by simply transcribing those sources. In Perrin's (1959) terms, nearly half the time the students were not *composing* from sources.

Quotation holds an essential place in academic discourse, bringing multiple voices to bear on the topic at hand, respecting the precise articulation of a source. We use quotation extensively in this chapter. Quotation does not, however, reveal how much the citer has engaged with the cited text. When a writer only copies from sources, the reader does not necessarily know whether or how well the source has been read. And this is a key question in assessing students' writing from sources.

The use of paraphrase in pedagogy dates back at least to Erasmus (Corbett 1971), and although 77.6 percent of the 174 students paraphrased at least once in the part of the paper we coded (Table 5.4), paraphrase occurred far less frequently than copying, with only 31.87 percent of the 1,911 citations being successful paraphrases (Table 5.3). Even if we combine the percentage of successful paraphrase (31.87 percent) with unsuccessful paraphrase—patchwriting—(16.01 percent), we are still left with less than half of the citations reflecting the kind of intellectual intensity David Maas (2002) describes as central to paraphrase. Further, if we review the numbers in the cumulative column of Table 5.3 again, we see that in 93.72 percent of these 1,911 citations the students were sentence-mining. Copying, paraphrasing, and patchwriting all work from isolated sentences. Only summary works beyond the sentence level.

Digested Source Material: Summary and Paraphrase

In their textbook *Writing Analytically*, David Rosenwasser and Jill Stephen (2006) go so far as to assert, "Summary is the standard way that reading—not just facts and figures but also other people's theories and observations—enters your writing" (117). Judging from the Citation Project findings, Rosenwasser and Stephen are, like Perrin (1959), articulating an ideal rather than describing students' practice. Summary accounts for only 120 (6.28 percent) of the 1,911 citations (Table 5.3). While it is true that 71 of the 174 students (40.8 percent) summarized at least once in their papers (Table 5.4), most of them did so *only* once. Using Perrin's terminology, only 40.8 percent of the papers showed evidence that the student had "digested" *any* of the ideas of the source by summarizing them. It is important to remember that "summary" here can mean something as small as "summary of three consecutive sentences." It also includes one-sentence general plot summaries of works of literature that may have been read for the class. Even with that expansive definition of "summary," we found only 120 incidences of it in 800 pages of student-researched writing (Table 5.3).

Location of Cited Material Within the Source

When we saw the data in Tables 5.3 and 5.4, we wanted to think that surely they did not reflect the best of the students' abilities. Surely, far more often than these data show, the students *did* understand the source and simply weren't demonstrating it by paraphrasing or summarizing. One can engage with the entire source even if one only quotes from it; however, in many such cases we would expect those quotations to be taken from strategic places within the text. Table 5.5 challenges that optimism. Not only are students deciding to use quotation to incorporate the majority of their source material, but those quotations usually come from the first or second page of the source. Of the 1,911 citations, 46.31 percent are to the first page of the source, and a further 23.18 percent to the second page (Table 5.5).

As with our other data, this finding does not prove that students are not reading the entire source. The first two pages of most academic texts provide some form of summary of the material to follow in the form of an abstract or set of introductory paragraphs that include a thesis or findings to be discussed. In this chapter, we have quoted or paraphrased material from the first page of some of our sources, a notable example being our footnote describing the halo effect in research. In most cases, though, we also reproduce material from elsewhere in the source. To provide only a series of thesis statements or major findings is to fail to provide nuance; readers do not know how the thesis was reached, what constraints surround it, or what role it played in the argument of the source. When students do not include that information, at the very least they reveal that they do not understand its significance. We suspect that this lack of understanding may be at the heart of the problem. While some students may not understand what they read, others may simply not understand what will be gained from reading an entire source, when all the "evidence" they need is right there in the introduction. In other words, our data may be revealing that students do not know how to read academic sources or how to work with them to create an insightful paper.

Our data reveal this tendency to sentence-mine from the first two or three pages from each source text regardless of the overall length of that source. While two of the 174 papers do provide quite extensive summaries of an article that is more than six pages in length (one in each paper), and a few more provide plot summaries of works of fiction, very few of the papers quote or paraphrase from several different pages in one source or draw on one or more sources throughout.

Conclusion

When 93.72 percent of the citations in 174 students' researched writing papers from 16 disparate U.S. colleges and universities are working only with sentences from the sources and are drawing those sentences from pages 1 or 2 of the source 69.49 percent of the time, we can conclude that these papers offer scant evidence that the students can comprehend and make use of complex written text. Maybe they can; but they don't.

Our data raise the question of whether first-year students who are asked to write college-level researched papers have a full understanding of what that means. If they are told that their task is to make an argument and provide evidence supporting it from a number of sources, as Head and Eisenberg (2010) found many of our assignments require, then reading and engaging with those sources may seem counterproductive to the students. A reader who was sentence-mining this chapter might skip our methodology section entirely (indeed, in many disciplines this might be appropriate if the data are sufficiently clear); however, if that writer also skips the discussion, he or she might end up using our data as evidence for a claim that it cannot support.

Similarly, like several other authors in this collection (for example, see Purdy and Silva in Chapters 6 and 7, respectively), we do not present a thesis or finding until several pages into the chapter. A reader expecting a thesis on the first page might simply skip the entire chapter. Or, if challenged to summarize the argument in this chapter, an inexperienced reader of academic texts might report that we argue that writers "should be able to *talk* about the subject before [they] *write* about it" (a claim we quote from one of our sources on our first page). Another reader, having learned that we work on plagiarism, might search this document for terms such as "patchwriting" and use this article to provide a definition of that term or a statistic about its frequency, or maybe that reader would quote our recommendation that patchwriting be considered misuse of sources rather than plagiarism. Is any of that wrong? Not in the least. Would the reader have "digested" the broader argument? Not at all.

If writing instructors' goal in assigning the research paper is to use it as a vehicle to teach information literacy skills, synthesis of ideas, or argumentation, we seem to be failing. Our data, we believe, reveal a problem that our pedagogy should address. These and other Citation Project findings suggest a compelling need to overhaul the teaching of researched writing in college classes; what we are doing right now is producing results that no one can celebrate.

We hope that our campus librarians and our faculty colleagues in writing programs and across the disciplines will take these findings as a mandate for instructional change. For example, we believe that we must offer instruction designed to bring students to a deep engagement with sources, of the sort that enables them to talk *with* and *about* a source rather than merely mine sentences from it. This involves walking students through texts and modeling for them the kind of engaged reading and rereading that we expect of them. It also involves teaching and assigning summary-writing and the process of building summaries into a text. As Head and Eisenberg (2010) recommend, it means providing careful instructions for the researched paper that focus on the purpose and method rather than the punishment for failure to correctly cite sources. This research has led us as teachers to replace the end-of-semester researched paper with shorter papers that are source-based, but that use fewer sources and require students to engage with their arguments and build them into a conversation. At the very least, we urge our colleagues to focus attention not on the ethics of plagiarism, but on source use as "a sign of good workmanship, part of the morality of writing" as Perrin (1959, 636) puts it.

Endnotes

1. While the two of us, as principal researchers, have shepherded the work described in this article, many able, dedicated compositionists have worked as our co-researchers and are listed at www.citationproject.net (2012).

2. "Patchwriting" stands between quotation and paraphrase; it is neither an exact copying nor a complete restatement, and scholars such as Howard (1992) and

Pecorari (2003) have argued that it typically results from an incomplete comprehension of the source.

3. Examples of this include research on student information literacy skills by members of the library sciences and second language studies disciplines, and research on source use (and misuse) by psychologists and anthropologists.

4. Linda Smith (1981) elegantly describes what this type of research accomplishes: "In general, a citation implies a relationship between a part or the whole of the cited document and a part or the whole of the citing document. Citation analysis is that area of bibliometrics which deals with the study of these relationships" (83). See also Howard White (2004).

5. We give special thanks to Drew University Professor of Statistics Sarah Abramowitz, who generously advised us in this process.

6. We wish to thank Drew University for two faculty research grants, the McGraw-Hill corporation for an additional research grant to support the coding of data, and Binghamton and Syracuse Universities for providing staff and material support.

7. Like Mary Ann Gillette and Carol Videon (1998), we found tracking down these sources to be a challenge. In some cases we had to go through 30 papers to get 10 whose sources we could locate. That process taught us a lot about how much students struggle to identify the components of sources gathered electronically: Who is the author? What is the title? Who is the publisher? These things are far from clear to the majority of students whose papers we source-searched. But not all of the problems with source retrieval were because the student was at fault. Some institutions make available to their students collections of sources in databases such as the Opposing Viewpoints Series, to which our coders did not have access. This aspect of source selection is another finding of this research that we will explore elsewhere.

8. We have made our methods and training materials available to help people understand our data. The reliability and validity of Citation Project data comes from a methodology developed over half a decade and from careful training and calibration of coders. We believe that citation analysis can be a valuable pedagogical tool, a very effective part of faculty development, and a useful component in course and program assessment as we discuss at the end of this chapter. We do not, though, invite people to use our methods and identify them as Citation Project research without our permission.

9. Statistical Package for the Social Sciences (SPSS)—renamed Predictive Analytical Soft Ware Statistics (PASW), but still generally referred to as SPSS—is a series of integrated computer programs that allow researchers to record and review data and produce various forms of statistical analysis and reports. Tables 5.3, 5.4, and 5.5 in this chapter were generated by SPSS using the data we entered. Although PASW includes a mechanism to test for inter-coder reliability and variation

among coder's decisions, we only entered final data once coding pairs had reconciled their coding sheets. For this reason we do not have PASW inter-coder
reliability data. Because this research requires human judgment and interpretation, it is essential for coders to reach consensus on each individual citation.
Where there were disagreements, one of the principal researchers joined the conversation to ensure consistency. The data for calibration papers coded by all
coders therefore show 100 percent agreement rather than capturing the nuance
of that conversation.

10. The Halo effect in empirical research, first described by Edward Thorndike in
1920 (25), occurs when one trait (in his case, physical attractiveness; in our case,
effective writing) influences researchers' assessment of other traits (in his case,
character; in our case, use of sources). More recent studies confirm his finding and
add that the effect "extends to alteration of judgments about attributes for which
we generally assume we are capable of rendering independent assessments,"
including in one example, students' writing (Nisbett and Wilson 1977, 250, 251).

11. For those unfamiliar with SPSS output tables, figures listed under "Valid Percent"
are the percentages excluding any missing data. If any citations had been counted
but not coded, that count would have been recorded in "Frequency" along with a
percentage under "Percent," with the adjusted percentage of the five relevant traits
appearing in "Valid Percent." In this case, all incidences of source use were counted
and coded as one of the five traits, so "Percent" and "Valid Percent" are the same.

12. See the Council of Writing Program Administrators' Best Practices document for
the differences between *plagiarism* and *misuse of sources* (www.wpacouncil.org/
node/9). We agree that examples of cited patchwriting such as those presented in
Table 5.2 should be defined as a misuse of source material, as should examples
where the student omits to block or otherwise mark a cited quotation.

References

Anson, Chris M. 2008. "The Intelligent Design of Writing Programs: Reliance on
Belief or a Future of Evidence?" *WPA: Writing Program Administration* 31 (3):
11–38.

Brown, Ann L., and Jeanne D. Day. 1983. "Macrorules for Summarizing Texts: The
Development of Expertise." *Journal of Verbal Learning and Verbal Behavior* 22:
1–14.

Buranen, Lise, and Denise Stephenson. 2008. "Collaborative Authorship in the
Sciences: Anti-Ownership and Citation Practices in Chemistry and Biology." In
Who Owns This Text? Plagiarism, Authorship, and Disciplinary Cultures, edited by
Carol Peterson Haviland and Joan Mullin, 49–79. Logan, UT: Utah State
University Press.

The Citation Project. 2012. Accessed September 17, 2012. www.citationproject.net.

Corbett, Edward P. J. 1971. "The Theory and Practice of Imitation in Classical Rhetoric." *College Composition and Communication* 22: 243–250.

Council of Writing Program Administrators. 2003. "Defining and Avoiding Plagiarism: The WPA Statement on Best Practices." Accessed September 17, 2012. www.wpacouncil.org.

Gillette, Mary Ann, and Carol Videon. 1998. "Seeking Quality on the Internet: A Case Study of Composition Students' Works Cited." *Teaching in English in the Two-Year College* 26 (2): 189–194.

Head, Alison J., and Michael B. Eisenberg. 2010. "Assigning Inquiry: How Handouts for Research Assignments Guide Today's College Students." *Project Information Literacy Progress Report.* Accessed September 17, 2012. www.projectinfolit.org/pdfs/PIL_Handout_Study_finalvJuly_2010.pdf.

Howard, Rebecca Moore. 1992. "A Plagiarism *Pentimento.*" *Journal of Teaching Writing* 11 (2): 233–246.

Howard, Rebecca Moore, Tricia Serviss, and Tanya K. Rodrigue. 2010. "Writing from Sources, Writing from Sentences." *Writing and Pedagogy* 2 (2): 177–192.

Maas, David. 2002. "Make Your Paraphrasing Plagiarism-Proof with a Coat of E-Prime." *et Cetera* 59 (2): 196–205.

Nisbett, Richard E., and Timothy D. Wilson. 1977. "The Halo Effect: Evidence for Unconscious Alteration of Judgments." *Journal of Personality and Social Psychology* 35 (4): 250–256.

Pecorari, Diane. 2003. "Good and Original: Plagiarism and Patchwriting in Academic Second Language Writing." *Journal of Second Language Writing* 12: 317–345.

Perrin, Porter, with Karl W. Dykema. 1959. *Writer's Guide and Index to English*, 3rd ed. Chicago: Scott Foresman.

Rosenwasser, David, and Jill Stephen. 2006. *Writing Analytically*, 4th ed. Boston: Thomson.

Smith, Linda. 1981. "Citation Analysis." *Library Trends* (Summer): 83–106.

Thorndike, Edward L. 1920. "A Constant Error in Psychological Rating." *Journal of Applied Psychology* 4 (1): 25–29.

White, Howard D. 2004. "Citation Analysis and Discourse Analysis Revisited." *Applied Linguistics* 25 (1): 89–116.

CHAPTER 6

Scholarliness as Other: How Students Explain Their Research-Writing Behaviors

James P. Purdy

Beyond Catch and Release

Attend nearly any meeting with faculty across campus who teach research-based writing and stories frequently turn to attribution problems and plagiarism. Such discussion can be contagious;[1] faculty member after faculty member bemoans having to spend time marking every citation error or tracking down sources from which students plagiarized. The understandable frustration teachers feel with this approach signals its futility—and the need for a change.

Rather than focus discussions of student research around potentially plagiarized products, I argue we should direct our attention to students' research practices. A product-centered approach problematically makes plagiarism detection services an attractive "solution." When the teacher's job is to find and mark product errors (e.g., citation mistakes, copied text), arguments for tools that expedite those activities are persuasive. Leading plagiarism detection service Turnitin indicates that, as of December 2011, over 1 million teachers from over 10,000 high schools and colleges use its services, which translates to Turnitin processing over 300,000 papers per day (Turnitin 2012). These statistics show that attempts to discourage use of plagiarism detection services have been of limited success—at least outside of writing studies. As long as teachers approach students' research-based texts as markers of error, such efforts will continue to be hampered as means to make mistakes quickly visible will continue to be attractive.[2]

Focusing primarily on product violations or flaws also counters writing studies' proclaimed valuation of process and its advances in writing pedagogy and theory. This approach treats research processes much as textbooks treated writing processes prior to the writing process movement, as linear, discrete, prescribed, quantifiable steps (Purdy and Walker 2012, 19–23). It also fosters "a universalized conception of plagiarism" that diminishes the social and contextual nature of writing (Robillard and Howard 2008, 2) and ignores the culpability of academic institutions that reify "originality while ignoring the complexity of knowledge-building" (Haviland and Mullin 2009, 165). This approach leads students to experience "originality despair" (Haviland and Mullin 2009, 162) and focus on "error avoidance" rather than learning (Yancey 2008, 158; see also Purdy 2009, 73). A primarily error-focused view diminishes research-writing's complexity, recursivity, and situatedness, and thereby perpetuates an inaccurate and damaging view of research-based writing.

Perhaps most damaging, this seek-out-product-error approach offers research instruction as a means to reveal students' inadequacies rather than to build on their capabilities. In other words, it constructs instruction as a way to gate-keep rather than produce knowledge. Teachers thereby assume roles other than teacher, such as cop, warrior, or detective, that can be counterproductive because the focus shifts from teaching and learning to detection and punishment (Anson 2008; Howard 2001; Purdy 2005; Warnock 2006). Certainly, intentional unethical source use needs to have consequences. As Thomas S. Dee and Brian A. Jacob (2010) argue, however, students are more likely to change their source use practices in response to instruction instead of threats (3, 27). Carol Peterson Haviland and Joan A. Mullin

(2009) agree that "when positioned as readers and writers rather than as punishment avoiders, students can describe ownership and citation practices in readerly-writerly terms" (172). These scholars support the idea that education ultimately proves more effective than punishment. Teaching appropriate and ethical source use is an important component of research instruction in writing classes, but doing so through the lens of plagiarism detection neither matches our theoretical underpinnings nor proves an effective means to shape student behavior.

We should instead refocus our attention to study students' predilections and practices for research-based writing tasks, particularly what students say they do and what they actually do. The premise for this approach is that a more productive way to address anxieties about students as researchers is to find out what they are doing and how they represent and explain what they are doing rather than to focus only on their written products and technologies of detection. Instead of concentrating on the text after it has been written, as a focus on plagiarism detection does, we are better served to focus also on students' processes in writing their research-based texts, particularly their use of digital resources.[3]

Studying Student Research Practices

In this section I discuss a study that begins to achieve this goal of learning more about how students use and say they use available tools, particularly digital resources, to complete research-based writing tasks.[4] The project is especially interested in the ways in which student perceptions match—and do not match—what students do for academic projects.

This project comprises several parts:

1. The first is a questionnaire on students' thoughts about their research practices and identities. To encourage honest feedback, I instructed students to complete questionnaires anonymously, unless they indicated interest in participating further in the study (e.g., being interviewed). Questions, as

shown in Appendix A, addressed two aspects of student approaches to research: attitudes and activities. In addition to asking for background information, such as major and year, the survey included 10 questions that provided a mix of qualitative and quantitative data. Seven were open-ended, short-answer response questions. Three asked students to rate or select from available choices.

2. The second is a research log asking students to record the steps they followed in finding sources for course projects over an entire semester.

3. The third is an essay asking students to reflect on their research logs, what they learned, what worked and what did not, and why they did what they did.

4. The fourth is a digital research skills assessment asking students to find particular information online. The skills assessment was an in-class search modeling activity that asked students to locate information for four different online sources. As shown in Appendix B, each of the four questions comprised multiple parts, asking students to record specific details about the text they found (e.g., publication date, the first sentence) and the steps for how they found that information.

For this chapter, I studied these four categories of texts for students at one university.[5]

All instructors teaching the second semester writing course at a mid-sized Midwestern university were asked to distribute the questionnaire to students in their classes. Of 1,169 questionnaires distributed, 523 were returned. The corpus for the research log/reflection and research skills assessments was texts from one class of 17 students. Both groups were mostly first-year students with majors from across campus. The study focuses on students enrolled in first-year writing classes because these classes are often the site of instruction in research-based writing for the majority of students in postsecondary education. These writing classes, therefore, take on particular importance in student research training and identity formation.

Tensions in What Students Say and Do

This chapter shares three results from the study that highlight tensions regarding students' perceptions and actions. All point to students' sense of scholarliness as "other," something foreign and external to the digital spaces they inhabit.

Result 1: Google and Context

Google was students' preferred research tool and starting place. Students, however, showed some context awareness in deciding when to use Google and when to use other research resources.

What Students Said

Students said they like Google and use it often. On the surface, this result is expected. Examining it further, however, yields some surprises. In the questionnaire, 312 students listed Google as their favorite digital research tool. One student even noted using Google "about 20 times a day" for nonacademic research tasks. This total is more than three times the total for the next resource, which is Google Scholar: 94. Taken together, both Google-affiliated resources account for 73.6 percent of students' favorite digital research resources (406 of 552[6]). Clearly, students preferred this search engine as a means to find information when conducting research.

Not only did students identify Google as their favorite research tool, but they also identified it as the first place they go, particularly when doing nonacademic research. Google was listed by 231 students as the first site they visit for nonacademic research tasks. Google was far and away the top vote getter—receiving eight and a half times more votes than the second place resource, Wikipedia (with 27 votes). Students claimed to use Google more for nonacademic research tasks than academic research tasks, however. When it comes to academic research, students, perhaps because they thought they should, indicated that they start with library databases more often than Google: 230 to 190 votes, respectively. This result shows that students in the study, who came from diverse majors, behaved in a way consistent with the humanities and social science majors Alison J. Head (2007, 2008) and Head and Michael B. Eisenberg (2009) studied who said that they start academic research projects with library-related resources or course texts more frequently than public search engines like Google.

Even those students who indicated that they start academic research with Google shared that they often use Google and library resources together. They gathered background information on their topic with Google and then turned to the library to find more specific and credible information. Several students, for instance, explained, "[I] google [the] topic at first—to get ideas—then use library databases to get specific reliable facts," "I usually begin with google [*sic*] to get simple questions answered and then I use the library database to find scholarly articles," and "[I] start at Google to get a general sense of the topic; then I go to Google Scholar and the library's website to find credible information." These responses illustrate that Google was one step, not the only step, in students' research processes for academic writing tasks. Their non-mutually exclusive use of Google and the library reinforces Purdy and Walker's finding (2007) that students use nonacademic and academic online resources together. This combined use also challenges concerns that students ignore the library in favor of Google—or that they use only Google all of the time.

These results indicate context awareness: Students reported that they used Google more for nonacademic research and used it together with the library, rather than alone, for academic research. Because students conceive of Google itself as nonscholarly, they recognized a need to (say they) use it differently depending on the research task. Two students aptly summarized this larger idea: "It really depends on what I am researching" and "what I am doing research on ... directly relates to where I start." Comments such as these show that students were sensitive to purpose in deciding how to use their favorite research tool.

What Students Did

Students' academic research activities to some extent illustrate what they said about Google. In the digital research skills assessments, all but one student used Google at some point to find information, which reinforces questionnaire results regarding students' affinity for Google. Students, however, ultimately used Google as a starting place more than library databases—even though in the questionnaire most claimed that they use the library first for academic research tasks. Google was the most common first step for all four questions. Students used library databases first for only one question, though they could have used them first for all four. They still used library resources, though; 11 of 16 students[7] consulted the library website at some point during the assessment.

In the research logs, however, Google did not dominate. Students used proprietary library databases more. For course assignments requiring outside sources, students indicated that they used Google 11 times, Google Scholar 10 times, and library databases 26 times. That is, students used library databases over twice as many times as Google, action consistent with what they said they did for academic research tasks. They also started with the library website and library databases more than Google—12 students started with the library as opposed to four who began with Google—a result consistent with what they said in their questionnaires.

Time, therefore, was seemingly an important factor (Chapter 10 further discusses effects of time constraints on students' practices). Students used Google more frequently when they had less time to find sought materials, as they did with the research skills assessment that they completed in class. When they had more time to complete research tasks, as they did with the research logs and reflections that they completed outside of class, they used library resources more often than Google.

Conclusions

These data show that students were aware (at least superficially) of which resources are best suited for academic and nonacademic research tasks. Students knew academic tasks require scholarly sources and that Google does not necessarily or reliably return these sources. Thus, they framed Google, a resource they use frequently, as nonscholarly—suitable for academic work only in its Google Scholar instantiation or in conjunction with the library. Such results suggest that students know the limitations of Google (even if they use it in spite of them).

These data also suggest that we need to pay serious attention to Google as a research resource. As a primary gateway to students' academic and nonacademic research, it plays an important role in shaping their practices and determining which sources they consult, whether they use it alone or in conjunction with library resources. We should, therefore, exploit possibilities for linking Google to library resources, explicitly teach students ways to take advantage of Google's advanced search features, and acquaint them with the Google Scholar option. Given students' response to time constraints, we might also reinforce that source retrieval need not be fast to be successful and clarify that a time-intensive search is not necessarily bad.

Result 2: Valuing Scholarliness

Students valued scholarly sources but could not necessarily identify them.

What Students Said

In their research log reflections, students indicated that a primary reason they use particular resources for academic research is that those resources return scholarly sources. Thirteen of 15[8] students offered this reason a total of 26 times, which tied for the most identified reason. When explaining their choice of a resource, most students indicated how it reliably provides access to scholarly texts: "I also searched JSTOR and Project Muse, where I knew I would find scholarly sources," "The best part about JSTOR is that I do not even have to worry about validity of the article because all articles stored on the JSTOR database are scholarly and peer reviewed," and "Because I like the set up of google.com, I use googlescholar.com to find my scholarly sources for papers. Google Scholar works just as Google would, but they only give you scholarly papers and results." As these responses reveal, students chose resources based on confidence that those resources return only scholarly results.

Questionnaire responses likewise reinforce that "scholarliness" was a primary criterion in research tool selection. Students, for instance, indicated that they use Google Scholar because "you know its [sic] scholarly;" it is "great at weeding out the crap" and leads to "easy, reliable sources;" it "tells you what is scholarly;" and it is "already checked for being scholarly." Google Scholar was well received and frequently used because students saw it as already vetting the scholarly sources. They could trust its results are scholarly without doing additional evaluating.

This trust showed in students' rating of research resources. As Figure 6.1 illustrates, when asked in the questionnaire to rate on a scale of 1 to 10 the relative importance of different resources in their research, students rated scholarly resources highly. They gave scholarly search engines (e.g., Google Scholar) an average rating of 7.05, which was the second-highest average (behind public search engines like Google); 91 of 520[9] students, or 17.5 percent, gave it a 9, which was the most frequent score. The resources with the third- and fourth-highest averages also are commonly labeled as scholarly sites: library online journal databases and books, earning average scores of 5.79 and 5.41, respectively, with 23.7 percent (123 of 520) answering 8 or 9 for databases.

Other questionnaire results further signal this privileging of scholarliness. In response to the first two survey questions about where they begin their searches for academic and nonacademic research, respectively, students clearly signaled that they value and use what they see as scholarly resources. They, for instance, responded to the first question, "I try to search for articles from reliable sources like PBS or the NY Times [sic]. I also look at google scholar [sic]. Truthfully, I do look at Wikipedia to get a general idea, but I never end my research there

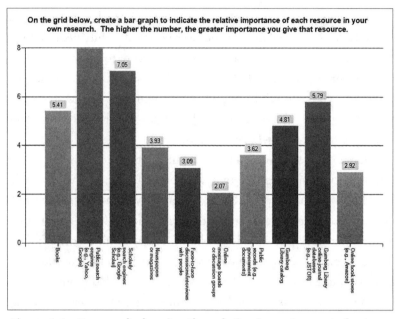

Figure 6.1   Bar graph showing the relative importance students gave research resources[10]

because I know it's not credible," I "search Wikipedia or google [*sic*] to gather basic understanding then move to databases (pubmed [*sic*], etc.) for the real cited research," and "I use Google to find a good website. Never Wikipedia!" Notably, this last student indicated that she or he frequently uses Wikipedia as a starting place for nonacademic research. Several others did, too, and were sure to designate Wikipedia as non-scholarly: "Wikipedia has great nonacademic info!" and "I first browse Wikipedia to get a general overview, then I proceed to sites that are more legitimate." These students positioned Wikipedia as a gateway to "legitimate" and "real" academic sources. Apologies for using resources like Google and Wikipedia, along with caveats that students knew these sources were nonscholarly, characterized students' responses.

In their questionnaire responses, students also associated their weaknesses and strengths as a researcher with the use or nonuse of scholarly resources. For instance, numerous students identified as a weakness their use of Wikipedia, which they represented as nonscholarly:

"Tendency to use Wikipedia," "Still research from Wikipedia," and "I like Wikipedia." Others noted as weaknesses: "Finding a large/appropriate amount of scholarly sources" and "trouble distinguishing what is best article/if they are scholarly." Similarly, students identified as strengths: "I don't use Wikipedia or blogs," "Finding scholarly articles about my topic," and "I know how to identify if a website is credible and applicable." Overall, 78 students identified their ability to find scholarly/credible sources as a strength (the second-highest total) and 46 students identified their inability to find scholarly/credible sources as a weakness (the fourth-highest total).

Notably, as shown in Appendix A, the survey question about strengths and weaknesses asked students about being a researcher in general, not about doing academic research specifically. It reads, "What would you say is your greatest strength as a researcher? What is your greatest weakness?" That students so frequently responded in terms of scholarliness shows that they associated being a good researcher with being adept at finding scholarly sources. These responses and totals illustrate that students saw use of scholarly resources not only as a positive aspect of being a researcher, but also arguably as the defining quality of being a researcher. In other words, they defined researchers as those who work with scholarly sources and believed that the work they do in Google does not make them researchers.

What Students Did

Despite valuing scholarly sources, students did not necessarily retrieve scholarly sources even when looking for them. For the research skills assessment, for instance, only six of 15 students (fewer than half) found the correct article when asked to find a scholarly article on the Piraha tribe. Most listed one of two articles from serious periodicals (rather than peer-reviewed academic journals). For this question, moreover, most students (nine of 15) started their search with a scholarly resource: Google Scholar, JSTOR, other scholarly databases, or the university library. Of these students, only five (33 percent) found a scholarly source. In research logs, students similarly erred. One student, for example, labeled as "scholarly critiques" of Jorge Luis Borges two .com websites without references and with content copied from Wikipedia. While these data reference only a few scholarly source retrieval tasks, they reinforce students' larger confusion about what constitutes a scholarly source and an overreliance on search resources in deciding for them.

Conclusions

Based on these results, students seemed to associate the scholarly label with a database or resource rather than with the specific texts it returned. They tended to designate Wikipedia as nonscholarly and Google Scholar as scholarly and all the sources each returns as nonscholarly and scholarly, respectively. Said another way, students ostensibly assumed scholarly resources (e.g., Google Scholar, online databases) always return scholarly results. This finding coincides with that of Angela Weiler (2005), who likewise affirms that students privilege information source classification over content. She reports that for "Generation Y" students "[t]he source of the information (i.e., information from a 'good authority') takes precedence over the information itself" (51).[11] Students' approach might reflect how in earlier years of schooling students frequently were permitted to use only sources already vetted by others and were not allowed to use other internet sources and, therefore, did not gain experience in evaluating sources on their own. That they are used to being told what to use is exemplified by one student's compliment that her or his school was "good about informing students ... about which internet sources are good to use." Our charge, then, may be helping students respect but not blindly rely on "scholarly" and "nonscholarly" labels. Scholarly activity can be found in many different venues and is not necessarily found in particular publications or databases.

While this finding outwardly seems to be in tension with the finding I describe previously that students showed context awareness in the use of Google, both illustrate that students assigned significant weight to resource designations. They placed trust in the scholarly label, as it was nonscholarly resources that they treated contextually. Because they tended to label Google as nonscholarly, they recognized a need to use it differently for different research tasks (e.g., in conjunction with library resources for academic writing). But when they labeled resources like Google Scholar and library databases as scholarly, many carried that label to all sources these resources returned.

These results might also signal that students thought it was important to say that they privilege scholarly sources. That is, they knew they are supposed to use and want to use scholarly sources in academic contexts. Amy E. Robillard (2008) reinforces that "self-reporting carries with it students' desires to meet our expectations in asking the questions in the first place. The very fact that it is teachers who are asking questions of students about their motivations with regard to academic writing shapes students' responses significantly" (30). Because the questionnaire, research log and reflection, and skills assessment were all associated with academic classes and activities (even if they were not used for a grade), perhaps students responded in ways that they thought academics want to hear. Still, these responses usefully signal that students have learned that they are supposed to value scholarliness. These results suggest that it is not that students do not value (or think they should value) scholarly resources; it is that they have difficulty identifying them.

Result 3: Student Self-Perceptions

Students saw themselves as open, focused, and interested researchers but reported that they do not particularly enjoy research or see what they do as unique.

What Students Said

In the questionnaire, as shown in Figure 6.2, when asked to select from a list of 10 words those that apply to their identity as a researcher, students selected *open*, *focused*, and *interested* most frequently: 298 (of 518,[12] or 57.5 percent[13]), 271 (52.3 percent), and 248 (47.9 percent), respectively. Relatively few students selected *linear* and *tangential*: 39 (7.5 percent) and 45 (8.7 percent), respectively. These responses suggest that while students did not think of themselves as following straight, step-by-step paths, they also did not see themselves as diverging or proceeding haphazardly. Indeed, 174 students (33.6 percent) selected *structured* as descriptive of their identity, perhaps indicating that they imposed (or saw themselves imposing) structure on their research activities.

While these designations may be seen as idiosyncratically characteristic of the student population from one school, students in the pilot study, which was conducted at another university with a different student population, selected the same three top terms and same two bottom terms in the same order of frequency. The consistency of these responses indicates a common self-perception among students that opposes prevailing approaches to research instruction in writing classes, which emphasize linearity and assume student disinterest.

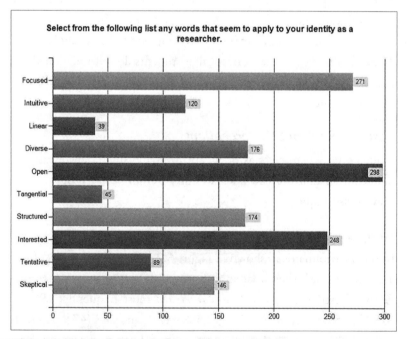

Figure 6.2   Number of students who selected given words to describe themselves as researchers

What students identified as their strengths and weaknesses as researchers reinforces their view of themselves as open researchers. Twenty-five times students listed strengths related to openness, such as "Being open to any information found," "openness to new ideas," "my openness to many views and opinions," "being open to all types of resources," "openness regarding different search tools," and "I am open to different ways a topic is presented in research." As these example responses illustrate, students saw themselves as open to different ideas, viewpoints, resource types, and search tools.

References to strengths of focus and interest were likewise common. Students made 19 and 34 references to focus and interest, respectively. These included, "focused and know what I am looking for in the beginning," "staying focused," "concentration," "being focused enough to find a lot," and "focus on accomplishing tasks." References to interest included, "staying interested in a topic I don't like," "interested to learn," "interest in finding info," "I often get excited and interested in topics," "If the topic interests me I can spend days sifting through evidence and research material," and "I'm naturally interested." These responses reveal students' interest extended to the research process, research sources, and learning in general.

Despite this openness, focus, and interest, most students indicated that they do not enjoy research. Figure 6.3 illustrates how, when asked to rate on a scale of 1 to 5 how much they enjoy doing research, 208 students (of 523, or 39.8 percent) selected 3, 163 (31.2 percent) selected 2, and 85 (16.3 percent) selected 1. Only 67 (12.8 percent) chose 4 or 5, which indicates most students took a neutral to negative stance toward their enjoyment of research activities.

This lack of enjoyment coincides with a perception of banality. The majority of students (278 of 523, or 53.2 percent) indicated that there is nothing unique about their research practices. They either explicitly answered *no* or left the question blank. Two, for instance, responded, "no, I tend to follow the ways I was instructed" and "I was taught a process in high school so it's not unique." Such responses signal that students viewed the processes they were taught as universally

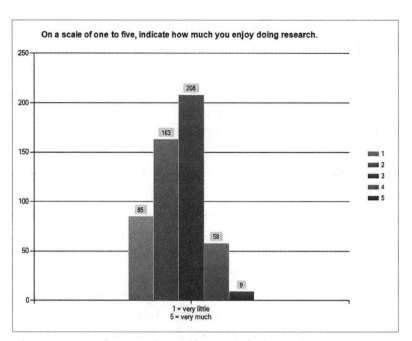

**Figure 6.3   Students' ratings of how much they enjoy
doing research**

applicable; for them, following prescribed instructions limited possibilities for flexibility.

What Students Did

Students did approach research tasks differently. No two students' research logs were the same (see Chapter 8 for more evidence of students' search individualization). Even when students found the same sources, they often did so via different means. For instance, according to their logs, several students used the same essay, "The End of Technology" by Jeffery Pence, as a secondary source for a compare and contrast writing assignment, and they found this essay in different ways: One student retrieved it from the Project Muse database through the library, two students went directly to the Project Muse database (i.e., bypassed the library), another reached it from JSTOR through the library, and six others found it from the course's Blackboard site (which linked to the library's databases). Students also accessed proprietary databases themselves differently: Eleven reached databases through the library website and seven reached them directly from doing a Google Scholar search or typing in the database URL (if done from campus, these methods provided students direct admission to the databases to which the library subscribed).

In the digital research skills assessment, moreover, while many students started with or used Google, their paths sometimes diverged significantly from there. For question 3, for instance, four students started with Google (with two then going immediately to Google Scholar), three students started with Google Scholar, three started with JSTOR, three started with the university library website (with one using it as a link to Google Scholar), one started with Blackboard (the host of the class's website), and another started with the university homepage (using it as a link to the library). This diversity of approaches shows that students do have unique approaches to research, even if they do not recognize this uniqueness.

Conclusions

Students' seemingly contradictory characterization of themselves as open, focused, and interested researchers but not as enjoying research suggests that students, at least in the first couple years of their college careers, approach research tasks with interest but find doing the research itself irksome. Perhaps the process through which they are required to work ultimately makes research less enjoyable for them. Or this tension might mean that students see enjoyment as antithetical to scholarliness. That is, for them research is not meant to be enjoyable. There is, of course, a difference between interest and enjoyment—we can be interested in things we do not enjoy—but such a finding challenges the notion that students inherently and automatically hate research. Rather it reinforces that students do not have a proclivity toward research in academic contexts. Connecting students' nonacademic research activities to their academic practices may lessen this "enjoyment gap" and make assuming the role of researcher more interesting and feasible for them.

This finding may also mean that students do not see research processes as adaptable, that they believe there is only one correct research process to follow. In other words, these results potentially indicate that they do not see uniqueness and flexibility as valuable. We might, therefore, do well to explain to students that research processes are indeed variable and contextual. As with writing, no two people research exactly the same way—and that is OK.

Conclusion: Moving Beyond a Scholarly/Nonscholarly Binary

Though small scale and thereby tentative,[14] this study provides insight into students' research practices that can help us understand how students think about research, conceive of themselves as researchers, and produce research-based texts. The results point to underlying tensions in students' approaches to research-based writing: Students have a strong proclivity for Google but sometimes recognize its limitations for scholarly work; value scholarly sources but have difficulty recognizing them; and characterize themselves as open, focused, and interested researchers but claim not to enjoy research or do anything unique. Taken together, these results indicate that students hold scholarliness as "other," something external to themselves. They associate scholarliness with texts found outside the online spaces they normally inhabit (e.g., Google), and they trust that those resources others label as scholarly (e.g., library databases) necessarily act as a gateway to scholarliness. For many of them, the identity of "scholarly researcher" is disjunctive with their role as digital searchers.

These results show that we as teachers have succeeded in emphasizing for students the importance of using scholarly texts in academic research-based writing—perhaps too well. Students have internalized the scholarly/nonscholarly binary to the point that, at least early in their college careers, they structure their approach to research around where they see themselves and their sources falling in this binary. Their sense of their strengths and weaknesses as researchers correlates with their ability to successfully find and use the right scholarly resources.

Instead of focusing so much on this binary, we need to help students recognize that different types of sources work in different contexts so that "scholarliness" is less an abstract text or database label and more a recognition of use value of particular kinds of knowledge-making. In other words, rather than make scholarliness about identifying particular textual forms, we need to make it about engaging in particular kinds of activities. We might accomplish this goal by encouraging students to apply their contextual approach to Google to other resources (including scholarly ones) and to move beyond a rigid association of scholarly with "good" and citable and nonscholarly with "bad" and noncitable. We need to channel and build on students' openness, focus, and interest so that they see flexibility and uniqueness as valuable aspects of scholarliness.

In doing so, we can likely also help to discourage plagiarism. Some students will regrettably always seek ways to avoid the work necessary for research-based writing. However, if students see knowledge-making through writing as more a process of responding to and building on scholarly texts—that is, of demonstrating their interest in and openness to multiple ideas, viewpoints, and sources—rather than regurgitating the right answer(s) as already presented in other scholarly texts, then they might be less compelled to plagiarize. The value of plagiarized work diminishes when re-presenting "correct" scholarly sources becomes not an end in and of itself but a means to develop new ideas. When we use plagiarism detection services as advertised, we reinforce the notion of scholarliness as "other," positioning it as something students must work toward but can never quite attain. On the other hand, when we represent scholarliness as a set of practices toward which students have already begun to work with their nonacademic research activities, we can make being a scholarly researcher seem more attractive, possible, and relevant.[15]

Endnotes

1. I choose the word "contagious" consciously as discussions of plagiarism are often couched in terms of disease (see Howard 2000).

2. Whether these services accurately identify citation mistakes and plagiarism is questionable, as I argue elsewhere (Purdy 2005) and as Victoria Brown, et al. (2010) report in their study of Turnitin use and faculty concern with its high number of "false positives" (119). Scholars have explored the potential ethical and functional problems of plagiarism detection technologies from a range of perspectives—writing centers (e.g., Brown, et al. 2007), textbook publishers (e.g., Carbone 2001), journalists (e.g., Dehnart 1999), writing program administrators (e.g., Gillis, et al. 2009), writing instructors (e.g., Marsh 2004; Purdy 2009), and librarians (e.g., Royce 2003).

3. For literature reviews of past studies of students' research and research-writing practices, see McClure's Chapter 1, Eliason and Jenks's Chapter 3, and Mirtz's Chapter 8 in this volume.

4. The study was designed by Joyce R. Walker and me, and received IRB approval.

5. For purposes of the study, students' questionnaires and research log reflections represent what students said they do, and students' research logs and research skills assessments represent what they did. Distinguishing what students say from what they do is to some extent artificial, but doing so helps to isolate some illustrative tensions. The logs and assessments, of course, are also forms of self-reporting; as in the questionnaires and reflections, students still framed their activities for an audience. The logs and assessments, however, were assigned as records of students' actual practices and, though potentially a flawed approach, I accept them as such for this study. Robillard (2008) rightly cautions that in using student surveys "we must remember that [students'] responses are contingent and contextual" (30). Self-reports are limited when used in isolation but are an important component of a larger research agenda concerned with student practices and perceptions. Thus, in this chapter I consider them alongside students' research logs and research skills assessments.

6. This number exceeds 523 (the total number of questionnaires) because some students listed two or more research tools as their favorite; 552 is the total number of favorite research resources students listed.

7. This total is 16 rather than 17 students because one student did not complete the assessment.

8. This total is out of 15 rather than 17 students because two students did not complete the research log reflection correctly (i.e., they did not reflect on their own practices).

9. Three students did not answer this question, so the total is 520 rather than 523 students.

10. Graphs were generated by SurveyMonkey online survey software: www.survey monkey.com.

11. There are exceptions. One student, for example, indicated in the questionnaire, "I think the library databases are pretty reliable, but I check them anyways. When using print sources I read only a small amount to determine if I can use it, and I really inspect internet [sites] to make sure the sites are relevant." Such responses, however, were rare.

12. This number is less than 523 because not all students answered this question.

13. Percentages here and following are calculated based on the number of students responding to the question (518) rather than the total number of students (523).

14. The study is limited by its size. The corpus of texts, particularly of research logs/reflections and skills assessments, is not representative or large enough to draw definitive conclusions about students' research practices. It does, however, begin to provide insight into ways in which students are using—and say they are using—digital resources for academic research-writing tasks. Such insight is invaluable in helping us design effective research-based writing tasks and pedagogies.

15. This research project was funded, in part, by a Wimmer Grant from Duquesne University. Research assistants Erin Rentschler and Melissa Wehler provided invaluable assistance with compiling and coding questionnaires, research logs and reflections, and skills assessments.

References

Anson, Chris M. 2008. "We Never Wanted to Be Cops: Plagiarism, Institutional Paranoia, and Shared Responsibility." In *Pluralizing Plagiarism: Identities, Contexts, Pedagogies*, edited by Rebecca Moore Howard and Amy E. Robillard, 140–157. Portsmouth, NH: Boynton/Cook.

Brown, Renee, Brian Fallon, Jessica Lott, Elizabeth Mathews, and Elizabeth Mintie. 2007. "Taking on Turnitin: Tutors Advocating Change." *Writing Center Journal* 27 (1): 7–28.

Brown, Victoria, Robin Jordan, Nancy Rubin, and Gladys Arome. 2010. "Strengths and Weaknesses of Plagiarism Detection Software." *Journal of Literacy and Technology* 11 (1): 111–131.

Carbone, Nick. 2001. "Turnitin.com: A Pedagogic Placebo for Plagiarism." *Bedford/St. Martin's Tech Notes: Technology and Teaching*, June 13. Accessed September 17, 2012. www.bedfordstmartins.com/technotes/techtiparchive/ttip060501.htm.

Dee, Thomas S., and Brian A. Jacob. 2010. "Rational Ignorance in Education: A Field Experiment in Student Plagiarism." *NBER Working Paper Series*. Cambridge, MA: National Bureau of Economic Research. Accessed September 17, 2012. www.swarthmore.edu/Documents/academics/economics/Dee/w15672.pdf.

Dehnart, Andy. 1999. "The Web's Plagiarism Police." *Salon*, June 14. Accessed September 17, 2012. www.salon.com/tech/feature/1999/06/14/plagiarism.

Gillis, Kathleen, Susan Lang, Monica Norris, and Laura Palmer. 2009. "Electronic Plagiarism Checkers: Barriers to Developing an Academic Voice." *WAC Journal* 20: 51–62.

Haviland, Carol Peterson, and Joan A. Mullin. 2009. "Conclusion: Rethinking Our Use of 'Plagiarism.'" In *Who Owns This Text? Plagiarism, Authorship, and Disciplinary Cultures*, edited by Carol Peterson Haviland and Joan A. Mullin, 156–177. Logan, UT: Utah State University Press.

Head, Alison J. 2007. "Beyond Google: How Do Students Conduct Academic Research?" *First Monday* 12 (8). Accessed September 17, 2012. www.first monday.org/issues/issue12_8/head/index.html.

———. 2008. "Information Literacy from the Trenches." *College and Research Libraries* 69 (5): 427–445.

Head, Alison J., and Michael B. Eisenberg. 2009. "Lessons Learned: How College Students Seek Information in the Digital Age." *Project Information Literacy Progress Report*, December. Accessed September 17, 2012. www.projectinfolit.org/pdfs/PIL_Fall2009_Year1Report_12_2009.pdf.

Howard, Rebecca Moore. 2000. "Sexuality, Textuality: The Cultural Work of Plagiarism." *College English* 62: 473–491.

———. 2001. "Forget about Policing Plagiarism. Just Teach." *Chronicle of Higher Education*, November 16. Accessed September 17, 2012. www.chronicle.com/weekly/v48/i12/12b02401.htm.

Marsh, Bill. 2004. "Turnitin.com and the Scriptural Enterprise of Plagiarism Detection." *Computers and Composition* 21 (4): 427–438.

Purdy, James P. 2005. "Calling Off the Hounds: Technology and the Visibility of Plagiarism." *Pedagogy: Critical Approaches to Teaching Literature, Language, Composition, and Culture* 5 (2): 275–295.

———. 2009. "Anxiety and the Archive: Understanding Plagiarism Detection Services as Digital Archives." *Computers and Composition* 26 (2): 65–77.

Purdy, James P., and Joyce R. Walker. 2007. "Digital Breadcrumbs: Case Studies of Online Research." *Kairos: A Journal of Rhetoric, Technology, and Pedagogy* 11 (2). Accessed September 17, 2012. kairos.technorhetoric.net/11.2/binder.html?topoi/purdy-walker/index.htm.

———. 2012. "Liminal Spaces and Research Identity: The Construction of Introductory Composition Students as Researchers." *Pedagogy: Critical Approaches to Teaching Language, Literature, Composition, and Culture* 13 (1): 9–41.

Robillard, Amy E. 2008. "Situating Plagiarism as a Form of Authorship: The Politics of Writing in a First-Year Writing Course." In *Pluralizing Plagiarism: Identities,*

Contexts, Pedagogies, edited by Rebecca Moore Howard and Amy E. Robillard, 27–42. Portsmouth, NH: Boynton/Cook.

Robillard, Amy E., and Rebecca Moore Howard. 2008. "Introduction: Plagiarisms." In *Pluralizing Plagiarism: Identities, Contexts, Pedagogies*, edited by Rebecca Moore Howard and Amy E. Robillard, 1–7. Portsmouth, NH: Boynton/Cook.

Royce, John. 2003. "Trust or Trussed? Has Turnitin.com Got It All Wrapped Up?" *Teacher Librarian* 30 (4): 26–30.

Turnitin. 2012. "About Us." iParadigms, LLC. Accessed November 3, 2012. turnitin.com/en_us/about-us/our-company.

Warnock, Scott. 2006. "'Awesome Job!'—Or Was It? The 'Many Eyes' of Asynchronous Writing Environments and the Implications on Plagiarism." *Plagiary* 1 (12): 1–14.

Weiler, Angela. 2005. "Information-Seeking Behavior in Generation Y Students: Motivation, Critical Thinking, and Learning Theory." *Journal of Academic Librarianship* 31 (1): 46–53.

Yancey, Kathleen Blake. 2008. "Beyond Plagiarism." In *Pluralizing Plagiarism: Identities, Contexts, Pedagogies*, edited by Rebecca Moore Howard and Amy E. Robillard, 158–170. Portsmouth, NH: Boynton/Cook.

Appendix A: Research Practices Questionnaire

Please answer the following questions regarding your research practices. Your identity will remain anonymous, unless you choose to participate further in the study.

Background Information

Major/minor:

Year (e.g., freshman):

How many years have you been taking courses at this school?

Please list any other institutions where you take (or have taken) courses for your degree:

Questions

1. When you are doing research for a scholarly project (i.e., research you are asked to do for school), where do you begin your searches (e.g., library database, specific website, library

book catalog)? What is the first thing you are likely to do? Please be specific.

2. Do you ever do nonacademic self-directed research (i.e., research that is not part of a school or work assignment)? If so, how often and on what topics (e.g., research to find airfare packages, shopping bargains, your favorite band's concert schedule)? Where do you begin your searches? What is the first thing you are likely to do? Please be specific.

3. On the grid below, create a bar graph to indicate the relative importance of each resource in your own research. The more blocks you fill in, the greater importance you give that resource.

Books										
Public search engines (e.g., Yahoo!, Google)										
Scholarly search engines (e.g., Google Scholar)										
Newspapers or magazines										
Face-to-face discussions/interviews with people										
Online message boards or discussion groups										
Public records (e.g., government documents)										
Library catalog										
Library online journal databases (e.g., JSTOR)										
Online book stores (e.g., Amazon)										

4. On a scale of 1 to 5, indicate how much you enjoy doing research.

5. Select from the following list any words that seem to apply to your identity as a researcher:

Focused

Intuitive

Linear

Diverse

Open

Tangential

Structured

Interested

Tentative

Skeptical

6. What would you say is your greatest strength as a researcher? What is your greatest weakness?

7. What is your favorite online research tool or resource (e.g., Google, Google Scholar, Furl, Wikipedia, Amazon, the library website)? Why? How did you learn to use it? Describe a specific situation in which you used this resource.

8. What about the way you do research would you consider unique?

9. What is your general impression of the University library database? What do you find effective? What frustrates you? Please be specific.

10. When searching library databases, how do you assess which sources you will use? When searching print resources, how do you assess which ones you will use? What about when searching the internet?

Appendix B: Digital Research Skills Assessment

Part of the research process is knowing where and what you are searching when you are looking for information. To help to measure this awareness, you are being asked to complete this digital research skills assessment. Please answer all parts for each question. The final part asks you to list the steps that you used to locate your answer. For example,

1. I started with the search engine Yahoo!.

2. I entered the search term "library subject headings."

3. I clicked on the "Library of Congress" entry.

4. I went to "American Memory."

Please give the URL for the websites that you use. You may record your search process on this page or type it online. If you work online, save the file before you start and save it frequently!

The questions listed below should take approximately 10 minutes per question. If you can't locate a final answer, please make sure to list the search steps that you used to reach the point where you stopped. Don't worry if you are not able to find the answer. This assessment is as interested in learning how you use digital spaces as it is in having you reach the final correct answers. Finish as much as you can in class today.

Question 1: Find the text of an article that appeared in the *New York Times* on December 4, 2005 that discusses concerns about the online resource Wikipedia.

A. According to this article, where does the creator of Wikipedia live?

B. What keywords did you use to search for the answer?

C. List your search steps for locating this information.

Question 2: Locate *Galileo's Daughter: A Historical Memoir of Science, Faith, and Love.*

A. What is the date of publication?

B. Who is the publisher of the book?

C. What is the place of publication?

D. List one library that has a copy of this book.

E. List the search steps you used for locating this information.

Question 3: Locate a scholarly article on the language of the Piraha tribe.

A. List:
    article title:
    article author:
    publication title:
    date of publication:
    volume:
    beginning and ending pages:

B. Explain how you concluded that this article is scholarly.

C. What keywords did you use to search for the answer?

D. List your search steps for locating this information.

Question 4: Locate the article "The Only Gadget You'll Ever Need: Japan's Infatuation with Cell Phones Is Rapidly Turning Them into Devices that Can Do Everything," which appeared in the journal *New Scientist* on March 5, 2005.

A. Write the first sentence from this article.

B. What keywords did you use to search for the answer?

C. List the search steps you used for locating this information.

Can I Google That? Research Strategies of Undergraduate Students

Mary Lourdes Silva

College students' apparent lack of information literacy (IL) skills has been a subject of concern of late in many higher education circles. Research indicates that students struggle with locating and retrieving trustworthy source material (Jenson 2004; Knight 2006; Metzger, Flanagin, and Zwarun 2003), properly citing information and including documentation (Lunsford and Lunsford 2008), differentiating between primary and secondary resources and knowing when to reference (Ivanitskaya, O'Boyle, and Casey 2006), articulating the authority and bias of sources (McClure and Clink 2009), and integrating source materials without plagiarizing (Wood 2004). Despite the efforts of organizations like the Association of College and Research Libraries (ACRL) and American Library Association (ALA) to establish IL standards for academic research, one problem with IL instruction in higher education is that teachers and librarians enforce prescriptive guidelines, which primarily encourage superficial approaches to teaching and learning (Johnston and Webber 2003).

Recent theoretical trends in writing studies have foregrounded IL skills as vital for students in the digital information age to search, retrieve, evaluate, and integrate electronic resources. Norgaard (2003) warns that it may be "tempting to think of information literacy as 'applied' to the field of writing" rather than viewing "information literacy as 'shaped' by writing—writing theory, writing instruction, and the very writing process itself" (125). I would add that writing is "shaped" by IL. Both writing and IL are social, cognitive, rhetorical, technological, and situated processes of using language, tools, systems, artifacts, and people to construct knowledge and participate in communities of practice (Elmborg 2003; Kapitzke 2001; Lloyd 2005, 2007; Marcum 2002; Tuominen, Savolainen, and Talja 2005).

The challenge teachers face is that the practices and processes associated with writing and IL are mediated by a collection of technologies, tools, digital resources, and hyperlinked texts. In the digital age, there are a number of literacy skills and practices expert research-writers have internalized, which are not described explicitly in the ACRL IL standards. For instance, digital information retrieval is dependent on the use of a search engine, database, or digital archive; however, no two systems are identical. One database may be case sensitive and report no results, while a search engine designed to handle natural language queries would produce tens of thousands of results. A savvy researcher would likely identify this as a database limitation, whereas a novice researcher may perceive a no-results page as an indication of a topic's limited breadth.

Once a source item has been located within a database, whether it is a PDF of an article or HTML page, the source needs to be saved or bookmarked on a personal or school computer, then retrieved again for later use. This technical procedure mandates a degree of technological literacy, which involves knowledge about renaming files or lengthy web addresses, creating nested folders, or creating tags. In conclusion, a "one size fits all" IL curriculum does not address the technological idiosyncrasies of databases and the individualized needs of students in a general education class like first-year writing.

The Council of Writing Program Administrators (WPA) and organizations such as the ACRL have made pedagogical efforts to bridge the gap between writing and IL instruction; however, research in other concentrations, such as educational psychology, information science and technology, computer science, and cognitive science, suggests that conducting research online is a far more complex sociocognitive technical activity than suggested by existing methodological approaches. In a cross-disciplinary attempt to expand existing models that integrate the WPA first-year writing outcomes (writing literacy) and ACRL information standards (IL), the following three literacy practices have been included in these organizations' standards: technological literacy, digital reading literacy, and navigational literacy. In total, five literacies (IL, writing literacy, technological literacy, digital reading literacy, and navigational literacy) represent the basis of the multiliteracies model, which was used to frame the present study. There is scant research that uses a multiliteracies approach as a pedagogical framework for research-writing instruction. For an overview of all five literacy practices, refer to Silva (2011).

Objective

In the majority of studies examining IL and its relationship with writing studies, the interconnected complexities and challenges of sociotechnical landscapes and navigation are overlooked or oversimplified as a "cyberspace" problem. The primary objective of the exploratory study reported in this chapter was to present and assess the success of an intervention that draws on research traditions from both IL and writing studies, as well as cognitive psychology, computer science, and information science and technology. The study offers a holistic perspective of students managing their learning (i.e., multiliteracies practices) across various information and technological landscapes throughout an academic quarter-long process of writing a research paper. For the purpose of this chapter, I will only report on students' navigational and IL development. Two questions frame this chapter:

1. What are the navigational and IL strategies and skills students use at the beginning of a research-writing course?

2. After students receive training based on a multiliteracies approach (IL, writing literacy, technological literacy, digital reading literacy, and navigational literacy), how do navigational and IL strategies and skills change?

Data show that a multiliteracies instructional package can improve navigational literacy skills. As for IL strategies, interestingly, there was a decrease in the number used; however, there were qualitative differences in the way students used IL and navigational literacy strategies due to changes in the rhetorical situation and technological landscape.

Methods

Participants and Classroom Context

The present study is an examination of three students enrolled in a course titled Writing 50: Research Writing at a large West Coast university. Pseudonyms are used for each student. The first student, Ethan, was a junior and a computer science major. The second student, Isabel, was a sophomore and a Spanish major. The third student, Ana, was a freshman and a business economics major. The three participants felt confident using the internet and were comfortable using their personal laptops. In the course, students were expected to write a research proposal that included at least one reference; an annotated bibliography that included six sources (one book, two popular sources, and three peer-reviewed journal articles); a five-page paper; and a 10-page paper, which was expected to be an expansion of the five-page paper (four additional sources were required).

Design

A single-subject design across three participants, referred to as a multiple baseline design, was used to assess whether a multiliteracies instructional package would result in increased levels of strategy use. In a single-subject design, the subject serves as his or her own control. A multiple baseline design allows for comparative analysis between participants and controls for "the principal weakness of the simple phase change" when the intervention is introduced and when the participants are observed or assessed after the intervention—the independent phase (Hayes, Barlow, and Nelson-Gray 1999, 203). Data included surveys, semi-structured interviews, self-reports, research paper drafts, and screen-capture videos of student navigational practices.

Materials

All recordings of students' online navigational behaviors and strategies were completed within a 30-day subscription of Camtasia, which was downloaded on the participants' personal laptops. In addition, each student received a digital folder that contained seven video tutorials, each 4 to 6 minutes in length, designed to provide the strategy instruction. In addition, students received two handouts that delineated and categorized the strategies discussed in the video tutorials (see Appendices A and B).

Procedure

Baseline

In the first week of the academic quarter, before students received any form of class-based instruction on library research, baseline data were collected. For Isabel, data were collected for 3 days; for Ana, 4 days; and Ethan, 5 days. During the baseline period, the students conducted research online for 20 to 30 minutes on their personal computers using the research assignment handout assigned by the professor of the research-writing course. Students were expected to locate six sources: one book, two popular sources, and three peer-reviewed journal articles. I provided no assistance or instruction. Using Camtasia, students conducted a think-aloud protocol of their research processes during the entire 20- to 30-minute session. (For more discussion on the think-aloud protocol and instructional strategies based on this protocol, see Chapter 16 in this book by Janice R. Walker and Kami Cox.)

Intervention

During the second week of the academic quarter, I delivered a multi-literacies instructional package, which included a repertoire of strategies for students to locate and retrieve information within various information systems; evaluate web-based content; process and integrate information for a specific disciplinary rhetorical purpose; and finally, monitor and regulate learning of domain knowledge, sociotechnical knowledge, and strategy use. Individualized face-to-face training sessions occurred on 4 to 5 consecutive days during 30-minute appointments depending on each participant's availability. A second face-to-face training was scheduled during the fifth week of the academic quarter. It included a 1-hour review session with each student. Prior to each training session, students were expected to view 4- to 6-minute video tutorials that I designed to provide instruction on a strategy (e.g., how to interpret a bibliographic reference and use various online databases to retrieve it). Once students viewed the tutorials and handouts, the objective of the training session was to review the content discussed and provide face-to-face modeling, which allowed me to review student application of the strategies and prompt students to self-regulate their learning within the hypermedia environment (e.g., see Azevedo, Greene, and Moos 2007). For a complete list of questions, refer to Appendix B.

Independent Phase

During the sixth week of the quarter, students were expected to complete three 25- to 30-minute screen-capture recordings of their online research on their personal computers. At this point in the academic quarter, students had received their feedback and grades for their five-page paper. The objective of the 25- to 30-minute sessions was to locate four requisite sources for the final 10-page paper.

Results and Discussion
Navigational Literacy (Week 1—Before Training)
Hub and Spoke Method

Each student was unique in managing his or her navigation within multiple information landscapes; however, each student engaged in some variation of the hub and spoke method, which is the technical process of going back and forth between the search results page and a target page using the back button (Cutrell and Guan 2007). A typical search for Ana and Isabel consisted of a three-step recursive process. First, these students would enter keyword phrases (e.g., "farm workers and pesticides") into either the Yahoo! or Google search box. Next, the students would read and evaluate the results page or source material. Last, they would return to the results page or revise the keywords. Ethan also engaged in a similar method, yet he applied it differently, using a fan approach. After he entered keyword phrases, he would open three to four search results as new tabs, like opening a fan, then proceed to read and evaluate the results before he closed each one from right to left, returning to the search results page to repeat the process.

The multiple baseline design across participants showed that Ana and Isabel initially engaged in low levels of navigational literacy strategies. During Week 1 for Ana, 45 percent of total navigational strategies involved the use of the back button. For Isabel, 40 percent of total navigational strategies involved the use of the back button. Embedded hyperlinks and navigational aids were seldom used. As a result, Ana and Isabel did not experience the levels of disorientation often experienced by learners in hypermedia environments (Last, O'Donnell, and Kelly 2001). This may have been due to the fact that the search process only involved about three steps. However, Ana did experience high levels of frustration and confusion because she could not find any source material to answer her inquiry. As Ana's level of frustration and confusion escalated, she continued to use the same navigational literacy strategies, repeating the same three-step process.

Although Ana and Isabel engaged in the hub and spoke method, Isabel varied her navigational literacy strategies in three ways. First, she also used the address bar to navigate to different information databases. Second, she used filters like "Academic Journals" to narrow her results. And last, she often added a single keyword or phrase into the Google search box to narrow results, as opposed to Ana who used the back button to return to the main results page before revising her keywords. Although Isabel used the back button often (40 percent of total navigational literacy strategies), she explored using the tools within her environment.

Ethan engaged in high levels of navigational literacy strategies during Week 1 with an average of 22 navigational literacy strategies per session and a range of 43. The high level of navigational literacy strategies was partly due to two sessions: 45 navigational strategies during Session 3 and 39 during Session 5. In Session 3, Ethan clicked on several hyperlinks because he could not figure out how to retrieve a library source. In Session 5, he clicked on various library bookmarks, only to discover none worked, so he repeated the search process to re-retrieve all his sources. He believed that he resolved the problem by using the library email function; however, he was left frustrated later on when his email contained only the citation, not the full description available on the library site.

When Ethan did not have problems with accessing or retrieving a source item, he averaged only eight navigational strategies per session, similar to Ana who averaged only nine per session and Isabel who averaged eight per session as well. In sum, although Ethan differed from Ana and Isabel in the way he managed his search results page, all three students primarily engaged in the hub and spoke method, seldom clicking on embedded hyperlinks or using other strategies to acquire more information. Furthermore, high or low levels of navigational literacy strategies did not equate to better or worse navigation. Frustration and disorientation were experienced by both Ana and Ethan; however, the qualitative difference in navigational literacy strategies between Isabel and the two other participants may have factored into participants' attitudes or perceptions about the search process.

Information Literacy (Week 1—Before Training)

Information Need

For Ethan, Ana, and Isabel, the average use of IL strategies during Week 1 was 15.60, 25.00, and 22.33 strategies, respectively. The majority of IL strategies involved students identifying their information need, entering keywords into Google or Yahoo!, then evaluating the relevance of a results page or source material. At the beginning of the search process, students' information need was structured by their topic of interest and the research prompt, which specified that students needed to find one book, two popular sources, and three peer-reviewed journal articles. Ethan (Google), Isabel (Google), and Ana (Yahoo!) chose to start with their favorite search engine in order to locate general information about their topic, or what Ana described as "overview information." For example, Ana did not want source material on a specific food policy in the United States; she wanted information *about* food policies in the United States.

In some instances the participants used Wikipedia to fulfill this search objective. As described in Alison Head and Michael Eisenberg's (2009, 2010) comprehensive research on college student research practices, students were aware that sites such as Wikipedia lacked credibility, yet they used it anyway as a way to get "unstuck." The problem students had with searching for "overview information" was that they expected to find the "perfect source" (Head and Eisenberg 2009) that pretty much answered their research question—in other words, a legitimate version of Wikipedia. This perfect source would then function as the backbone of their paper. The search objective from there would be to "stretch out" this perfect source by locating whatever remaining sources were specified by the prompt.

Relevance

Limited criteria for evaluating the relevance of search results appeared to hinder students from framing the information need. Students often made general comments, such as "I hope this is helpful" and "I think this is good" to assess the value of a source (participants may have had more complex criteria for evaluating the relevance of a source, yet they only articulated whether it was "good" or "helpful"). When students ignored or selected a source, students often drew upon false assumptions or their prior knowledge. For instance, because Isabel assumed that children no longer worked in orchards, she interpreted an article as "unhelpful." Ethan's prior knowledge of labor movements disgruntled with the loss of jobs due to mechanization or digitalization dictated an entire session in which he repeatedly discounted Google and Google Scholar results because they did not focus on arguments against computers in the food industry. It was during this session when he engaged in a high level of navigational literacy strategies (39 total).

Currency, Accuracy, and Reliability

Student evaluation criteria also included evaluation based on currency, accuracy, and reliability. However, consistent with other studies (Hung 2004; McClure and Clink 2009; Metzger, Flanagin, and Zwarun 2003), students did not possess a well-defined and rigorous set of criteria for evaluating source material. For instance, Ana excluded sources like blogs in her Yahoo! search, believing that blogs were not reliable or trustworthy. However, she only excluded the blog source when "blog" was listed in the title or within the page. In one blog about the Bubba Gump Shrimp Company, Ana failed to recognize the URL, which included "blogspot" within the address, and failed to recognize the typical archive layout of most blogs.

Of the three participants, Ana used more advanced IL strategies to evaluate the reliability of sources; however, this may have been due to the fact that she used generic keywords (e.g., *fast food, media, movies, food industry*) that elicited numerous commercial sites. Although she had the most "questionable" source material to work with, she did not identify the relationship between her keyword choice and the commercial nature of the source material due to the use of the popular search engine. She attempted to resolve her problem through query reformulation. As for Isabel, in her evaluation of sources, she focused predominantly on their currency, probably because most were retrieved from the library, which organizes book titles chronologically, and where she appeared to retrieve the most recent titles, only to find out later that the sources did not hold up to the standard for currency. To her misfortune, it was not until the last session when she recognized that all of her sources were outdated. Ethan only communicated his evaluation of sources according to relevance, but not according to currency, accuracy, or reliability. For instance, in one session, he used the library catalog to locate books on computers in the food industry, yet he never noticed that the books were published in the '80s and '90s. Clearly, much has changed in computer technology over the past 25 years.

These findings allude to two problems. First, students who use search engines require more instructional support regarding the sociotechnical and discursive architecture of the web. Second, library websites may do little to prompt students to evaluate sources according to currency, accuracy, or reliability. Students may assume that sources retrieved from a library site do not necessitate a rigorous set of criteria for evaluation. In fact, by Week 6, none of the students communicated any evaluation based on currency, accuracy, or reliability, and all of the students used Google Scholar, EBSCOhost, JSTOR, or the library catalog. In Chapter 6 of this book, James P. Purdy reports a similar finding in which students used the "scholarliness" of a research tool as a primary criterion.

Navigational Literacy (Week 6—After Training)
Mining a Reference

The primary navigational strategy for the participants was to start with a reference page from a source they had used for the five-page paper, which was located within a nested folder in the students' hard drive. Next, students copied and pasted the citation information into Google Scholar or a library database, engaged in reading and evaluating the results page or source material, then located more references from either the original journal article, the new journal article, or from a "Cited by" link. This navigational literacy strategy was referred to as mining a reference within the instructional materials provided. As a navigational literacy strategy, it required the management of and movement between multiple windows. The participants preferred this strategy to fulfill their information need. To students, starting with a published article rather than keywords from their prior knowledge gave them more control of the research process.

The multiple baseline design across participants showed that Isabel had a 92 percent increase, Ana a 75.5 percent increase, and Ethan a 65 percent increase in the average number of navigational strategies per session from Week 1 to Week 6. The effect size of the intervention was 0.75, 0.78, and 0.37 for Isabel, Ana, and Ethan respectively. The results suggest that Isabel and Ana benefited most from the instruction on navigational literacy strategies, whereas the intervention had little effect on Ethan's use of navigational literacy strategies.

Ana's navigational literacy strategies increased during Week 6, partly due to her confusion about interpreting a citation within a reference page. Students had received training on how to interpret a citation; however, if students only engaged in the technical process of copying and pasting a citation into a search box without carefully interpreting the citation in order to use the correct database, then they were left confused and frustrated about a strategy that worked previously. Similar to Ethan, Ana repeated the process two to three times before she modified her plans:

> Okay, I searched for it. Why won't it come up? I searched for it twice and it still won't come up ... How about the article I just found. Maybe I could get something off of there. Okay, go back. I found it so I can go back to it anytime I want and just search for it.

Although Ethan and Ana repeated the mining a reference strategy and ultimately failed to access their target source, they became far more invested in finding a target source because the strategy had worked for them in the past. During Week 1, on the other hand, students were more apt to abandon a source after a single attempt. In sum, Ana and

Ethan appeared to have more effective navigational literacy strategies for retrieving relevant and credible sources, yet their misreading of citations or misuse of databases led to higher levels of navigational literacy strategies. Whether students resolve these problems on their own requires further research.

Hub and Spoke Method

Based on the total number of navigational literacy strategies, the use of the back and forward buttons decreased for Isabel and Ana. For Isabel, there was a 17 percent decrease in the use of the back button from Week 1 (40 percent) to Week 6 (23 percent). For Ana, there was a 27 percent decrease in the use of the back button from Week 1 (45 percent) to Week 6 (18 percent). Whereas in Week 1, the primary navigational strategy was the hub and spoke method, by Week 6, Ana and Isabel relied on three other navigational strategies: 1) using the bookmarks toolbar, filters, and scroll bar to locate the reference section of journal articles; 2) selecting PDF hyperlinks; and 3) using the Ctrl F function to isolate a single concept and navigate through a source item to evaluate the relevance of the source. Although the navigational literacy strategies may have aided Isabel in her search for relevant material, Ana struggled to locate source material for other reasons described in this chapter, which suggests that a pedagogical approach centered on a single literacy practice cannot account for the multiple literacy activities interwoven throughout the research-writing process. Thus, the increased use of navigational literacy strategies does not necessarily equate to "better" research practices.

Similar to Week 1, Ethan's primary method of navigation was the hub and spoke method, which involved the use of multiple tabs. Moreover, as in Week 1, when Ethan struggled to access a source, he engaged in an iterative process of clicking on hyperlinks to locate the source. One reason for Ethan's high use of navigational literacy strategies (an average of 36.33 per session) and difficulties with accessing sources was his search objective to find a PDF of articles: "I don't really get this. I don't know why I'm having so much trouble getting to this article right now. (Sigh)." As mentioned earlier, his negative experience of losing all his bookmarks and only receiving the citation information from the library led him to focus only on PDF versions of articles. In one situation, he found an HTML version of the source and disregarded it after repeated attempts to locate the PDF version. Furthermore, because Ethan had success during his training sessions in using the mining a reference strategy, he unsuccessfully repeated the strategies for retrieving a source two to three times, which increased his average use of navigational literacy strategies from approximately 22 per session to 36 per session. This finding indicates that the medium of a source can affect students' attitudes toward the content of the source, thereby influencing their search and navigational activities.

Information Literacy (Week 6—After Training)

Currency, Accuracy, and Reliability

Overall, the average use of IL strategies decreased by approximately 2 percent for Ethan and 13 percent for Isabel. For Ana, the average number of IL strategies increased by 21.32 percent. During Week 1 there was some evidence of evaluation of sources based on currency and reliability. During Week 6, none of the participants evaluated sources based on currency or reliability. Their use of Google Scholar, EBSCOhost, JSTOR, or the library catalog may have factored into the lack of evaluation criteria. Evaluating the authority and validity of a source is an important critical thinking skill (D'Angelo 2001; McClure and Clink 2009) in IL development that should not disappear altogether simply because students are using information databases regarded as "safe" and trustworthy.

Relevance

The participants did, however, have an evaluation criteria based on relevance, which did exhibit some qualitative changes by Week 6. To my surprise, each of the participants started the search process with the instructor's marginal feedback on the five-page paper as a sort of checklist. In Isabel's case, the instructor advised her to locate information about health programs for farm workers in regard to pesticide exposure. Throughout Sessions 1–3, she used "health programs" as the major lens for evaluating source materials. In Session 3 she commented, "Now that I think about it, self-management is not an actual program. I feel like this one would be helpful. I have to find information on actual programs that have taken place, why or why not."

Ana made a similar move by starting her session with a goal to find a source for each teacher comment: food and image, food and relationships, and the role of food for women. The instructor had listed these topics in the margins as a way to illustrate the various topics (and lack of organization) in Ana's paper. Ana, on the other hand, interpreted the feedback to mean that she needed to find source items to support each disparate topic. As a result, the majority of source materials were evaluated as relevant or irrelevant based on the instructor's feedback. This finding suggests that instructors should view their feedback as part of a larger discursive and technological context in which words on the page could also be used as words in a search box.

Mining a Reference

As described earlier, students preferred the mining a reference strategy to locate and retrieve sources. I describe this strategy as both a navigational technique (managing multiple windows) and an IL strategy (fulfilling an information need). Although each participant used the strategy, participants did vary slightly in its application. Both Ethan and Ana used a downloaded PDF of an article from an earlier search attempt to initiate the search process for the 10-page paper. Isabel primarily used online reference sections or "Cited by" links to mine for references. One reason students preferred the mining a reference strategy was due to the fact that Google Scholar and JSTOR could instantly retrieve the pasted source. Even if the source item was not available in Google Scholar or JSTOR, the information systems were sophisticated enough to find related sources. EBSCOhost and the library catalog, however, were not as successful and would produce a zero-results page if the specific source could not be located. This may have affected students' attitudes about the two library databases.

Although students found success with the mining a reference strategy, they often engaged in an iterative search process that led to confusion and frustration if they could not locate or access a PDF of an article. As mentioned earlier, student misinterpretation of a citation led students to the wrong database (e.g., within the library website, there are two navigational options for locating a journal article title, one being far more difficult, yet a book source cannot be retrieved through the Electronic Journals database). In some ways, students' favorite search tool during Week 1 (Google or Yahoo!) was now replaced by Google Scholar or JSTOR—a problem if a book citation was misinterpreted as a journal article. These findings suggest that students have a limited understanding of the relational, hierarchical, and technological structure of electronic information systems and require further instructional support. Moreover, further research is needed to determine whether students eventually resolve these problems with practice and experience.

Implications

The instructional materials and method of instruction that I have developed have been in a recursive and iterative process of revision and evolution. From the results of this study, I make the following suggestions for the development and implementation of a multiliteracies approach to teaching research-writing:

- Students need assistance with generating keywords that are relevant to a disciplinary field or situated context (see Eagleton, Guinee, and Langlais 2003). Often students struggled to generate keywords and relied primarily on their prior knowledge, which often led to frustration. As a result, students would abandon their original inquiry and write a paper based on what they *could* find. Moreover, teacher feedback on drafts could also play a significant role in assisting students with keywords.

- Students would benefit from understanding the limitations of information databases and search engines. An aggregate of keywords relevant to a discipline or topic of interest can be rendered ineffective in the wrong database or search engine. Students do not realize that popular search engines like Google or Google Scholar only contain a percentage of the total number of sources, not *all* source material (see Scott and O'Sullivan 2005). As a result, when students use a favorite information database or search engine and obtain irrelevant results, students assume that there is nothing on their topic. In the following chapter of this collection, Ruth Mirtz advises writing instructors to view search databases rhetorically and understand how these databases influence students' topic selection and writing development. According to Mirtz, assignments such as a library database review allow students to develop a critical awareness of search databases.

- Students require instructional support in creating a well-defined and rigorous set of criteria for source evaluation. Providing a generic rubric that asks students in general to question the currency, accuracy, relevance, coverage, and authority of online source material is not helpful when category definitions are vague and universal. Generic rubrics do not consider disciplinary conventions, values, beliefs, and methodologies.

- According to students in the present study, the most successful strategy was the mining a reference strategy in which students learned the genre features of a citation and the corresponding databases that store the source material. Ironically, researchers have relied on this low-tech strategy for hundreds of years. The affordances and convenience of digital environments (i.e., copying and pasting citation titles, hyperlinks to source material, or digitalized archives) can create confusion because each information system welcomes a new user with a search box. As mentioned earlier, instruction on the limitations of databases can make the mining a reference strategy more effective.

Although these suggestions are based on the results of the present study, generalizations about student research practices and online search behaviors cannot be made without further replication studies. Furthermore, additional research like that offered in other chapters in this book is required across disciplines and throughout various writing research courses (i.e., writing intensive courses, linked courses, and first-year writing). Finally, further research is needed in the use of the multiple baseline design as a procedure for measuring student progress. From this study, we can infer that instructional support throughout the research-writing process results in some improvement in student online search practices, although longitudinal studies may be needed to determine the lasting impact on student learning and writing.

References

American Library Association. 1998. "Information Literacy Standards for Student Learning: Standards and Indicators." Accessed September 17, 2012. www.ala.org/acrl/standards/informationliteracycompetency.

Azevedo, Roger, Jeffrey A. Greene, and Daniel C. Moos. 2007. "The Effect of a Human Agent's External Regulation Upon College Students' Hypermedia Learning." *Metacognition Learning* 2: 67–87.

Council of Writing Program Administrators. 2008. "WPA Outcomes Statement for First Year Composition (Amended)." Accessed September 17, 2012. www.wpa council.org/positions/outcomes.html.

Cutrell, Edward, and Zhiwei Guan. 2007. "What Are You Looking for? An Eye-Tracking Study of Information Usage in Web Search." Paper presented at the CHI: Proceedings of the SIGCHI Conference on Human Factors in Computing Systems, San Jose, CA.

D'Angelo, Barbara J. 2001. "Using Source Analysis to Promote Critical Thinking." *Research Strategies* 18: 303–309.

Eagleton, Maya, Kathleen Guinee, and Karen Langlais. 2003. "Teaching Internet Literacy Strategies: The Hero Inquiry Project." *Voices from the Middle* 10 (3): 28–35.

Elmborg, James K. 2003. "Information Literacy and Writing across the Curriculum: Sharing the Vision." *Reference Services Review* 31 (1): 68–80.

Hayes, Steven C., David H. Barlow, and Rosemary O. Nelson-Gray. 1999. *The Scientist Practitioner: Research and Accountability in the Age of Managed Care*. 2nd ed. Boston: Allyn and Bacon.

Head, Alison J., and Michael B. Eisenberg. 2009. "Finding Context: What Today's College Students Say about Conducting Research in the Digital Age." *Project Information Literacy Progress Report.* Accessed September 17, 2012. www.projectinfo lit.org/pdfs/PIL_ProgressReport_2_2009.pdf.

———. 2010. "How Today's College Students Use Wikipedia for Course-Related Research." *First Monday* 15 (3). Accessed September 17, 2012. www.firstmonday. org/htbin/cgiwrap/bin/ojs/index.php/fm/article/view/2830/2476.

Hung, Tsai-Youn. 2004. "Undergraduate Students' Evaluation Criteria When Using Web Resources for Class Papers." *Journal of Educational Media and Library Sciences* 42 (1): 1–12.

Ivanitskaya, Lana, Irene O'Boyle, and Anne Marie Casey. 2006. "Health Information Literacy and Competencies of Information Age Students: Results from the Interactive Online Research Readiness Self-Assessment (RRSA)." *Journal of Medical Internet Research* 8 (2): e6.

Jenson, Jill D. 2004. "It's the Information Age, So Where's the Information? Why Our Students Can't Find It and What We Can Do to Help." *College Teaching* 52 (3): 107–112.

Johnston, Bill, and Sheila Webber. 2003. "Information Literacy in Higher Education: A Review and Case Study." *Studies in Higher Education* 28 (3): 335–352.

Kapitzke, Cushla. 2001. "Information Literacy: The Changing Library." *Journal of Adolescent and Adult Literacy* 44 (4): 450–456.

Knight, Lorrie A. 2006. "Using Rubrics to Assess Information Literacy." *Reference Services Review* 34 (1): 43–55.

Last, David A., Angela M. O'Donnell, and Anthony E. Kelly. 2001. "The Effects of Prior Knowledge and Goal Strength on the Use of Hypertext." *Journal of Educational Multimedia and Hypermedia* 10: 3–25.

Lloyd, Annemaree. 2005. "Information Literacy: Different Contexts, Different Concepts, Different Truths?" *Journal of Librarianship and Information Science* 37 (2): 82–88.

———. 2007. "Learning to Put Out the Red Stuff: Becoming Information Literate through Discursive Practice." *Library Quarterly* 77 (2): 181–198.

Lunsford, Andrea A., and Karen J. Lunsford. 2008. "'Mistakes Are a Fact of Life': A National Comparative Study." *College Composition and Communication* 59 (4): 781–806.

Marcum, James W. 2002. "Rethinking Information Literacy." *Library Quarterly* 72 (1):1–26.

McClure, Randall, and Kellian Clink. 2009. "How Do You Know That? An Investigation of Student Research Practices in the Digital Age." *Libraries and the Academy* 9 (1): 115–132.

Metzger, Miriam J., Andrew J. Flanagin, and Lara Zwarun. 2003. "College Student Web Use, Perceptions of Information Credibility, and Verification Behavior." *Computers & Education* 41: 271–290.

Norgaard, Rolf. 2003. "Writing Information Literacy: Contributions to a Concept." *Reference & User Services Quarterly* 43 (2): 124–130.

Scott, Thomas, and Michael O'Sullivan. 2005. "Analyzing Student Search Strategies: Making a Case for Integrating Information Literacy Skills into the Curriculum." *Teacher Librarian* 33 (1): 21–25.

Silva, Mary L. 2011. "Can I Google That? A Study of the Multiple Literacy Practices of Undergraduate Students in a Research-Writing Course." PhD diss., University of California, Santa Barbara.

Tuominen, Kimmo, Reijo Savolainen, and Sanna Talja. 2005. "Information Literacy as a Sociotechnical Practice." *Library Quarterly* 75 (3): 329–345.

Wood, Gail. 2004. "Academic Original Sin: Plagiarism, the Internet, and Librarians." *Journal of Academic Librarianship* 30 (3): 237–242.

Appendix A: Handout on Navigational Strategies

Focusing Search

- Use Ctrl F or Command F, which highlights the keyword, sentence, or phrase throughout an active window.

- Via Ctrl or Command F, locate buzz words around keywords of interest (e.g., critique, criticism, analysis, thus, in sum, in other words, concludes, etc.).

- Click the Advanced Search link or button.

- Click the Modify Search Results link or button.

- Use Filters (e.g., click on Peer Reviewed Journals, Magazines, Books).

Generating Keywords

- Skim titles from search results to see what words are synonymous to or associated with the concept you're interested in.

- Look for outlines (e.g., Wikipedia) to see how others organize and label your topic of interest.

- Skim for hyperlinks to find synonyms or important concepts related to your interests.

- Type in a general question to see how a search engine interprets the question.

- Use a Boolean Search (and, or, but).

- Look for the subject terms section or keyword section on library webpages.

- Search within YouTube and watch videos/lectures on your topic and take note of keywords.

Mining Sources

- Look over the references page of a source you love for other sources.

- Look over the references page of a source for peer-reviewed journal titles.

- Visit a professor's website and look for publications to retrieve those sources.

- Visit an organization's website and look for a References page or section.

- Look for sources titled Bibliography, Annotated Bibliography, Review, or Overview.

- Because introductions provide an overview of the subject and issue, read an introduction of a source to locate sources referenced.

- Search Amazon.com and locate books there, then search for a specific title in our library.

- Use a source you love and type it into Google Scholar to determine who cited that source (Cited by) and determine other Related Articles.

- Copy and paste any citation into Google Scholar to see if it links you directly to the PDF.

- Use Google Scholar to find sources, then within the source, see how authors are summarizing the info to gain an understanding of how people represent the information.

Organization of Information

- Bookmark the web with specific tags or labels to skim through that information later.

- Download PDFs, create PDFs yourself, or print articles or webpages; create either digital or nondigital folders and label every source thoroughly by author's last name and source title.

- Email articles or links to yourself.

- Take notes, journal ideas, label information.

- Use graphic organizers or aids.

- Copy and paste important ideas onto a document. Don't forget to place quotes around it so you can summarize or paraphrase later, and don't forget to copy and paste the source information: title, author, year, publication, etc.

Reading Strategies

- Pay attention to web layout or structure to see how information is organized (hierarchical relationships, causal relationships, correlational relationships, conceptual relationships, categorical, etc.).

- Pay attention to words repeated; authors/organizations, institutions referenced; hyperlinks, graphic captions, tags, visual and audio content.

- What do you already know about this topic? Did your knowledge derive from experience, books, instructors, religious institutions, parents, peers, etc.?

- Think of a metaphor/simile to understand the new concept (e.g., activity theory is like theories on social historicism except that ...).

- Watch videos/lectures on YouTube or Ted.com to acquire more context on your topic.

- Visit Wikipedia to acquire more context on your topic.

- Google your research question and visit message boards to acquire more context on your topic.

- How do the different modalities and media shape the way you understand the topic and the significance of the information?

Mapping

- Would another search engine do a better job of organizing and filtering the results?

- Would another library database best serve your cognitive and disciplinary needs?

- Are you in the wrong library database?

- Are you unknowingly on a commercial site or blog? You may notice all the ads, the web layout, or the URL, which are indicators of commercial sites or blogs.

- Would popular sources on sites such as Time.com or Psychology Today best answer complex questions before looking at more theoretical or empirical sources within a discipline?

- Is it time to email a professor or a specialist for trustworthy authors, key concepts, notable journals, library databases, or websites?

- How do the different databases and websites shape the way you understand the publications and the way you understand the topic?

Evaluation of Information for Validity

- Confirm an author's credentials by visiting the institution website that s/he is associated with.

- Read a large number of sources on the same topic to determine the consensus of knowledge, what counts as evidence, what kinds of claims are being made, what topics are discussed in depth, which topics are glossed over, and what is not discussed.

• Who paid for the research study or the program/ organization? Is the information associated with a political, religious, or commercial institution?

• If you are on a .org, .gov, or .edu site, do these institutions function as an authority on the topic?

• Pay attention to the year of publication to determine the relevance of that source.

Evaluation of Information for Rhetorical Purposes

• How have you repurposed or transformed the source material to support the claims you're trying to make in your paper?

• How does the information align with other sources or perspectives in the paper?

• What rhetorical structures best organize your sources, hence your paper (most to least influential, compare/contrast, hierarchical, categorical)?

• If the objective is to explore a topic and challenge your thinking, how does the information "complicate" your argument (i.e., instead of black and white, pro and con, positive and negative, you present information that shows the complexity of the situation)?

• In what ways does the information meet the needs and expectations of the audience you're writing for?

Appendix B: Handout on Self-Regulated Learning Strategies
SPEWLS

• What's the *situation*?

• What's your *plan*?

• How are you going to *execute* that plan? What knowledge, skills, and resources will help you execute that plan?

- What's *working* and *not working*? What needs to change?

- What are you *learning*? How does the new information connect to what you already know?

- Which *strategies* or methods can be re-used in new situations?

SPEWLS are not linear or sequential. You can go in any order at any time. It's just important to know what you're doing and why.

At the Beginning of Research

1. What would you like to accomplish within the next 20 minutes? How would you like to use this time?

2. Where would you like to start? Why there?

3. What would you like to look for? Why that?

   a. Peer-reviewed article

   b. General information from a website (e.g., Wikipedia, About.com, TED)

   c. A video (e.g., YouTube, TeacherTube, TED, etc.)

4. What keywords, phrase, sentence, or question comes to mind for the search box? Why those words? How are they related to your current understanding of the topic? How are they related to other sources you've found?

5. Are these words a revision of an earlier attempt? What worked, didn't work, or almost worked with that attempt?

Navigation

1. What are the factors that affect your reading of a screen/ window? What are you reading or what are you looking for or how are you reading? What do you anticipate to find on the screen?

2. What are the factors that affect your movement on the screen?

   a. Are you looking for the navigation bar? Why?

b. Are you looking for hyperlinks? Why?

c. Are you looking for global structures like titles, headings, subheadings, captions, bolded words, etc.? Why?

d. Are you looking for the "Advanced Search" or "Modify Search Results" link to narrow your search? What do you want to exclude to narrow the search? How does the excluded material relate or not relate to your topic of interest?

3. How effective or ineffective is the site in helping you navigate the page? What are ways to manage any disorientation you may have?

Technologies in Action

1. What resources can you use to manage the volume of information that you're encountering?

a. Email sources to yourself

b. Bookmark sources

c. Tag or label sources

d. Create PDFs of sources or print sources

e. Take notes by paper or Microsoft Word

f. Use graphics or a concept map to manage the volume of information

g. Copy and paste text with citation information into a document to later summarize

h. Use "cited by" and "Related Articles" to narrow your search

i. Use "Advanced Search" or "Modify Search Results" to narrow your search

j. Share sites, sources, or materials with others for discussion

Evaluation of Sources and Content

1. How have the sources/sites answered some of the questions you had about the topic?

2. How have the different databases, websites, or journals shaped your understanding of the topic?

3. How have the different authors shaped your understanding of the topic? Do you notice particular authors being used repeatedly?

What Do You Know and Don't Know Now

1. What keywords/phrases, sentences, or questions can you use for your next search? If it's the same as before, what do you anticipate finding using the same words as before?

2. What have you learned about your topic of interest?

3. Which sites, databases, or journals worked for you? Which didn't? What would you do differently or the same next time? Why?

4. Of the sources or sites you came across and liked, downloaded, emailed to yourself, or bookmarked, how would you rank them?

5. How would you structure them?

   a. Do sites/sources represent a pro/con perspective, a range of perspectives, negative/positive, hierarchical structure, causal relationships, correlational relationships, etc.?

   b. How do these sites/sources inform the way you plan to organize, write, or revise your paper?

CHAPTER 8

Encountering Library Databases: NextGen Students' Strategies for Reconciling Personal Topics and Academic Scholarship

Ruth Mirtz

While most writing instructors are pleased with the relative ease with which their students can access information and scholarly articles in modern university libraries, significant attention needs to be paid to the way that digital tools, such as library databases, shape students' research-writing processes. For example, writing instructors might not be aware that many library databases, such as Gale's Academic OneFile or EBSCO's Academic Search Premier, are not neutral tools that constitute a quick stop in the research process. Often due to the ways in which they are constructed, library databases present real obstacles, and thus become a shaping force in students' research processes. In the same way that writing assignments can mark out a limited territory for students to exert their authority as writers, library databases define search patterns that discipline how and what our students find.

This chapter presents the findings from an action research study of 18 first-year college students' processes of searching for scholarly articles for use in a first-year writing course. The findings suggest that students' online search strategies in library databases "box in" their topics, that both luck and persistence play a role in their searching process, and that topic choice may have more influence than any instruction on how they do research and make writerly decisions based upon the findings of that research.

Literature Review

Apart from the chapters in this book, surprisingly little research has been done that observes actual searching behaviors of undergraduate students in the process of composing academic research papers. As teachers and researchers, we have concentrated instead on the writing of the research paper, perhaps not realizing how much the act of searching for sources affects the writing. Current conversations about undergraduate research involve how to construct students as developing experts in what Laurie Grobman calls a "continuum of scholarly authority" (2009, W177). In addition, many studies of students' citation methods have been conducted in order to gain insight into students' processes of incorporating sources into their papers (e.g., see Carlson 2006). These studies tend to highlight the difficulties students have navigating and evaluating the enormous amount of information they encounter in databases and on the internet. Other citation studies conclude that students need more instruction and rely uncritically on Google and Wikipedia (Head and Eisenberg 2009), and that students consider convenience and availability as or more important than the reliability of the source (Twait 2005).

In the attempt to make undergraduate research-writing a useful and yet rhetorically sophisticated activity, compositionists have often invoked the social nature of knowledge and described what students do during collecting research as "entering the conversation" on a topic, in midstream (e.g., see Harris 2006). Unfortunately, most library databases have dislocated the article as an artifact from the context of the journal, and they have wrenched chapters from monographs and made them digital, usually without any accompanying illustrations, indexes, or front matter. Michelle Sidler (2002) describes these articles as "disembodied texts," existing in online discourse that is "immediate and without origins" (60). Thus, the conversational give-and-take of scholars on a subject is not as obvious. The ease with which students can access material is confounded by the absence of physical mediation that used to guide and slow down the process.

Another result of this dislocation of information sources is that students are blamed for being lazy researchers because of their attachment to Google and their apparent lack of interest in a complete and robust research process (e.g., see Thompson 2003). They are characterized as technologically adept and labeled the "Google generation," but they are often considered unsophisticated evaluators of online information. Sue Bennett, Karl Maton, and Lisa Kervin (2008) question many of the claims made about "digital natives" and their abilities, and Tara Brabazon (2006) feels students' use of Google actually "flattens" their abilities by dumbing down their searches.

If we don't blame students for superficial, plagiarized research papers, then we blame the assignments for which they are written. Plenty of compositionists have complained about the problems with the classic research paper (e.g., see Larson 1982). As Karen Kaiser Lee explains in Chapter 2 of this volume, the traditional research paper assignment has been criticized as busywork, a fact-finding, formulaic, regurgitation activity that students dislike writing and teachers dislike assigning. Lee also explains that, despite problems with plagiarism, the assignment persists because of its perceived benefit for students later in their academic careers and as a knowledge-making, expressive activity.

Other research into searching behaviors shows that if students are lazy researchers, they are simply doing what most researchers do. Studies have shown that often researchers of any kind (not just academic) use strategies and sources they are familiar with rather than ones they know are of higher quality. David Ellis and Merete Haugan

(1997) studied engineers and scientists in Norway and found that engineers in particular tended to rely on verbal communication with colleagues and librarian-assisted searches of their field's literature, and they fashioned their searches based on whatever research was most easily available within the project's timeline. Similarly, students fashion their searches on the most readily available full-text sources, by using Google, even when they may be fully aware of library databases and interlibrary loan. Kyung-Sun Kim and Sei-Ching J. Sin (2007) found from surveying 225 undergraduates that accuracy and trustworthiness were preferred characteristics for information just slightly more than accessibility when choosing among web portals, print sources, and family and friends as sources of information. Michelle Twait (2005) conducted think-aloud protocols with 13 students as they did online searches and concluded that the students ranked relevant content as the most important selection criteria, but with familiarity and reliability being rated higher than availability or accuracy. Studies such as these help us understand students' preferences, but the studies neither explain why students rank some features so highly nor whether library databases provided the relevant, familiar, and accessible information that they preferred.

While library databases require significant time and effort in most research-writing assignments, very few studies have looked at how the search for material affects the writing. One of the most relevant research studies on research processes involving library skills was conducted by Barbara Fister (1992), who interviewed students extensively about their research processes. She found that most students don't follow the traditional general-to-specific rule of thumb for undergraduate research; they use a variety of browsing techniques rather than targeted keyword searches, and they integrate their searching, focusing, and writing processes. Fister's study also points out why traditional general-to-specific library instruction doesn't work: Students in most courses already have some background in the subject matter and rely on their instructor, not an encyclopedia or handbook, to guide their topic choice. Chandra Prabha, Lynn S. Connaway, Lawrence Olszewski, and

Lillie Jenkins (2007) identified the most prominent reason why undergraduates decide to stop their searches, which they call "satisficing": Students reach the requirements of the assignment, have enough material to write the assignment, and/or their allotted time runs out. Most students don't have time to embrace a topic fully and do a methodical search of sources when the results may be unpredictable and the goals ambiguous.

The lack of research on the effect of searching databases on students' writing processes may be caused by the assumption among both students and instructors that the databases are neutral, transparent tools, requiring only one-shot library instruction to use well and effectively. If databases are thus the equivalent of a handy tool which simply requires some practice to use well, then instructors and librarians hardly need to spend their time improving how they support students in their searches. However, Kathleen Yancey (2010) mentions library databases as one of the new locations of undergraduate research, a location along with library buildings that are not designed specifically for undergraduates or for single semesters. According to Yancey, undergraduate research in such new locations can help students participate in forming a scholarly identity by giving them greater independence.

If certain locations of research, such as library databases, support students as they begin to enter the scholarly conversations in their fields, then those databases deserve our greater attention. This research study shows how library databases and the ways students navigate them significantly impact students' writing. Databases shape how students engage with, and often abandon, topics as well as how, and whether, they consciously view searching as part of the drafting process. The data collected shows a number of individualized exploratory methods used by students for online academic research, which included a mix of Google-associated practices, typical satisficing behaviors, and even misunderstandings of how article databases work.

Methods: Following Students' Searching Processes

This chapter presents the findings from an action research study conducted in the fall of 2008 of 18 first-year college students' processes of
searching for scholarly articles as part of a research-writing assignment.
The students were enrolled in one of two sections of a first-year writing course, and both sections met regularly in a computer classroom.
As the instructor and researcher, I used screen capture software to
record and evaluate students' searches at several points: pre-instruction
(before demonstrating the features of scholarly articles and library
databases), post-instruction, and in a follow-up session. I also consulted students' written self-reports of their searching strategies and
their final research papers. All of the students included in the study
were traditional 18- to 19-year-olds, attending a regional comprehensive university with average ACT scores of 21. All students previously
had a library orientation session in a required first-year seminar course,
and four students (22 percent) said they had used a library database
before this course.

Their assignment was a one-source reaction paper, designed to provide an early exposure to research-writing. The assignment asked students to find one professional or scholarly article (but not necessarily
peer-reviewed) of at least four pages with which they had some reason
to engage. Students were allowed to choose any topic with which they
had some kind of direct personal experience, and they were encouraged
to connect the assignment to issues they were studying in other classes
to give them some background knowledge of the topic.

The assignment called for a response paper rather than a typical
research paper, and it asked students to analyze the article carefully
and then agree, disagree, interpret, and/or explain the importance of
the main points of the article for an audience of their peers. Because
the focus of the entire paper was one professional or scholarly article,
a great deal of the success of the students' papers rested on finding the
right kind of article. Students were to use paraphrasing and quoting,
avoid plagiarism, use an online library resource, and practice basic
documentation.

As the first step of the assignment, students made a list of 10 possible topics. Second, students worked at their computers (purposely with no guidance) to find some "good" articles for the assignment. After students recorded what process they followed, I demonstrated how to access and perform a keyword search in Academic OneFile (a large, multidisciplinary database of journals, magazines, and newspapers). Students then returned to their computers to continue searching for possible articles for the assignment. In the next class meeting, students continued searching, discussed the differences between using Google and using library databases, and investigated the characteristics of formal scholarly articles. Based on this assignment process and using analytic transcripts of the screen capture videos as well as students' papers and self-reflections, I studied students' screen movements, looking particularly at the sequence of moves that got students to articles that they considered acceptable enough for their papers.

Results: Library Databases as Mazes

As might be expected, every student in this study used a different strategy for finding articles that fit the assignment. In general, though, these students had at least three approaches in common for finding articles in library databases: trying new topics as opposed to trying more varied kinds of searches; persisting in long scans of one narrow topic; and rethinking their interests in a topic to allow for a broader range of articles.

Trying New Topics
The largest group of students encountered the maze of the library database by looking continually for new openings. This included nine (50 percent) of the students. These students only looked at one page of search results and did not try alternate terms after initial unsuccessful searches. In their self-reflections after the class, these students said they didn't find anything in which they were interested. On average, these students spent 80 percent of their searching time looking at results lists

that were only tangentially related to their topics. They spent a lot of time slogging through lists of article titles, and they made decisions about what to write about based on these seemingly irrelevant search results, often dismissing articles that I would have recommended as excellent choices. The first hour of searching appeared exploratory, but this exploratory searching limited their ideas while not focusing them or redirecting them to other possibilities.

In fact, there seemed to be no correlation between what students did in their searches and their success at finding articles. Narrowing a very broad topic worked sometimes, and other times it didn't. Trying various keywords worked sometimes, and other times it didn't. For instance, searching for research articles on the interesting question of "whether younger teens could be trusted to drive responsibly" (in other words, could the driving age be lowered) yields few results that a first-semester college student would likely find engaging. The keywords "driving age" brought a student to the subject "motor vehicle driving laws," yet the subtopic "laws, regulations, and rules" brought up articles about distracted driving and the problems of older drivers, moving the student farther and farther away from her true interest.

This random "findability" characteristic of library databases meant that students ultimately needed a different search strategy for every topic, but they used only one search strategy. For instance, Dustin[1] searched under the keyword "healthcare," was directed to the subject heading "medical care," then chose the subtopic "medical care insurance" and spent several minutes scanning a good article reviewing the reasons why health care costs have skyrocketed in recent years. He moved on, however, to the subtopic "finance" but was not interested in the articles that were presented (health equity in Malaysia, medical coding costs, HIPAA, and bounced checks). He then backtracked to new keyword searches on "economics" and "economic depression." The article titles in his results list were about the concept of open federalism, imperialism theory, and Latin America's liberal economics. Dustin ultimately rejected all of these topics and wrote about college students and credit card debt. As with the other students in this group, whose searches resembled looking for random openings in a maze of sources, he ultimately wrote, according to his self-reflection, about a topic he was less interested in, therefore allowing him to distance himself from the topic and turn the assignment into a routine paraphrasing activity.

The student described here spent less than 2 minutes searching any topic. When he got irrelevant results, he moved on to other topics. Students who used this strategy were more or less looking for black-and-white results. Either a search brought up a group of relevant articles immediately or they moved on to another topic. This strategy appears to be borrowed from Google searches, where the context and content of the search is quite different from library databases. Google searches are more likely to be successful upon the first try because students are often looking for the same information for which millions of other users are looking. Students in this group did try to use the limiting features of the database to narrow their topics and use the suggested subtopics and alternate subject terms; however, their lack of success using such features and strategies probably reinforced their reversion back to more Google-like approaches.

Sticking It Out With One Narrow Topic

Unsuccessful database searches forced one student to adapt the assignment rather than adapt his choice of topics. Mark tried in vain to find journal articles about college athletes turning professional. Because not much beyond opinion-based magazine articles has been published on this topic in the field of exercise science, he had a difficult time searching. This topic was one he had knowledge of and a purpose for writing about, and eventually he decided to write his paper in response to a webpage that did not meet the assignment criteria, rather than change his topic.

More persistent students had as little success as those who kept trying different topics. This second, much smaller group of students stayed true to their first choice of topics and tried, with random success, to make the database find what they wanted. Three students (15 percent) stuck with unsuccessful searches for more than 20 minutes and did not try alternate terms. For instance, one student in this group, Alicia, was a knowledgeable, persistent searcher who indicated she knew about library databases before being introduced to them again in this course. Alicia focused on just two topics: competitive swimming, in which she was currently participating, and the effect of strokes, from which her grandmother was recovering.

When she moved to Academic OneFile, she attempted all the techniques offered in the instruction session: basic and subject searches, alternate keywords, delimiter tabs, and even the article linker. Using a combination of these strategies, she repeated the same searches with the same search terms several times, never moving far away from the keyword "swimming," apparently trusting that she would see something in her results if she looked again. She downloaded only one article and did not use it for her paper. Most of the article titles she skimmed were irrelevant to her topic and interests, even though she had the right subject term and subcategories: Some were about swimming crabs in Australia, some were about experiments with rats, and so on. Alicia's self-assessment at the end of the assignment included a rather unreflective statement: "It took me a while to look through all the articles, but I finally came across two perfect articles that fit the topics I was looking for." One would imagine her searching process was simply "looking" until the right articles popped up, as opposed to the topic switching strategy.

Broadening a Topic

A third, also small, group of students broadened their keyword searches in order to adapt their topics to what they were finding in the databases. Two students (10 percent) tried broader terms during their searches (for instance, trying "violence" after trying "video game violence"). One student in this group, Alaina, quickly found usable articles on adoption. However, she entered the searching process with an attitude different from other students. In her final reflection, she explained:

> One main problem that I encountered was the fact that
> even though there was a vast amount of article results
> found, not many of them had to do with what I specifically
> wanted to write about. … To solve the first problem I had,
> I just changed what I specifically wanted to write about,
> and decided to just find an article that caught my interest
> in the same subject area.

Because Alaina was browsing for something interesting on the broad topic of adoption, she found many articles to download, read several abstracts, and saved at least four of them. She browsed in the journal *Child and Family Social Work*, when the article linker led her to the entire journal instead of just the article.

Overall: Proceeding Without Awareness of Strategies

Students in this study encountered obstacles mostly at the point that the detailed instruction of the database demonstration stopped. For some students, the database demonstration gave them a visual list or sequence of clicking for getting started, which allowed them to get to the library webpage; then access the database; then do keyword, subject, and subtopic searching. When they had to move ahead on their own, they didn't read very carefully or understand some of the lingo of databases. For instance, four students in the study (22 percent) stopped searching on a topic when they found an interesting article title but didn't understand how to access the full text immediately. In another instance, one student didn't realize that the function of the "search within these results" box was continuing to limit her search instead of broadening it.

Another pronounced feature of the students' searching was their lack of conscious strategies when searching databases. Fourteen of the students (80 percent) had no details to report on their searching strategies in their written self-reflections at the end of the research process. Even after several weeks of discussing research processes, including more in-class sessions searching databases, most students wrote something similar to what Ryan wrote: "I really only used one search strategy and that was searching on the databases in the school library." Ryan's comment points out the crucial nature of switching from Google to a library database as a strategy, but it also points out the students' feeling that searching databases was a matter of random finding.

Implications

If we assume that there are appropriate sources to be found in the library databases, then we also assume that more specific library instruction, more time to search, and more limited topic choices would solve the problem of the research paper. This set of assumptions rests on the belief that students have straightforward rhetorical tasks in front of them and that the database is a neutral tool for completing those tasks. Prior to conducting this research on research, I would have made similar assumptions, not knowing how the database searches were affecting the students' choice of sources and their subsequent papers. In the past, I was just happy that most of my students found "something" and wrote adequate papers. However, the high variability of students' search results according to topic (*seat belts* is a different kind of search from *hunting*, for instance) makes simply adjusting the instruction difficult. Students' encounters with the library database were highly individualized, even though their responses on paper were generic and vague, indicating that they didn't (and weren't encouraged) to problematize their searches or to see their searches as something other than random events governed by luck.

The library databases thus present a number of obstacles: technical jargon, confusing mixes of programs, assistive search algorithms that try to help, and a preponderance of technical articles intended only for experts in that field. The databases also made good results (appropriate articles for the assignment) look unappealing and confusing to students or, in some cases, simply overwhelmed them with too many results. Thus, the more fixated students were on a specific topic, the more they needed to luck upon the right keywords or to be persistent in their searching. With limited time, and with the encouragement of database vendors to put articles in folders for checking out later, the same way that they put items in carts in an online store as if they were shopping for knowledge, databases encourage students to use a more "consumptive" version of searching than a preferred exploratory version of searching. As Kelly Ritter (2010, 90) points out, writing a paper often becomes a "students versus sources" problem, as evidenced in her survey of about 400 students from two different universities that showed only 35–40 percent of students considered their academic writing to be an act of "authorship."

Library Database Searching as Discursive and Developmental

The way the students in this study used library databases indicates that they saw themselves as subjects with a linear, single purpose, one independent of variables. The students in this study apparently learned that database searching is like rummaging around in a stranger's attic full of random items saved over the years. Students' sense of authority, thus, becomes as disembodied as the articles in the database. Therefore, future versions of the response paper assignment need to show students how the databases are a kind of conversation among the scholarly community and are only apparently random, as one's personal Twitter feeds might look to a stranger. If instead we think of databases as a kind of discourse, as Mark Poster (1996) proposes, then we should include database searching as part of the rhetorical situation for any research-writing assignment. As Poster points out, discourse (including databases) has the power to constitute the subject in hidden ways. We need to make those constructive powers less hidden and more consciously a part of students' research processes.

If instructors and librarians see students' attempts to search library databases through a developmental lens, then they should redefine unsuccessful searches as developmental markers. Obviously, the influence of popular search engines such as Google has to be taken into account when designing research-writing assignments, the same way we consider any prior knowledge possessed by our students. Most of us use Google without instruction and with only one strategy—entering keywords and skimming the first set of results. Because this usually works on Google for nonscholarly topics, such as finding the local movie show times, students expect it to work elsewhere, and they are more resistant or just hesitant to develop search strategies needed for library databases. However, we don't want students to get stuck, developmentally, in these Google-ized searching behaviors. For example, as first steps toward more sophisticated searching, the students in this study learned a lot: how much persistence and time research takes, how library databases and Google differ, how influential the right research material is on the resulting paper.

Yet we don't have to assume students aren't interested in learning more. While students' searches are influenced by extensive practice with Google, they were shown to be mostly receptive to more academic resources and able to use Google as an additional strategy combined with library databases. Before they were given instruction about library databases, all of the students in this study used Google to find research articles, while afterward, 90 percent of them returned to the library databases and used Google as a secondary strategy. If there's a bad influence from using Google, it's the failure to read instructions around search boxes, such as the option to "search within these results." In this developmental vision, "not finding anything" (a constant refrain in my students' self-reflections) doesn't have to imply "not learning anything," and failed searches can be made a part of the research process.

Making Database Searching a Part of the Research-Writing Process: Suggested Assignments and Strategies

If we continue to value research-writing assignments in the university, we need to take into account the nature of library research databases. Students need safety nets, more chances to approximate research, and more time to read articles. As my students' experiences indicate, there's no such thing as a quick search for relevant scholarly articles because the databases are too big and complex.

An initial annotated bibliography, which is a traditional preparation step in many research projects, can be adapted to help focus first-year writers on shaping their topic. In the past, I have not assigned an annotated bibliography in first-year writing courses, in order to minimize the amount of work required for an assignment. However, minimizing the work may be more frustrating than maximizing the possibilities; in other words, asking students to find 20 articles vaguely connected to their topic has been more helpful, as a step in a longer process, than asking them to find one article to which they were certain they could respond. An annotated bibliography on a broadly conceived topic allows students some time and space for listening in on the conversation in the field, if not actually entering the conversation. A colleague of mine asks her students to prepare a bibliography of articles, all on different topics, but within the students' career field, simply to begin finding out what people on the job (teachers, corrections officers, nurses, graphic designers) are talking about in publications.

Other activities can make searching databases and using Google part of the conscious research-writing process, such as an assignment to write an analysis comparing the results from a Google search and library database search on one topic. I have also asked students to focus on how databases work by assigning a library database review, where students develop criteria for evaluating a database and then apply the criteria in a review paper. Many first-year writing courses include a website evaluation or website review; therefore, a database review would be a natural follow-up to other kinds of review-based assignments, providing solid, analytical writing practice, even if no research paper is to follow. I-Search papers, for instance, are process-intensive and encourage students to think carefully about how they are searching, as well as evaluating what they find (see Macrorie 1988; also see Lee in Chapter 2 of this volume).

Embedding librarians more completely into a series of research-based assignments has also proved invaluable. As Thomas Peele, Melissa Keith, and Sara Seely report in Chapter 14 of this volume, students at Boise State University learned more about research when information literacy, research, and writing were integrated in their coursework. More library instruction tailored specifically to the research project at hand has been more helpful than simply giving students more library instruction. Embedding a librarian in a writing course may include devising research paper assignments together along with inviting the librarian to attend class, offer regular feedback to students about topics, and help students through research obstacles during their drafting and revising processes.

Librarians have access to information about databases beyond the mechanics of how to get results. Their knowledge of the inner workings of databases, database costs in dollars as well as resources, and the uneasy relationship between traditional print materials and open access information can illuminate the power structure behind a simple keyword search in a database. I collaborate with my librarian as a "section designer" in all of my online writing courses so that she can anticipate research-writing problems, see patterns in questions from students, and provide individual as well as group instruction. Likewise, a required appointment for an individual consultation (face-to-face or online) with a librarian may be much more helpful to students than several hours of demonstrations on databases (although few libraries have sufficient staffing for such an assignment).

Finally, instructors can also work with librarians to develop a theme-based database demonstration on a topic of integral importance to the course, such as procrastination or documentation, which can then also act as a student's "second-choice" last-ditch topic. In my courses, the themed database demonstration has led to small group activities comparing database results or developing instant handouts to share with the entire class. When students have more thorough experience searching for articles about at least one workable topic, they can work independently on new topics with more confidence. Given the highly variable nature of topics, as shown by my students in this study, a demonstration that compares two topics requiring very different research strategies would also be helpful.

Conclusion

The fact that library databases are fast, accessible, and full of features for targeted searching might lead writing instructors to think that research is easier and thus less influential on students' research-writing. Instead, speed, accessibility, and search features give databases more shaping power over students' writing processes.

This study shows how database searching affects students' understanding of research as a process and how the databases change their concepts of what and how to write. The databases gave students the opportunity to conduct research independently and on topics of importance to their lives, but the databases also limited that independence and reduced their choice of topics. Most significantly, the topics over which they held the most personal authority were often the ones least likely to be supported by accessible scholarly articles.

Robert Davis and Mark Shadle (2000) encourage assigning "alternative" research papers that insist on mystery and exploration, but as long as library databases and Google are part of the research process, searching for secondary sources of support for their papers will feel like an arbitrary maze to be navigated for a short period, rather than part of the discovery process. Students may have an "itch," as Davis and Shadle describe it (423), but those itches are reduced to something less fascinating by the mediation of the database. This rhetorical situation exemplifies one of the many discursive relationships students should be able to understand.

Teachers and librarians need to continue researching what students do online as they search for supporting materials for their compositions. With better information about student searching strategies, instructors can balance writing and researching tasks without letting research tasks overwhelm the core goal of the writing assignment. Classroom research could tell instructors how much time students need for research and what kind of library database instruction students need: detailed database feature instruction, sample searches as models (including how to do nonlinear research and what to do with unsuccessful searches), more advanced searching skills such as citation chasing even at lower undergraduate levels, or more inquiry-based classroom activities.

If we believe the research paper assignment has value for NextGen students, it is worth our time to more intentionally study student research processes and to extend our teaching methods to include database searching processes within the varied research processes introduced to the new digital scholar.

Endnote

1. All student names are pseudonyms.

References

Bennett, Sue, Karl Maton, and Lisa Kervin. 2008. "The 'Digital Natives' Debate: A Critical Review of the Evidence." *British Journal of Educational Technology* 39 (5): 775–786.

Brabazon, Tara. 2006. "The Google Effect: Googling, Blogging, Wikis and the Flattening of Expertise." *Libri: International Journal of Libraries and Information Services* 56: 157–167.

Carlson, Jake. 2006. "An Examination of Undergraduate Student Citation Behavior." *Journal of Academic Librarianship* 32 (1): 14–22.

Davis, Robert, and Mark Shadle. 2000. "'Building a Mystery': Alternative Research Writing and the Academic Act of Seeking." *College Composition and Communication* 51 (3): 417–446.

Ellis, David, and Merete Haugan. 1997. "Modeling the Information Seeking Patterns of Engineers and Research Scientists in an Industrial Environment." *Journal of Documentation* 53 (4): 384–403.

Fister, Barbara. 1992. "The Research Processes of Undergraduate Students." *Journal of Academic Librarianship* 18 (3): 163–169.

Grobman, Laurie. 2009. "The Student Scholar: (Re)Negotiating Authorship and Authority." *College Composition and Communication* 61 (1): W175–W196.

Harris, Joseph. 2006. *Rewriting: How to Do Things with Texts*. Logan, UT: Utah State University Press.

Head, Alison, and Michael Eisenberg. 2009. "Lessons Learned: How College Students Seek Information in the Digital Age." *Project Information Literacy Progress Report*. Accessed September 18, 2012. www.projectinfolit.org/pdfs/PIL_Fall2009_Year1 Report_12_2009.pdf.

Kim, Kyung-Sun, and Sei-Ching Sin. 2007. "Perception and Selection of Information Sources by Undergraduate Students: Effects of Avoidant Style, Confidence, and Personal Control in Problem-Solving." *Journal of Academic Librarianship* 33 (6): 655–665.

Larson, Richard L. 1982. "The "Research Paper" in the Writing Course: A Non-form of Writing. *College English* 44 (8): 811–816.

Macrorie, Ken. 1988. *The I-Search Paper*. Portsmouth, NH: Boynton/Cook Heinemann.

Poster, Mark. 1996. "Databases as Discourse: Or, Electronic Interpellations." In *Computers, Surveillance, and Privacy*, edited by David Lyon and Elia Zureik, 175–192. Minneapolis: University of Minnesota Press.

Prabha, Chandra, Lynn S. Connaway, Lawrence Olszewski, and Lillie R. Jenkins. 2007. "What Is Enough? Satisficing Information Needs." *Journal of Documentation* 63 (1): 74–89.

Ritter, Kelly. 2010. *Who Owns School? Authority, Students, and Online Discourse*. Cresskill, NJ: Hampton Press.

Sidler, Michelle. 2002. "Web Research and Genres in Online Databases: When the Glossy Page Disappears." *Computers and Composition* 19: 57–70.

Thompson, Christen. 2003. "Information Illiterate or Lazy: How College Students Use the Web for Research." *Portal: Libraries and the Academy* 3 (2): 259–268.

Twait, Michelle. 2005. "Undergraduate Students' Source Selection Criteria: A Qualitative Study." *Journal of Academic Librarianship* 31 (6): 567–573.

Yancey, Kathleen Blake. 2010. "Afterword." In *Undergraduate Research in English Studies*, edited by Laurie Grobman and Joyce Kinkead, 245–253. Urbana, IL: NCTE.

Pedagogical Solutions to Enrich the Research and Writing Practices of NextGen Students

Undergraduate Research as Collaborative Knowledge Work

Christa B. Teston and Brian J. McNely

Our students, regardless of major, can and should contribute new knowledge to the programs, professional domains, and broader disciplines within which they work as undergraduates. "Knowledge work," R. Stanley Dicks (2010) argues, relies on professionals who "can do many tasks well and can analyze and synthesize information" (53). Knowledge work likewise demands the understanding and regular implementation of multiple approaches to analysis and synthesis; knowledge workers should be as adept at human subjects research as they are at performing traditional forms of undergraduate inquiry.

Undergraduates' knowledge work is complicated by anecdotally based assumptions about the ways digital spaces and technologies impair students' ability to read, complete tasks, and think. Nicholas Carr (2010), for example, argues that web-based literacies are leading to a crisis of attention and a dearth of critical, deep-reading experiences. Implicit in many of these arguments is the Heideggerian (1977) notion of technological determinism: "Everywhere we remain unfree and chained to technology, whether we passionately affirm or deny it.

But we are delivered over to it in the worst possible way when we regard it as something neutral" (4). Bonnie Nardi and Vicki O'Day (1999) detail a similar ethos in their discussion of predominant technology metaphors that position technology as tool, text, or system; they argue that "technologies are not neutral—at the very least, they invoke in us certain kinds of responses" that are "intrinsic features" of the technologies we use and deploy (38). We ask: How do contemporary undergraduate researchers construct new knowledge while navigating dominant cultural assumptions about the supposed unreliability of digital information?

While this chapter will not explicitly attend to the issue of assessing the reliability of digital information (see Chapters 1 and 4 in this volume for more information on this issue) or the complexities of properly citing said information (see Chapter 5 in this volume for more information on this issue), it will provide one approach on which writing instructors might model students' departure from the Heideggerian fear and anxiety so often associated with conducting research in digital environments. Specifically, we detail one curricular and pedagogical approach to empowering students in their collaborative constructions of knowledge—collaborations made possible through, and afforded by, the digital technologies available to them. Moreover, we attend to issues related to students' digital agency as emerging researchers and knowledge workers and detail the means by which writing instructors might explicitly position them as such. Here, digital agency, following Carl Herndl and Adela Licona (2007), is *enacted* rather than possessed. This means explicitly positioning students as researchers who create new knowledge. In order to accomplish this, we describe and critique the results of a qualitative study that took place in one institution's introductory course to writing as a major.

In this chapter, we offer what we believe is a fundamental shift in thinking about what it means to ask students to do research, as we encourage the harnessing of students' digital agency toward the creation (not just the discovery) of new knowledge. Our final pedagogical recommendation (following Kaptelinin and Nardi 2006), therefore, includes asking students to *position themselves* as knowledge workers and to develop and investigate researchable questions that do not make transparent the technologies available to them, but instead place the people and practices surrounding these technologies as objects of study. Specifically, this chapter concludes with a set of suggested best practices for students as collaborative constructors of knowledge who recognize that technologies themselves are "tools with rhetorical constructions and implications" (Clark 2010, 86). Data from students' collaboratively written white papers and online survey responses inform our suggestions for best practices.

Looking at, Not Through, Technologies

One of the claims leveraged by critics of the vast amount of digital information available to student researchers is that they "tune it out" (Bauerlein 2008, 33) before being able to properly and adequately assess information toward some end. The fear, therefore, is that student researchers suffer from some brand of "information overload"—a construct invoked by Alvin Toffler in 1970 with his publication *Future Shock* (311). Interestingly, this construct, "information overload," was originated by consumer researchers Jacob Jacoby, Donald E. Speller, and Carol A. Kohn-Berning with their 1974 publication, "Brand Choice Behavior as a Function of Information Load: Replication and Extension." Jacoby, Speller, and Kohn-Berning investigated the ways in which participants—192 housewives, to be specific—experienced so-called "information overload" when faced with more brand options than were necessary for making a decision. The authors argue that in the face of this plethora of information, housewives were unable to make good decisions.

When we adopt the construct of "information overload" within the context of students' writing and digital research, we position students as little more than passive consumers of information who are expected to simply make surface observations of what is available to them, weigh those observations based on some implicit sense of need and appropriateness, and proceed accordingly. When students are reduced to information gatherers, they may not take the time to look *at* (versus *through*) the very tools, technologies, and information they use to research—whether that be source code and metadata, the reliability of an online journal article, or the note-taking capability of a mobile device. Toward these ends, we propose and then critique one curricular and pedagogical model that facilitates opportunities for students to conduct primary and secondary research of the practices surrounding particular contemporary writing technologies. In the next section, however, we trace the construct of knowledge work in a theoretically rich way in order to later operationalize it in a set of proposed best practices when adopting this particular pedagogical approach.

Positioning Students as Knowledge Workers

The notion of knowledge work has seen increased scholarly attention in professional and technical communication since 2005. Clay Spinuzzi (2006) defines knowledge work as that "in which the primary product is knowledge, information that is continually interpreted and circulated across organizational boundaries" (1). We argue that knowledge work is a construct that should inform writing curricula and pedagogy and can be productively articulated with recent trends in undergraduate research (as detailed, for example, in Karukstis and Elgren 2007). Positioning undergraduate students as knowledge workers is, in large measure, to position them explicitly as *researchers* (for example, see McNely 2010), since many knowledge work practices involve the exploration of problems within both local and distributed environments, with attention to the technologies that mediate such interactions.

A knowledge work approach to curricula and pedagogies, therefore, necessarily enlarges the potential for students' enactment of agency, placing upon them the responsibility to actively engage one another while addressing real-world problems via both distributed and *in situ* research and collaboration. Both Johndan Johnson-Eilola (2005) and

Jason Swarts (2007) see the foundations of knowledge work in Robert Reich's (1992) figurations of the symbolic-analytic, where professionals work "within information, filtering, rearranging, transforming, and making connections to address specific, specialized problems" (Johnson-Eilola 2005, 19). Cynthia Selfe (1999) argues that Reich's ideas supported the Clinton administration's push for the National Information Infrastructure (NII) by focusing on the types of information economy skills that would be necessary in the 21st-century workforce.

Johnson-Eilola (2005) argues that "symbolic analysts are people we might think of as *technical rhetoricians* working in the datacloud" (19). This perspective is crucial, since it necessitates that student researchers as knowledge workers will learn to think and act rhetorically, while constantly renegotiating their enactment of agency within contemporary work and school structures. These contemporary social structures are in turn mediated by people acting intentionally with technologies (Kaptelinin and Nardi 2006), by "the human-made, purposeful, rhetorical, and political choices" that people make in local environments (Haas 1996, 216). Not coincidentally, the initial item in Spinuzzi's (2006) list of what we should teach about knowledge work is rhetoric. Rhetoric, therefore, is both an essential aptitude and critical perspective within a knowledge work approach because of the contemporary realities and possibilities of collaborative, technologically mediated research and practice in a wide variety of fields.

We suggest that positioning students as knowledge workers helps to counter some of the fears and anxieties digital researchers might have about conducting real-time research of the ways that writing technologies shape knowledge construction. Rather than reinforcing (tacitly or otherwise) the cultural myths of a transparent or all-powerful technology, positioning students as knowledge workers, we argue, requires them to explicitly confront the rhetorical, social, and subjective relations imbricated in contemporary digital research. Student researchers as knowledge workers strive to uncover human action and intentionality by looking *at*, rather than *through*, technologies; more importantly, these researchers, working collaboratively to *create* new knowledge about writing technologies, foster rich possibilities for enacting agency.

In the following sections, we explore the ways one particular pedagogical approach affords student researchers the opportunity to empirically investigate writing tools, technologies, people, and practices in a specific, local environment. We provide specific, local information relative to this curricular and pedagogical approach and make explicit where and when these local practices might be generalizable or applicable to both the undergraduate or graduate writing classroom. We are also critically reflective, however, of the ways students could have been better positioned as knowledge workers and had more meaningful experiences as researchers in digital environments.

One Pedagogical Approach

As a way to explore how students negotiate the complexity of conducting *in situ* research of writing technologies, we investigated a course required of all incoming writing arts majors at a midsized, state-funded institution on the East Coast. This particular course, "Introduction to Writing Arts," has three separate modules through which students cycle over the 15-week semester. The "Technologies and the Future of Writing" module has as a pedagogical goal—by the end of the 4-week cycle—of students' completion of a collaboratively written white paper that involves primary and secondary research regarding a particular information ecology (see Appendix for the assignment description). Students, therefore, spend approximately 1 full week conducting real-time, *in situ* research of the people, practices, values, and technologies within a local environment. For the majority of students, this is their first foray into human subjects research and is the first time they have had to draw on primary research in order to construct an argument.

The White Paper Research Experience

The assignment description (see Appendix) is provided to students as a way to guide their development of a researchable question, a set of investigative methods, and the development of prose toward their collaboratively written white paper. What is advantageous about this pedagogical approach is that students gain firsthand experience with conducting primary research about writing technologies and the practices surrounding them—technologies and practices that may have, at least up until this point, remained mostly invisible or transparent to them. Additionally, by asking student researchers to write their white papers in teams of four or five, they gain experience with collaborative constructions of knowledge and the writing technologies that facilitate these collaborations. Moreover, by using the IMRAD format (Introduction, Methods, Results, Analysis, and Discussion), many students learn a new writing genre that is prevalent in a variety of fields. Finally, the white paper experience affords opportunities for students to gain familiarity with a wide range of research methods. Students from our sample deployed a range of methods and approaches. Some of them conducted observations of technological practices, while others solicited participants for surveys. Still others developed small-scale case studies of actual users and their practices surrounding a particular technology. Some also chose to deploy a mixed-methods approach by combining observation with interviews or surveys.

One Pedagogical Approach, Critiqued

Despite the affordances of this pedagogical approach toward the positioning of undergraduate researchers as knowledge workers, we now turn to a critical review and reflection of the struggles had by students. In so doing, we hope to develop a set of generalizable best practices for future renditions of the white paper experience, and, more broadly, of undergraduate researchers engaging in human subjects research under a knowledge work model. Because this was the first time this particular module was designed in this way, and because this was the first time students were asked to conduct actual, real-time, *in situ* human subjects research within their second year of higher education, the collection and analysis of data is useful not so much for the purpose of assessing student success, but to better understand what pedagogical improvements might be made in subsequent renditions of this module, and in deploying a knowledge work approach more generally. As such, the following data and analysis is useful not because it warrants generalizable claims about students' research habits, but because it can help inform writing instructors' knowing-in-action (Schon 1987), thereby providing the grounds by which pedagogical best practices might be proposed—best practices that may be implemented in a range of writing classrooms.

Our research spans three semesters of the "Technologies and the Future of Writing" module and includes an analysis of 11 student white papers composed by a total of 38 students. In addition to the detailed and systematic analysis of 11 collaboratively written white papers, we developed an online survey available to all students who had completed the white paper assignment, and 20 of the 80 students enrolled in the "Technologies" course completed the survey. We also collected a small sample of students' in-progress collaborative work that took place in a web-based, collaborative text editor. This was primarily brainstorming work.

White papers were analyzed based on the following inductively derived codes for instances of the following occurrences: a) explicit consultation of outside sources or research, b) explicit stating of research question, c) explicit description of research method deployed, d) explicit statement about contributions the study makes to a broader argument, e) explicit statement of claim or argument. The total number of sources in the References section was also noted. Evaluative remarks were withheld for this particular analysis. Quality of prose, grammatical errors, and other kinds of surface errors were not considered for the purposes of coding and analysis for this particular study.

In general, student researchers struggled with two primary activities related to the white paper experience:

1. The development of a researchable question

2. The rhetorically effective incorporation of extant scholarship or research related to their investigation

The articulation of a research question is an important starting point for the generation of new knowledge about practices surrounding a particular technology. In addition, being able to consult—and join the scholarly conversation—in extant research is central to the building of an argument and subsequent contributions to broader intellectual, cultural, or technological debates. How can we facilitate opportunities for students to grow in these two respects? Moreover, how might students be challenged to do this kind of work while calling attention to the ways our tools and technologies shape the collaborative construction of knowledge?

The Development of a Researchable Question

Because more than half of the white papers we analyzed seemed to ask different research questions at the beginning of the paper than at the end, we chose to drill down on instances of explicitly articulated research questions. The informed modification of research questions is a necessary activity when conducting primary research; however, these students' peripheral research questions did not seem to be modifications of research questions based on findings or observational experiences, but a result of not feeling comfortable with the narrowing of their investigative gaze to specific practices. For instance, one white paper explicitly articulated their research question at the beginning as "What are the effects of Multimedia Messaging Service (MMS) usage in professional writing?" but then moved on to two peripheral research questions: "Does MMS usage 'sneak into' professional, academic writing?" and "Is there a trend of students noticing text language appearing in academic work?" Another collaborative group asked, "How do people in the public eye develop their persona through Twitter?" but later in their paper they asked two peripheral research questions: "Are people judging public figures based on what those public figures are tweeting?" and "How do different types of Twitter users utilize the microblogging tool?" Each of these three questions requires entirely different data sets and ways of analyzing said data. Sometimes students' research questions shifted throughout the course of the paper, but often students loaded their introduction with layer upon layer of research questions—all seemingly pertaining to the same "topic," but not necessarily investigating the same *question*.

Evidence of students' struggle with the development of a researchable question, and not simply a topic upon which they could write a paper, is also available in participants' responses to the online survey. Specifically, we asked participants, "How did you develop the research question for your white paper?" Interestingly, students seem to describe their answer to this question by including words like "topic," "technology," "idea," or "interest." For instance, one respondent wrote, "Our research question came from our personal *interests*" (emphasis added). Another wrote, "We developed the research question for our White Paper by brainstorming the general *topics* that we discussed in class. We all thought of one *topic* to research, put them together, and chose one as a group. We then modified it to fit the guidelines of the assignment" (emphasis added). A final representative response includes: "Through some discussions we had during our module, my group and I decided on our question because it was something we were *interested* in. The idea that new technologies are not evil, but the way that people use them makes it seem that way, was primarily what *interested* us. Therefore, we sought to prove this" (emphasis added).

The majority of all responses include students interchangeably referring to what was asked of them to describe—the "research question"— as some kind of topic, technology, idea, or interest. While the assignment description explicitly asks them to develop a research question about a particular *set of practices* engaged in by people surrounding a writing technology, students seem more comfortable with using language like "topic," "idea," or "interest." This language, however, clearly shaped what it is they set out to accomplish with their research. Within this particular white paper assignment, topics facilitate a broad-based exploration of a particular thing or idea, whereas engaging in human subjects research by asking a specific research question should yield some kind of new knowledge about a particular practice or set of practices. While students' attention was, indeed, directed at a certain technology, and while they no longer *saw through* it, they seemed unable to remain committed to a particular motivating query or investigation because of their overwhelming focus on a "topic" instead of a "question."

Data from this sample of students also seem to suggest that more pedagogical effort is necessary with respect to the ways that students find, assess, and invoke outside, secondary sources in conversation with their primary research. While several of the students' white papers demonstrated some rather rigorous attempts at the collection of data (i.e., the development of codes and heuristics for investigation), they do not substantiate broader claims or contributions to a larger conversation with the persuasive consultation of outside sources. Most white papers included only cursory references to outside knowledge either at the very beginning or the very end. Moreover, the majority of the white papers from our sample did not create conversation among the sources they invoked in those sections. They peppered in a quote or a scholar's name and moved on. Lack of rigor with respect to consultation and integration of secondary sources may have resulted because the assignment description (because of the emphasis on learning primary research) did not explicitly require a certain number of outside sources. One pedagogical approach, however, is to resist artificially requiring a certain number of sources necessary for the successful completion of research. And yet it is clear that students need more explicit instruction on the rhetorical necessity of incorporating extant scholarship relevant to the research question at hand.

The Incorporation of Extant Research

Evidence toward students' struggle with the rhetorical incorporation of extant research or outside sources relevant to their research is also available in participants' responses to the online survey. Specifically, we asked participants, "How did you know when to consult outside sources when writing your White Paper?" Representative responses included the following:

- "When writing our White Paper, we consulted outside sources when we came upon a stumbling block, needed clarification of an idea, or simply wanted to provide examples to verify our findings."
- "We knew we needed to use these outside sources when we needed to back up a point we had. Our points needed to be solid, and the outside sources solidified them."
- "When we needed to back up and have evidence to support our paper/point."

Responses seem to indicate that students perceive the act of consulting outside sources as having the fundamental aim of *verification*. They see the consultation of outside sources as a way to "back up," "clarify," or "solidify" their points or ideas. While some students' responses are more rigorous—"In order to give our research data meaning, we had to compare it to the class readings," for example—the students whose white papers we analyzed definitely struggled with the rhetorical integration of outside sources.

Based on these two struggles experienced by students during the white paper assignment, we now propose generalizable best practices with respect to guiding student researchers in digital environments. We propose that one possible pedagogical intervention that might facilitate the construction of researchable questions and the rhetorically effective incorporation of extant research related to their investigation includes the positioning of students as active knowledge workers, not passive consumers of information. Again, while the white paper research projects afforded students experience with collaboratively constructing knowledge, writing in a new genre, deploying qualitative research methods, and looking *at* and not *through* writing technologies, their learning experience could have been improved were they more effectively positioned as knowledge workers.

Students as Knowledge Workers

Were students more effectively explicitly positioned as knowledge workers while conducting primary and secondary research of digital writing technologies, they may a) more readily embrace their role as active constructors of questions that do not have immediate answers, and b) feel more empowered to contribute to broader, previously published conversations surrounding their research questions. In general, therefore, a pedagogical approach to inculcating effective collaborative knowledge work involves

1. Questions, not topics

2. Conversation, not verification

Writing instructors should aim to encourage student researchers to develop, articulate, and remain committed to a researchable question as opposed to reporting on a particular "topic." In order to see themselves as co-creators of new knowledge, it is important that they ask questions that invite investigation rather than reinforce generally accepted truths, cultural lore, or assumptions about technology. Were students more explicitly positioned as knowledge workers—that is, were they invited to better understand the construct itself and then asked to adopt that role in their research—they might be more apt to understand the rhetorical difference between asking and investigating a question instead of reporting on a topic. Asking a question does not always presuppose that there be an answer, either. Students, when invited to ask researchable questions rather than report on fixed topics, might more readily embrace the ways in which knowledge does not exist *a priori*, but is actively and collaboratively constructed.

Writing instructors should also challenge student researchers to create conversations with the consultation of outside sources. This is a markedly different task than invoking extant scholarship as a way to prove, verify, or support ideas or predetermined points. Were students more explicitly positioned as knowledge workers, they might better perceive their researcher role as one that contributes to a broader conversation instead of simply cherry-picking facts or dropping names at the beginning or end of their research, as was the case with the majority of our sample student white papers.

We argue that both of these best practices could be better accomplished upon the deliberate and intentional pedagogical positioning of students as knowledge workers. In order to accomplish this, we propose that students develop the core competencies of knowledge work by a) becoming fluent in theoretical definitions of and characteristics implicit in the construct "knowledge work," b) publicly vetting researchable questions that encourage looking *at* and not *through* technology (perhaps in a web-based, collaborative text editor), and c) practicing the incorporation of pre-existing ideas, theories, and research into their primary research. With these core competencies, students may more effectively conduct primary and secondary research while making real contributions to broader investigative inquiries. Table 9.1 displays these core competencies in knowledge work across three stages: establishing a theoretical baseline, developing questions, and creating conversations. We propose a set of pedagogical activities to

Table 9.1   Proposed Pedagogical Model for Positioning Undergraduate Researchers as Knowledge Workers

	Knowledge Work Stage I: Establishing a theoretical baseline	Knowledge Work Stage II: Developing questions	Knowledge Work Stage III: Creating conversation
Pedagogical goal	Become fluent in theoretical definitions of and characteristics implicit in the construct "knowledge work"	Develop researchable questions that encourage looking *at* and not *through* technology	Practice the incorporation of pre-existing ideas, theories, and research into primary research
Pedagogical activity	Read, write about, create schematics of, and collaboratively discuss Drucker (1988), Spinuzzi (2006), Spinuzzi (2007), Emig (1982), and Grabill & Hart-Davidson (2010)	Publicly vet individual articulations of research questions in a web-based, collaborative text editor	Draft and publicly vet (in a web-based, collaborative text editor) a "theoretical framework" as a living document that will undergo continual revision throughout the research

coincide with each of the pedagogical goals associated with all three stages.

Stage I: Establishing a Theoretical Baseline

We recommend as a standard introductory reading assignment Peter Drucker's (1988) "The Coming of the New Organization" paired with Spinuzzi's (2006) "What Do We Need to Teach About Knowledge Work?" During class, students might collaborate in small groups about answers to the following questions: Which of Drucker's predictions came to fruition? What are the differences between data and information? What are the differences between modular work versus knowledge work? What is black-boxing? What does Spinuzzi recommend for nascent knowledge workers? We suggest that the second reading pairing—Spinuzzi's (2007) "Guest Editor's Introduction: Technical Communication in the Age of Distributed Work" and Janet Emig's (1982) "Inquiry Paradigms and Writing"—be accompanied by a reflective response, due before the following class. Specifically, students might be asked to make connections across the four sources and create a working definition for the construct of knowledge work.

Stage II: Developing Questions

In addition to reading and responding to key outside sources that define knowledge work as a construct, we recommend that students publicly vet their research questions as a class and then in more focused, collaborative writing groups. Here, Emig's (1982) distinction between "inquiry" and "research" is enacted. Conducting Stage II in an online, web-based text editor such as Google Docs or a wiki is useful in that these early questions can be publicly displayed, responded to, commented on, and revised in real-time. In a pilot study wherein this pedagogical activity was deployed, we found it important to continually remind students to ask research questions that do not beg a "yes" or "no" answer. Asking "Is creative writing being changed by the internet and technology?" for example, is a markedly different question than asking "How do we define creative writing in the age of microfiction?" Again, we encourage writing instructors to challenge students to move beyond topic-based reporting. Instead, students should enact their digital agency by asking questions that require research of practices surrounding technologies. These questions do not have ready-made answers. As a result, students collaboratively construct knowledge.

Stage III: Creating Conversation

Stage III in the development of core competencies in knowledge work involves the creation of conversation across primary and secondary sources. While it is sometimes commonplace to require students to have a certain number of sources in their final research papers or products, we propose based on the results of our study that students should draft and publicly vet their white papers' theoretical framework at three different moments during their investigation. That is, rather than use a certain number of sources, students must engage in the consultation of sources at three different moments: when they are developing their research questions, during their actual investigations, and then after their investigations are complete. One pedagogical activity sometimes deployed in order to achieve this goal is an annotated bibliography. However, our strategy in Stage III—one where students do smaller, more focused consultations of outside sources at least three times and during markedly different periods in their investigations— might help them to see the ways conversations build over time.

The pedagogical model we propose in Table 9.1 and Figure 9.1 is but one example of the ways that writing instructors might position undergraduate researchers as knowledge workers.

Conclusion

In many ways, the best practices described herein are not necessarily unique to best practices for *digital* research; asking researchable questions and contributing to broader, knowledge-building conversations are heuristics for research broadly defined. An undergraduate digital research experience that focuses on the articulation of researchable

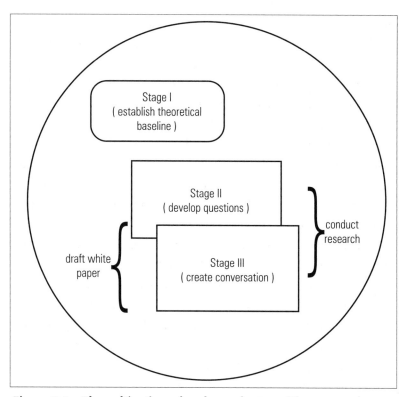

Figure 9.1   The cultivation of undergraduate writing researchers as knowledge workers in three stages

questions, the deployment of qualitative research methods, and the weaving together of primary and secondary data sources toward the building of a broader conversation empowers undergraduate researchers to critique, investigate, and *do* writing.

In sum, we encourage writing instructors to adopt a "student researcher as knowledge worker" approach in their classrooms. First, we encourage writing instructors to invite student researchers to become fluent in the very role they are to inhabit and enact. This means dedicating class time to exploring knowledge work as a construct. Second, rather than approve students' individually motivated research topics, we encourage writing instructors to facilitate opportunities to publicly negotiate researchable questions that do not invite yes or no answers. Instead, these researchable questions should open up possibilities for inquiry of actual, real-time practices surrounding certain technologies. Finally, rather than expecting students to complete an exhaustive review of secondary sources in a single document (like a literature review) before beginning their real time research, we encourage writing instructors to ask students to dip into the secondary source pool at least three separate times during each phase of their research. This means students should consult secondary sources once the research question has been articulated, during their actual *in situ* research, and after their research has been conducted. Here, conversation across sources and among their primary research experiences may be more readily facilitated. Consultation of secondary sources becomes more than mere verification or ethos-building for the writer. When secondary research is meaningfully incorporated in at least three different moments, sources act as both the theoretical framework motivating the study as well as the scholarly fuel that continually generates new ways to make students' research matter to a broader audience.

We have argued for (what may be for some) a paradigm shift with respect to what it means to ask undergraduates to be researchers. We propose that research tasks be framed as ongoing constructions of knowledge rather than mere reports of already created knowledge. We encourage writing instructors to empower and facilitate opportunities for students to not just search out or discover *a priori* knowledge, but to actively construct or invent it.

References

Bauerlein, Mark. 2008. *The Dumbest Generation: How the Digital Age Stupefies Young Americans and Jeopardizes Our Future (or, Don't Trust Anyone Under 30)*. New York: Penguin Books.

Carr, Nicholas. 2010. *The Shallows: What the Internet Is Doing to Our Brains*. New York: W.W. Norton and Company.

Clark, Dave. 2010. "Shaped and Shaping Tools: The Rhetorical Nature of Technical Communication Technologies." In *Digital Literacy for Technical Communication: 21st Century Theory and Practice*, edited by Rachel Spilka, 85–102. London: Routledge.

Dicks, R. Stanley. 2010. "The Effects of Digital Literacy on the Nature of Technical Communication Work." In *Digital Literacy for Technical Communication: 21st Century Theory and Practice*, edited by Rachel Spilka, 51–81. London: Routledge.

Drucker, Peter F. 1988. "The Coming of the New Organization." *Harvard Business Review* 66: 45–53.

Emig, Janet. 1982. "Inquiry Paradigms and Writing." *College Composition and Communication* 33: 64–75.

Enos, Richard, and Janice Lauer. 1992. "The Meaning of Heuristic in Aristotle's *Rhetoric* and Its Implications for Contemporary Rhetorical Theory." In *A Rhetoric of Doing: Essays on Written Discourse in Honor of James L. Kinneavy*, edited by Steven P. Witte and Neil Nakadate, 79–87. Carbondale: Southern Illinois University Press.

Grabill, Jeff and William Hart-Davidson. 2010. "Understanding and Supporting Knowledge Work in Everyday Life." *Language at Work: Bridging Theory and Practice*. Accessed December 12, 2012. www.languageatwork.eu/articles.php?cat_id=2.

Haas, Christina. 1996. *Writing Technology*. Mahwah: Lawrence Erlbaum Associates.

Heidegger, Martin. 1977. *The Question Concerning Technology and Other Essays*. New York: Harper.

Herndl, Carl G., and Adela C. Licona. 2007. "Shifting Agency: Agency, *Kairos*, and the Possibilities of Social Action." In *Communicative Practices in Workplaces and the Professions: Cultural Perspectives on the Regulation of Discourse and Organizations*, edited by Mark Zachry and Charlotte Thralls, 133–153. Amityville, NY: Baywood Publishing Company.

Jacoby, Jacob, Donald E. Speller, and Carol A. Kohn-Berning. 1974. "Brand Choice Behavior as a Function of Information Load: Replication and Extension." *Journal of Consumer Research* 1, 33–42.

Johnson-Eilola, Johndan. 2005. *Datacloud: Toward a New Theory of Online Work*. Cresskill, NJ: Hampton Press.

Kaptelinin, Victor, and Bonnie A. Nardi. 2006. *Acting with Technology: Activity Theory and Interaction Design*. Cambridge, MA: MIT Press.

Karukstis, Kerry K., and Timothy E. Elgren. 2007. *Developing and Sustaining a Research-Supportive Curriculum*. Washington, D.C.: Council on Undergraduate Research.

McNely, Brian J. 2010. "Cultivating Rhetorical Dispositions through Curricular Change in Technical and Professional Communication." In *Undergraduate Research in English Studies: A Sourcebook*, edited by Laurie Grobman and Joyce Kinkead, 229–244. Urbana, IL: NCTE.

Moore, David R. 2011. "Technology Literacy: The Extension of Cognition." *International Journal of Technology and Design Education* 21: 185–193.

Nardi, Bonnie A., and Vicki O'Day. 1999. *Information Ecologies: Using Technology with Heart*. Cambridge, MA: MIT Press.

Reich, Robert B. 1992. *The Work of Nations: Preparing Ourselves for 21st Century Capitalism*. New York: Vintage Press.

Schon, Donald. 1987. *Educating the Reflective Practitioner: Toward a New Design for Teaching and Learning in the Professions*. San Francisco: Jossey-Bass.

Selfe, Cynthia. 1999. *Technology and Literacy in the Twenty-First Century: The Importance of Paying Attention*. Carbondale, IL: Southern Illinois University Press.

Spinuzzi, Clay. 2006. "What Do We Need to Teach About Knowledge Work?" White paper. Accessed September 18, 2012. www.drc.utexas.edu/research/ what-do-we-need-teac-about-knowledge-work. [URL no longer available.]

———. 2007. "Guest Editor's Introduction: Technical Communication in the Age of Distributed Work." *Technical Communication Quarterly* 16: 265–277.

Swarts, Jason. 2007. "Mobility and Composition: The Architecture of Coherence in Non-Places." *Technical Communication Quarterly* 16: 279–309.

———. 2009. "The Collaborative Construction of Fact on Wikipedia." In *Proceedings of the 27th ACM International Conference on Design of Communication* (Bloomington, Indiana, USA, October 5–7, 2009). SIGDOC '09. ACM, New York, NY, 281–288.

Toffler, Alvin. 1970. *Future Shock*. New York: Random House.

WIDE Research Center. 2010. "The Writing Lives of College Students." White paper. Accessed September 18, 2012. www.wide.msu.edu/special/writinglives.

Appendix: White Paper Assignment Description

Technologies + the Future of Writing /
Collaborative White Papers

Rationale

Recall that on our first day of class we asked, and have continued to discuss, this question: In what ways do contemporary writing technologies and practices cause us to reconsider our definition of writing as well as constructs like audience, identity, originality, authority, ownership, materiality, and collaboration?

After having read and discussed Haas (1996), Moore (2011), Nardi and O'Day (1999), Enos and Lauer (1992), and reviewed Swarts (2009) and the MSU WIDE white paper (2010) as a model, your task is to collaboratively embark upon a small-scale investigation that will culminate in a white paper wherein you propose some possible answers to portions of the question that guided this module.

Objective

While you may choose to narrow your investigative gaze to a particular technological platform (i.e., Twitter, Chatroulette, Facebook, etc.), the focus of your investigation should not be the technology itself, but the practices and people surrounding it. That is, while you're asked not to ignore the materiality of the writing practices you're observing, you cannot make the focus of your analysis the technology itself. For instance, if you're narrowing your investigative gaze to Twitter only, you're researching what and how people microblog. The focus, therefore, is on the activity or practice, and not necessarily on one specific tool or technology.

What we're interested in here is observations and interviews of actual writers as they're working while using a particular technological platform. Your aim is to, based on your observations and interviews, make more grounded claims about what writing is now, and how that definition might shape or shift our ideas about constructs the field of Rhetoric and Writing Studies wrestles with (i.e., audience, identity, collaboration, etc.).

Parameters

This white paper should be collaboratively written in Google Docs by you and your fellow team members.

It should include the following components:

- 100- to 150-word abstract

- 5–7 keywords (i.e., "tags" or "labels")

- An Introduction that includes a description of the problem and any relevant research or sources we've read this semester or you've found on your own that might be useful for your reader to have as background

- A Methods section that describes *how* you encountered and collected your data

- A Results section that describes the specifics of your findings (screen captures or other images, tables, or figures are appropriate for this section)

- A Discussion or Conclusion section that explicitly attends to the question or problem you've identified in the Introduction

- References (in APA format)

Please feel free to use the Swarts (2009) or the MSU WIDE white paper (2010) we read as an example for how to set up and organize this kind of deliverable.

CHAPTER 10

Re-Envisioning Research: Alternative Approaches to Engaging NextGen Students

Rachel A. Milloy

What Students' Self-Assessments Reveal

At the beginning of each new semester, undergraduate students fill the first-year writing classroom at universities and colleges across the nation. They review the syllabus and become a bit dispirited. To their dismay, the course requires an extensive final researched writing assignment. Students send worried looks to each other that say, "This class won't be so easy."

I have taught first-year writing courses at four different institutions: two community colleges and two universities. While the locations and populations differed, students consistently expressed negative initial responses to research assignments. I wondered why and what I could do to help students become excited about research. Because today's NextGen students have grown up as digital learners,[1] educators must ask two important questions: 1) Do our research assignments appeal to the interests and needs of our digital learners? and 2) Do our assignments teach NextGen students the necessary skills for researching in a digital age? Teacher-research provided me with answers to these questions: By asking students to self-assess their own research strategies, I learned that their strategies for conducting research online lead to less-than-enthusiastic attitudes toward research.

Forty-seven of my own first-year writing students completed a research self-assessment (Appendix A) that I assigned during the 2009–2010 school year at a large land grant university.[2] Before beginning the course's major research assignment, 27 students in the fall 2009 semester and 20 students in the spring 2010 semester responded to the self-assessment prior to conducting research for their major course project. I reviewed and coded their responses to gain a sense of what students already knew about conducting research, their feelings toward research, and their processes for collecting information. The responses disclosed some surprising, but maybe typical, comments and reveal five common issues students encounter when conducting research in a digital age: 1) 70 percent admitted to turning to Google first when conducting research, 2) 68 percent admitted to using only one or two keywords before discontinuing their search for credible sources, 3) 57 percent claimed to feel overwhelmed by the amount of information available online, 4) 53 percent felt incapable of constructing original arguments because of the wealth of existing information, and 5) 89 percent confessed to struggling when attempting to determine an online source's credibility or relevancy to their topic. Due to these five issues, students described the research process as frustrating and uninteresting rather than enjoyable.[3]

These negative attitudes may stem from the "stigma associated with research" as a thesis-driven, formulaic process that today's students find dull (Pegram 2006, 18). Still, the five common issues forced me to examine how research assignments could better engage the interests of NextGen students while still teaching them the research skills they need. While this study replicates what many scholars have found about students' research strategies, it does not make generalizable conclusions about first-year writing students' research practices. Rather, this study aims to demonstrate how instructors can re-envision common research assignments so that they better appeal to digital learners' interests while still teaching the research skills necessary for the digital age.

Marc Prensky claims that digital natives *"think and process informa-tion fundamentally differently* from their predecessors" and that these learners "crave interactivity" in the learning process (2001a, 1; 2001b, 5; emphasis mine). As early as the 1990s, Michael Orr and Rae Fankhauser (1996, 2) noted the effects of the digital environments on students' research practices: "The advent of the digital information era has challenged and changed many of the traditional research sources, tools, practices and the premises on which [students] operate." Additionally, contemporary scholars have determined that, while they grew up in the information era, today's students have difficulty devel-oping effective research skills for an evolving digital age (Donham 2003; Fitzgerald 2004; Hignite, Margavio, and Margavio 2009; Owen 2010). In response to our NextGen students' needs and the digital age in which we live, writing instructors should re-envision research assign-ments so that they actively engage students in the process of research; lead to more creative, unique research products; and guide students through the process of navigating digital spaces for academic and pro-fessional purposes.

Accomplishing these goals requires that we remediate traditional assignments into new activities that incorporate Web 2.0 technologies and provide the interactivity our students crave. Such assignments challenge the traditional research model of finding and evaluating strictly alphabetic texts, submitting traditional annotated bibliogra-phies, and relying solely on already published sources to support an argument. These re-envisioned assignments not only require that stu-dents develop research skills for digital environments that "still depend on critical thinking, problem solving, and communicating" (Orr and Fankhauser 1996, 2), but also encourage students to contribute knowl-edge to discourse communities, collect primary data, and speak with authoritative voices on their research topics.[4]

After presenting my students' thoughts on research and the five common issues they face as researchers in a digital age, I will demon-strate how writing instructors can revise research assignments to more effectively engage students in the learning process. I share three research assignments developed in response to students' interests as NextGen learners and explain how these assignments aid teachers and students in addressing the challenges of researching in a digital age.

What Students Say About Research

The student responses collected for this study paint a picture of what students may experience as researchers in a digital age. Students communicated their general frustrations when researching in digital environments due to limited strategies for finding, evaluating, and responding to sources. Explained here are the five common issues students in this study encounter as digital researchers.

First Issue: Going to Google

First-year writing courses usually ask students to research current issues, problems, or local concerns, so it is not surprising that 70 percent of students in this study reported consulting Google first rather than library sources when conducting research.[5] Students often turn to the internet—rather than printed sources—when researching. Amelia wrote, "I love finding books and just sitting in the quiet in the middle of all that printed material. But, the only thing bad about books is that it's sometimes hard to find current information."[6] Amelia's response may represent her peers' feelings concerning print sources; when asked, only two of Amelia's peers said they planned to use books as resources. Students apparently value the internet for its quick access to current information. It is worth noting that students in this study used the terms "current" and "relevant" as synonyms when discussing online sources. Teachers therefore should explicitly define these terms early and often during the semester. Doing so may help students understand that a recently published source is not necessarily a relevant source.

In addition to consulting Google first, students' quest for information often ends with just this one search engine. Google turns out pages of information and students become overwhelmed by the number of choices; they stop seeking better information and may choose the first source Google lists. Lauren explains, "I just use the first source [that Google presents] because there's so much to choose from. All those sources are intimidating." Even more surprising than Lauren's comment is that not one student mentioned consulting other resources, such as Google Scholar, Advanced Google, library databases, or open-access journals when conducting research online.

Writing instructors should consider introducing students to a variety of search engines and databases before students begin the research process. By discussing the purpose of various resources, students may begin to think of sources in two distinct ways: for developing an idea and for supporting a claim. If students begin to think of online resources, such as Google, as a place to *learn* about topics, they may feel less intimidated by the amount of information they find. Additionally, if Google is used for idea development, students may be less likely to cite the first source they find in their final assignments.[7]

Second Issue: Limited Keywords

When researching online, students quickly encounter roadblocks due to the limited scope of their keywords.[8] In this study, 68 percent of students expressed frustration due to limited keywords. Julia wrote:

> Actually getting to those credible sources is ridiculous. Of course my first choice would be to go to the internet and type in a couple of keywords. However, most of the time that takes forever because ninety nine percent of the information that will pop up will be completely unrelated to your topic or just badly put together and probably not too helpful. After a few keywords it seems like I am just finding the same information over and over again.

Jonathan similarly wrote, "I have trouble coming up with a good key word [*sic*] to use. I usually just type my keyword in and click on the first result that would come up." It appears that limited keywords leave students with limited options. Scholars have noted the connection between lack of keywords and students' use of irrelevant sources

(Fitzgerald 2004; Freeman and Lynd-Balta 2010; Hignite, Margavio, and Margavio 2009). When students' initial keyword(s) fail(s) to produce useful sources, students likely use any available source "rather than wade through research results to find relevant, adequate, and accurate information" (Owen 2010, 21). In other words, students try to "make it work."⁹ It seems that teachers can provide more instruction on the purpose of keywords; determining what makes a keyword relevant; and how to read those initial sources to discover more, or better, keywords for further research.

Third Issue: Information Overload

Students' limited abilities to discover relevant keywords leads to information overload, again resulting in frustration. Due to the amount of information online and the time it takes to wade through that information, 57 percent of students claimed to feel overwhelmed when researching. Mathew described his frustrations when he wrote, "It's hard finding sources when there are so many to choose from." Maria likewise explained, "There is so much information available that now I have to pick which ones to use. The most frustrating aspect of research is getting the right information." In another response, Brandon wrote, "Getting the right information is pretty hard because there is a lot of information about the topic, but not the particular information that I need for my assignment." These students' responses suggest that perhaps just as important as finding the right keywords is the ability to quickly determine a source's relevancy to a particular research topic. Students struggle with sifting through large amounts of information, as Kathleen explained: "I know that I need to get as much information as possible, but some of the articles are 38 pages long and trying to read all of them is sometimes very time consuming." Adam reflected on the variety of online sources: "There's so much information on my topic so it is hard and sometimes time consuming to find the specific information I want to use. I have to choose between articles, videos, images, and lots of other stuff." These responses reveal that students encounter overwhelming amounts of information when researching; therefore, students need more instruction in making rhetorically informed choices about a source's relevancy, choices that take into consideration more than a source's length.

Fourth Issue: There's Nothing Left to Say

Due to the wealth of information that exists, students often feel incapable of adding new arguments to existing scholarship. In this study, 53 percent of students expressed concerns about feeling unoriginal when writing papers. In his response, Alex confessed the pressure he feels to have something interesting to say: "I don't know how to construct a legit thesis that maybe my audience would be interested in. It seems like all the sources I find already say everything." Teachers can help students build confidence by allowing them to produce original scholarship though primary data collection. Gary, when given the option, became excited about collecting his own data: "It's also kind of cool that we can do surveys, polls, interviews with other people for our research because that allows us to have interaction with others rather than just reading stuff off of an internet site, or out of a book." Gary later explains that primary data collection helps writers "have something to actually talk about." Primary data collection may build students' confidence in their abilities to contribute original arguments to existing scholarship.

Fifth Issue: Determining Credibility

Students have difficulty determining the credibility of digital sources, indicated by 89 percent of the responses analyzed for this study.[10] In a particularly insightful writing response, Jenna stated, "Because many different aspects of modern technology (such as the internet's acceptance of any website created by the average individual), it becomes exceptionally difficult for the average college student to determine validity in research." Students realize they must determine a source's credibility, but they are often confused about how to do so.[11] Jamie explained, "Finding credible sources is the hardest part about doing research. There are lots of facts on the internet in blogs, videos, websites, and other places. I just don't know what's true." As Rena Helms-Park and Paul Stapleton (2006) suggest, students—and teachers too—continually struggle to determine a web source's credibility and usefulness for academic papers. Elizabeth Daley (2003, 36) claims, "Multimedia, so ubiquitous to young people's experience, often seems to be particularly hard for them to analyze or deconstruct." Students' responses to the assigned writing prompt support these scholars' claims. It is wise for instructors, then, to model the process of analyzing digital sources. Instructors can discuss blogs, websites, wikis, and the other digital genres our students regularly encounter as forms of writing with distinct purposes, audiences, and exigencies. When students learn how to deconstruct these forms of writing, they become capable of making informed decisions about using online sources to support their own claims.

Re-Envisioning Research Assignments

Teaching students how to critique and use Web 2.0 technologies (technologies they already use socially) as part of the research process may help teachers address the five common issues presented earlier. Teaching students to use these technologies as research tools is important: "Computerized writing technologies," explain Heidi A. McKee and Dànielle Nicole DeVoss (2007, 3), "impact how and what we write ... and, certainly, computers and digital spaces affect our research approaches." Therefore, integrating Web 2.0 technologies into traditional research assignments may better engage NextGen students by incorporating their existing digital literacies into the research-writing process. James P. Purdy (2010, 48) suggests, "Rather than dissuade or forbid students from using the Web 2.0 technologies with which they may already be familiar, ... we should incorporate these technologies into writing instruction as objects of analysis and as writing and researching resources." Because "Web 2.0 is producing a read-write culture different from the read-only approach" (NCTE 2008, 17), students have the ability to engage in conversation with others while simultaneously conducting research. Research becomes an attractive, interactive, knowledge-producing process.

The three re-envisioned research assignments described later in this chapter incorporate Web 2.0 technologies and collectively address the five common issues previously discussed. The assignments strive to help students develop more effective keywords to use when seeking sources (Wordling Keywords assignment), better evaluate the credibility of sources (Digital Annotated Blogbiography assignment), and contribute original research to existing conversations through primary data collection (Digital Fieldwork assignment). While these assignments help students with the research process, they aid students in transitioning from consumers of information to creators of knowledge.

Assignment 1: Wordling Keywords

Helping students develop effective keywords is challenging, yet critically important. To address this issue, I designed a Wordling Keywords assignment (Appendix B) to help students see the variety of possible keywords available to them. Wordles visually represent themes from web content (websites, blogs, wikis) and can help students discover a variety of keywords related to a topic.[12] The assignment asks students to explore current online conversations about their topic; students copy and paste text from blogs, articles, websites, and video transcripts into a Wordle. The Wordle then produces a visual: Words used most often are bigger and brighter, suggesting to students that those words might be effective keywords for locating relevant sources through various search engines and library databases (see Appendix B). Through this process of exploring a variety of existing conversations about a topic, students begin to use Web 2.0 sources for idea development— as a way to fully investigate an issue before forming their own opinion or argument. An additional benefit to using this assignment is that, through reading a lot about an issue, students learn how to narrow their own research topics. In other words, by reading what other writers have said about a topic, students learn that broad topics can be broken down into many related issues. Students see that writers are capable of writing a lot about narrow, focused topics. This may ease students' fear about producing a lengthy research paper.

Students were excited about the Wordling Keywords assignment because it provided them with time to explore Web 2.0 resources they already find interesting. Students learned to view blogs, wikis, and other web sources as starting places for research. These digital sources also helped students become familiar with a particular community's discourse. Ryan, in his writing response, explained, "I find it cool to read blogs about topics because there are always people arguing online about different things and it helps to change your perspective on where you stand on different situations. That also helps me sometimes when I'm doing research to write papers." Learning the language associated with their topics may help students develop more relevant and focused keywords. Completing the Wordling Keywords assignment may reduce students' research-related frustration because the Wordle narrows their focus and reduces the time spent wading through irrelevant information.

Assignment 2: Digital Annotated Blogbiography

While the Wordling Keywords assignment helps students find relevant sources, students must still determine a source's credibility. Because digital environments change the ways in which audiences understand and make sense of information, observant teachers often witness students' lack of confidence when evaluating a digital text's credibility. Instructors can incorporate digitally adapted research activities that use Web 2.0 tools—such as blogs—to teach students to negotiate a source's credibility. Blogs allow for personal reflection and dialogue with peers, and using blogs for source annotations may give students agency and control over their own learning. The Digital Annotated Blogbiography assignment (Appendix C) can help students function as rhetorically informed decision makers in digital environments: The unlimited space of blogs allows students to reflect on their reactions to a source, engage in conversation about digital sources, determine the credibility of those sources, and make collaboratively constructed arguments for or against using a source.

Like a traditional annotated bibliography, the re-envisioned assignment asks students to cite, summarize, and make an argument for using each source. Unlike a traditional annotated bibliography, this digitally adapted assignment allows for interactive conversations with classmates about sources. By working collaboratively to negotiate criteria for online sources, students eventually arrive at a meaningful, informed decision about a source's credibility. Blogs thus are one way to help students form ethos as researchers, as these places are "informal collaborative knowledge-making spaces" (Graupner, Nickoson-Massey, and Blair 2009, 22). Re-envisioned research assignments, like the Digital Annotated Blogbiography, help teachers "move beyond a privileging of alphabetic text and embrace a multimodal approach" to teaching and learning (Graupner, et al. 2009, 21). Additionally, the blog records and reveals the social construction of knowledge. Such assignments may aid students in constructing knowledge about an online source's credibility while easing fears and frustrations in the development of this important information literacy skill.

I observed students' engagement with sources and with each other during the Digital Annotated Blogbiography assignment. When a student annotated a source in the blog, peers responded to the source by asking questions such as, "How do you plan to use this source?" and "What will this source contribute to your paper?" Through conversation, several groups developed their own lists of criteria for evaluating online sources. One group decided that if a source links to other sources, those linked-to sources must include a list of references; otherwise, the original source could not be used in the research assignment. Source annotations became interactive, rather than solitary acts characteristic of traditional annotated bibliographies.

Assignment 3: Digital Fieldwork Assignment

First-year writing courses should continue to teach students to find and incorporate scholarly, published information into their writing, but our courses can do more to help students understand how digital environments shape research practices. Primary data collection is an important part of what it means to be a successful researcher in a digital age, as digital environments present ripe opportunities for collecting primary data. Yet, first-year writing courses rarely teach students how to connect with online audiences or collect and use primary data. In this study, students expressed concerns about feeling unoriginal when constructing their own arguments based on what other writers have already said. Students felt incapable of adding new ideas to existing information. Such problems may only increase over time as the amount of published information continues to grow. Therefore, instructors should consider using digital fieldwork assignments that make effective use of Web 2.0 resources. Such assignments can help students produce original research and develop researcher identities. J. Elizabeth Clark explains that people are regularly "using publicly available resources to research and inform their opinions" (Clark 2010, 27). Through digital fieldwork assignments, students use public resources to pose research questions to a specific audience, collect data, analyze data, and produce original research.

The Digital Fieldwork assignment (Appendix D) I designed requires students to form a research question and determine whether a survey, interview, poll, or other instrument will effectively gather information from a target audience. The assignment asks students to identify a real-world problem, gather information about that issue, and then use that information to develop a solution for fixing the problem. The digital environment grants students access to many audiences, not just their instructor. Students must critically analyze Web 2.0 resources to determine which tools will best aid them in collecting primary data from friends, community members, and professors who have an opinion on a topic. This assignment grants access to real audiences, audiences that students analyze rather than construct, and writing and research become intertwined activities. Additionally, this assignment helps students learn to produce visual representations of their data, analyze that data, and interpret information for their readers. By conducting research in digital spaces with which they are already familiar and for real audiences, students become more engaged in the research-writing process.

Students found that Web 2.0 tools, such as social networking sites, could help them accomplish the assignment's requirements. For example, students posted their research questions and distributed surveys on Facebook. Facebook allowed the groups to gather large amounts of original data. I encouraged students to use their original data, combined with published library scholarship, to compose an original argument. In the final written papers, students used their own original research to comment on, confirm, and contradict other scholarly arguments found through traditional library research.

In addition to social media sites, students may choose to use other Web 2.0 tools, such as Skype, to collect original data for their academic research assignments. Students can use Skype to conduct multiple interviews with professionals in their fields, local politicians, or other willing participants who can answer questions about a student's research topic. The Skype video calling feature allows instructors to introduce focus groups as a research approach in college writing courses. Video calls can be recorded, allowing students to later transcribe and code the conversations for important issues or themes relating to their research topics. Armed with original data to analyze, students can then practice interpreting and representing data accurately and ethically for their audiences. When instructors incorporate digital fieldwork into traditional assignments, students learn to form a research question, more fully investigate what other scholars have already said about an issue, and contribute original research to an existing conversation. Perhaps most important, fieldwork assignments allow students to gain confidence with researching and writing, and the research process becomes much more relevant to students' lives as citizens and future professionals.

Conclusion

Digitally adapted research assignments that incorporate Web 2.0 technologies may better prepare students to be critically engaged citizens who question texts and make rhetorically informed decisions about how to communicate successfully inside and outside the academy. Doing so is even more important as digital environments continue to change and shape the ways we consume and produce information. By conducting primary research, students may begin to identify themselves as researchers and believe that they are contributing new knowledge to existing conversations. Web 2.0 technologies help writing instructors actively engage students in the process of research, providing students with the ability, power, and authority to make informed decisions in their academic, personal, and future professional lives. Employers increasingly look for digitally literate employees who can make informed decisions about how to use technology assiduously, search for information in a digital environment, discern the meaning of that information to make informed decisions, and even produce meaningful texts. Writing instructors can prepare students for these digital demands through the types of research projects assigned in first-year writing courses. In a digital age where students have access to a wealth of information, thoughtful teachers must determine which forms of research best serve their students; help students develop critical research skills; and prepare students for the expectations of their first-year writing courses, the university, and their future careers.

NextGen learners have digital literacies they use each day to achieve tasks they deem important. For instance, students search the internet for music files, communicate online with many audiences, read blogs for information, develop videos they upload to YouTube, and much more. My students' writing responses helped me understand that students are often less comfortable using their existing digital literacies for academic research purposes. The 47 writing responses helped me recognize a need for re-envisioned research assignments that build upon students' existing digital literacy and their research strategies.

Writing instructors can revise research assignments to incorporate Web 2.0 technologies so that students realize they *do* know something about researching and that they *can* learn to improve their strategies. As compositionists and librarians continue to redefine what it means "to research" and to be a "researcher," teachers can incorporate assignments that help students approach the vast world of digital spaces; that move away from the formulaic practices students believe research papers should imitate; and that move toward a research paradigm valuing creativity, exploration, and rhetorical choices appropriate for a digital age. Most important, Web 2.0 technologies nurture a researcher-writer identity and aid students in developing an authoritative voice for their own researched arguments.

Endnotes

1. See Marc Prensky (2001a, 2001b) for more information about digital learners.

2. This study received IRB approval. Students received final grades for the course before granting me permission to use their writing responses for this research.

3. Some students did describe research in positive ways; they found the process of learning something new to be enjoyable. See also Purdy (Chapter 6) in this volume. Purdy likewise discusses ways in which students think about research.

4. See also Teston and McNely (Chapter 9) in this volume. The authors argue explicitly for positioning students as knowledge contributors in the research process.

5. Once students learned of other resources, 88 percent of students said they would rather turn to library databases, Google Scholar, or Advanced Google as initial places to look for sources.

6. Pseudonyms are used for all student participants' quotations.

7. See McClure (Chapter 1) in this volume for information regarding students' prevalent use of Google.

8. See also Mirtz (Chapter 8) in this volume. Mirtz offers productive strategies that help students investigate topics through library databases.

9. This approach is likely due to the time constraints. Students may feel pressure to choose any sources available in order to complete an assignment.

10. See also Silva (Chapter 7) in this volume. Silva offers suggestions for improving students' information literacy skills.

11. Pamela Takayoshi and Cynthia L. Selfe (2007, 1) explain that "for the past 150 years ... formal assignments that many English composition teachers give to

students remain alphabetic." Digital sources are often nonlinear and not necessarily alphabetic, and the choices students must make about which content to view/use may be unclear to them.

12. Visit www.wordle.net for more information.

References

Clark, J. Elizabeth. 2010. "The Digital Imperative: Making the Case for a 21st-Century Pedagogy." *Computers and Composition* 27: 27–35.

Daley, Elizabeth. 2003. "Expanding the Concept of Literacy." *EDUCAUSE Review* (March/April): 33–40.

Donham, Jean. 2003. "My Senior Is Your First-Year Student." *Knowledge Quest* 32 (1): 32.

Fitzgerald, Mary Ann. 2004. "Making the Leap from High School to College." *Knowledge Quest* 32 (4): 19–24.

Freeman, Edward, and Eileen Lynd-Balta. 2010. "Developing Information Literacy Skills Early in an Undergraduate Curriculum." *College Teaching* 58 (3): 109–115.

Graupner, Meredith, Lee Nickoson-Massey, and Kristine Blair. 2009. "Remediating Knowledge-Making Spaces in the Graduate Curriculum: Developing and Sustaining Multimodal Teaching and Research." *Computers and Composition* 26: 13–23.

Helms-Park, Rena, and Paul Stapleton. 2006. "How the Views of Faculty Can Inform Undergraduate Web-Based Research: Implications for Academic Writing." *Computers and Composition* 23: 444–461.

Hignite, Michael, Thomas M. Margavio, and Geanie W. Margavio. 2009. "Information Literacy Assessment: Moving Beyond Computer Literacy." *College Student Journal* 43 (3): 812–821.

McKee, Heidi A., and Dànielle N. DeVoss, eds. 2007. *Digital Writing Research: Technologies, Methodologies, and Ethical Issues.* Cresskill, NJ: Hampton Press.

National Council of Teachers of English (NCTE). 2008. "Reading and Writing Differently." Accessed September 20, 2012. www.ncte.org/library/NCTEFiles/Resources/Journals/CC/0182-nov08/CC0182Reading.pdf.

Orr, Michael, and Rae Fankhauser. 1996. "Approaches to Research in a Digital Environment: Who Are the New Researchers?" Paper presented at the EdTech '96 Biennial Conference of the Australian Society for Educational Technology, Melbourne, Australia, July.

Owen, Patricia. 2010. "A Transition Checklist for High School Seniors." *School Library Monthly* 26 (8): 20–23.

Pegram, David M. 2006. "'What If?': Teaching Research and Creative-Thinking Skills Through Proposal Writing." *English Journal* 95 (4): 18–22.

Prensky, Marc. 2001a. "Digital Natives, Digital Immigrants Part 1." *On the Horizon* 9 (5): 1–6.

———. 2001b. "Digital Natives, Digital Immigrants Part 2: Do They Really Think Differently?" *On the Horizon* 9 (6): 1–6.

Purdy, James P. 2010. "The Changing Space of Research: Web 2.0 and the Integration of Research and Writing Environments." *Computers and Composition* 27: 48–58.

Takayoshi, Pamela, and Cynthia L. Selfe. 2007. "Thinking about Multimodality." In *Multimodal Composition: Resources for Teachers*, edited by Cynthia L. Selfe, 1–12. Cresskill, NJ: Hampton Press.

Appendix A: Writing Response Prompt

For this writing prompt, I'd like for you to reflect on the research experiences you've had during high school and college. You can reflect on all aspects of doing research, finding and choosing appropriate sources, or anything else. However, here are a few questions to consider:

1. How do you typically begin a research assignment? Where do you go to get information?

2. What are the most difficult aspects of doing research?

3. What do you find easy or enjoyable about doing research?

4. What issues or problems do you usually experience when conducting research?

Appendix B: Wordling Keywords Assignment

Objective

- To develop more effective keywords for finding sources for your research topic

Overview

Wordles are visual representations of texts. Wordles allow you to copy and paste text from a source, and then the Wordle produces an image of the most commonly used words in the text. Words that are used most often are bigger and brighter, and words used less often are smaller. A Wordle will help you determine which terms are most often associated with your research topic.

Instructions

Begin by finding two different texts that discuss your research topic. For instance, you might find a blog where people are discussing your topic. You can also find a wiki entry about your topic. You might even find a relevant website.

Visit www.wordle.net to begin, and click "Create your own." Copy and paste the text from those sources into a Wordle. The Wordle will produce an image of the most commonly used words related to your topic. Use these keywords to begin searching for more useful, credible sources for your research assignment.

Here's an example of what a Wordle looked like when I copied and pasted email conversations about multimodal research:

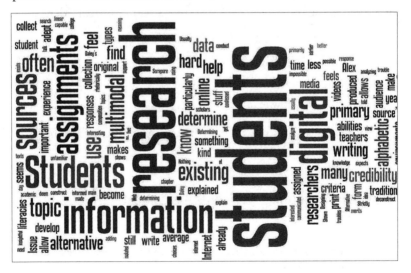

Appendix C: Digital Annotated Blogbiography Assignment
Objectives

- Locate and post multimodal sources to your blog.

- Engage in conversation with your peers about the credibility of those sources.

- Make arguments for or against using a particular source for your research project.

Overview

For this assignment, you will create a blog and work with three other classmates to determine whether or not the sources you find are credible and useful for your research project. You should locate and provide a link to one source each week on your blog. Each group member is responsible for posting to each blog about a source's credibility. Comment on features of the text based on the criteria you develop in your groups and listed in the course textbook.

Instructions

Begin by visiting www.blogger.com to register for and create your Digital Annotated Blogbiography.

Each week you should do the following:

Locate a multimodal source and post it to your blog. Then respond to three classmates' blogs about the credibility of the source they have posted. Make an argument as to why you believe the source is or is not credible enough to be used for the research assignment.

At the end of the week, once you've received feedback on the source you posted, review your peers' comments. Post a final comment that explains 1) if you plan to use this source for your research project, 2) why you plan to use this source, and 3) how it will add to your own argument for your research project.

Appendix D: Digital Fieldwork Assignment
Objectives

- To practice collecting primary data through observations, interviews, surveys, or polls

- To analyze and interpret that data for your audience in your final research project

Overview

How often have you thought, "What can I say about this topic? Everyone's already said everything there is to say!" Contributing to a scholarly conversation can be difficult, but conducting fieldwork is just one way to add original thought and information to an already existing conversation. Fieldwork includes observing; conducting interviews; and administering surveys or questionnaires, correspondence, and experiments. This kind of research will allow you to collect information that no one else has, and analyzing the results is just one way you can contribute new knowledge to what other scholars and researchers are already saying.

Instructions

By this time, you have developed a research question you want to explore for the final research assignment. Now you need to decide what audience cares about this issue. Do your peers care about it? Your professors? People in the community? Experts?

Deciding on an audience will help you determine how to collect information from them. Will you develop a survey to post on Facebook so that you can get information from friends? Or will you use www.surveymonkey.com to develop a survey instrument? Will you decide to conduct an interview with a professor? Your objective here is to draw a conclusion about your research question based on your observations, interviews, and other fieldwork methods. You will need to collect data through careful, detailed fieldwork.

Once you collect your data, you need to report on that data in the final research project for this course. Analyze and interpret that data for your readers for the research project. Tell your readers what the data means, why it is important, how it confirms or challenges existing research on your topic, and how it supports the argument you are trying to make.

CHAPTER 11

Embracing a New World
of Research

David Bailey

Envious of the half-erased theorems—the prestigious
signs—of the physicists, English teachers now compete by
chalking up theorems and theories of their own.

—Gore Vidal (1976, 76)

Echoes of the Fourth Paradigm

Research is the new zeitgeist for mainstream culture. We sit on the cusp
of a major shift in the accumulation and synthesis of knowledge. As
this shift challenges the scientific process, the effects will filter down
into culture in a way similar to the adoption of quantum mechanical
constructs, namely chaos theory and Heisenberg's uncertainty principle, into other areas of academia. The quote that opens this piece is a
favorite of mine because language and humanities instructors often
scour the world of science to inform their less scientific methods of
instruction, and it is obvious that Gore Vidal views the behavior as
ridiculous. Vidal's observation was particularly relevant in the 1970s,
as educators clumsily attempted to bridge the gaps between disciplines,
and it still applies to some extent today. This said, embracing and cod-
ifying scientific shifts in the writing classroom remains an important

endeavor in an attempt to preserve the relevance of writing studies as a discipline, and I believe the Fourth Paradigm of Science provides a potential unified theory of pedagogy missing in earlier attempts. The Fourth Paradigm builds information behaviors that are truly cross-curricular, reinventing a student's relationship with data and the educator's role within the classroom, thus providing research-writing pedagogy with a relevant and significant theoretical base suited for the digital age.

The new ground for Vidal's (1976, 76) codification of "prestigious *signs*" lies in the research realm. The Fourth Paradigm of Science is a fast-approaching revolution in data mining, and scholars have begun to apply its wisdom to various fields, including business, medicine, and marketing. The Fourth Paradigm of Science is the theoretical shift in the relationship a researcher has with data. Rather than forming initial hypotheses and engaging in years of research and experimentation, data is collected en masse, and the scientist pores through the data in search of patterns to form assumptions.

I became interested in this idea because of the immediate connections I could make to my writing classes, using writing and research to support students' interest in a multitude of professional identities. Jim Gray, the late researcher with Microsoft, characterized the Fourth Paradigm in a speech to the National Research Council and Computer Science and Telecommunications Board, two entities with joint government and private support for objective reporting and research. The following excerpt from Gray's speech was featured in the introduction of *The Fourth Paradigm: Data-Intensive Scientific Discovery*, edited by Tony Hey, Stewart Hansley, and Kristen Tolle (2009):

> The world of science has changed, and there is no question about this. The new model is for the data to be captured by instruments or generated by simulations before being processed by software and for the resulting information or knowledge to be stored in computers. Scientists only get to look at their data fairly late in this pipeline. The techniques and technologies for such data intensive science are

so different that it is worth distinguishing data-intensive science from computational science as a new, *fourth paradigm* for scientific exploration. (xxi)

Here, Gray emphasizes the need to differentiate the new scientific mode from "computational science," the dominant mode for research at the time of this writing. While this paradigm has been quite useful in embracing simulations to produce data, the amount of information produced in modern laboratories overwhelms the old hypothesis/test method and discoveries simply do not disseminate as quickly as modern technology allows. Data sets have overwhelmed the current publishing system, and Gray's Fourth Paradigm presents useful ways to move forward in the scientific community as well as in the writing classroom. Students approach writing from a traditional, scientific method–oriented organization that is quickly becoming outdated. This method preserves bias and orients students to search for information that conforms to their initial observations. The Fourth Paradigm offers a more open, exploratory format for research that is more appropriate for the NextGen student.

This information may at first seem limited to the scientific community, yet a shift of this degree in scientific thought often forecasts dramatic changes across areas of study. What has been especially intriguing about this shift has been the general public's apparent front-running of the process. Everywhere one looks, communication and data consumption tools receive astounding attention and popularity. In the classroom, students communicate with smartphones and laptops. Businesses scramble for marketing opportunities on platforms like YouTube and Twitter, while RSS feeds deliver posts from the latest blogs on every conceivable subject to devices of all kinds. This activity provides writing instructors many opportunities to engage their students in a new communication climate, one anticipating the coming Fourth Paradigm.

Yet a bit of resistance remains in regard to these opportunities. In some areas, it is quite understandable that traditional organizations are reacting aggressively against such intense innovation as many academic institutions are forced to radically redefine their roles in knowledge production, consumption, and communication. As written communication abandons classic, physical forms, the library itself, for example, has lost power to the masses who have leapfrogged the traditional method of research and cut out much of the library institution from the educational framework. All of this plays out as the library still picks at NextGen students' lack of research skills. Studies such as David Nicholas, Ian Rowlands, and Paul Huntington (2008) still define research primarily through a search engine framework that has grown more and more outdated:

> Much has been said recently about the apparent expertise of children using electronic resources, and there are claims that young people are using the internet more creatively and are becoming more proficient in their use than their teachers and that they are, in short, 'technologically savvy'. But there is no evidence in the serious literature that young people are expert searchers, nor that the search skills of young people has improved with time. (22)

The language of this piece shows the frustration and lingering contempt of the natural search behavior evolving within students. Rather than learn from the practices of the NextGen researcher, Nicholas, Rowlands, and Huntington (2008) instead struggle to maintain the importance of the library within the information literacy landscape. This culminates in the final recommendation that libraries conform to the research behavior of students rather than try to change it: "The main message of this report for research libraries is that the future is now, not ten years away, and that they have no option but to understand and design systems around the actual behavior of today's virtual scholar" (31). The language here almost sounds defeatist, a retreat from the lofty goal of *changing* research habits to model higher, more correct habits of information acquisition.

I propose we abandon this contempt of what appears to be an emerging Fourth Paradigm. To be sure, embracing less academic research skills will cause a great deal of discomfort for many among us. However, mounting evidence points to the paramount importance of Fourth Paradigm research skills. It is our responsibility to anticipate the writing of the future, and writing has actually proved to be a beautiful place to work with Fourth Paradigm concepts. In particular, Kathleen Yancey (2004) makes a pointed argument about the need to move more to the visual/social writing of NextGen students and how revolutionary the movement will become. In "Made Not Only in Words," Yancey highlights the opposition to academic writing and the radical creation of new texts: "Never before has the proliferation of writings outside the academy so counterpointed the compositions inside. Never before have the technologies of writing contributed so quickly to the creation of new genres" (298). Yancey speaks with urgency, seeing a deluge of radical new forms the academy must work to integrate, but she also laces this point with excitement and optimism. The integration of these radical new forms will demand a new pedagogical process that proves useful to the more visual and data-centric NextGen student.

I call this process aggregate integration analysis, and through it the Fourth Paradigm of Science and research can have an important place in the teaching of writing. Experimentation with aggregate integration analysis has changed the instruction of writing for me in many ways, and I believe the future of research instruction has its foundation in such a process.

Seeds of Aggregation and a Change in Philosophy

The current unstable nature of scientific discourse has created a hotbed of innovation in the basic conversation of research. At times, this innovation can cause problems due to a hyper-inflated sense of over-enthusiasm. Since I began teaching, I have been thinking in terms of redefinition. It is very easy in a world of iPods, Google, and

Chatroulette to think that traditional concepts of almost any form are outdated and in need of drastic revision. Revolutionary communication tools tempt us constantly with promises of new ways to define language and its creation, all the while quietly pushing us closer and closer to a new intellectual paradigm. A great deal of excitement waits for those willing to toss out old instructional methods and embrace the flashy devices students use to plan outings and send videos. Yet in this cabal of re-imagination, instructors can lose the pedagogical foundation that gives their classes direction. Often, this constant leap to reinvent can be somewhat shortsighted. The truth is that our plethora of new resources can be focused to both achieve traditional goals and lay a solid foundation for the creation of new ones.

These new goals should include arming students with the tools to access a growing data stream. Rachel Milloy explores this concept in Chapter 10, gathering data that demonstrates the frustration students feel for dull and formulaic research processes. The NextGen learner *desires* instruction that leads to a more empowering effect. Therefore, a writing instructor can capitalize upon that desire to achieve writing and research that better matches the overall demands of Gray's Fourth Paradigm. In fact, our students already operate as near natives in the Fourth Paradigm landscape. NextGen students need no help in discovering intellectual concepts, as a plethora of devices and services offer that level of exposure for free and contain no contingent demands. What they need is someone to show them a way to become "immersed" in those concepts. An instructor needs to demonstrate the various tools a student can use to parse resources, evaluate both the usefulness and validity of data, and construct true interpretations of that data for argument. One can do this by constructing visual representations of personal research and offering his or her own interpretations of that data.

It is a gross injustice to characterize this generation's information consumption as "lazy," as their cultural paradigm is based far more on contribution and creation of culture rather than the passive absorption defining the previous era. In fact, Don Tapscott's (2009) description of

NextGen suggests that students will quickly become bored with material that does not somehow invoke their natural creative urges. Tapscott offers an excellent psychological read of the digitally immersed group in his book *Grown Up Digital*. If anything, the current wave of students walking through our doors write and interact with culture much more than the past few generations due to the passing influence of history's greatest time thief: the television. NextGen students not only have a different relationship with television but also with other media. Tapscott thoroughly explores the behavior of this group and uncovers a very interesting pattern of behavior. They remix, discuss, share, and generally engage with many different forms of media, working on a laptop while television plays in the background (21).

It is important to look at the evasive, somewhat disrespectful behaviors of NextGen students, such as remixing material under copyright, not as a reflection of the negative influence of the web in writing skills, but as the total lack of engagement the traditional research assignment offers. It is easy for NextGen students to become belligerent or even combative when an assignment completely ignores their strengths in favor of outdated information practices. Traditional assignments often only get mediocre responses from this student population. These students are not turning their back on collegiate research because they lack the energy or drive to create documents and gather information; rather they are pushing back against an educational system that insists it play the dominant role in "exposing" them to concepts they are more than capable of discovering on their own.

One challenge will be moving beyond the refusal to adapt to the data stream laying the foundation of Fourth Paradigm constructs. Tapscott (2009) explains the failings of traditional academic research in regard to its relationship with the almost blinding world of information and the new literacy evolving to navigate its complicated virtual space. The problem with both secondary and postsecondary instruction is closely related to Cynthia Selfe's (1999) conception of intellectual exposure. Students in high school (and college) find themselves dashing from room to room, shifting mental gears in an almost preindustrial effort to cram as much data into their brains as possible. I think we have all experienced the day Tapscott describes in *Grown Up Digital*:

> For one period, they're memorizing formulas on related rates in calculus from one teacher in the math department; the next period they're regurgitating marine life taxonomy in biology from another teacher in the science department. (128)

The schedule of the American college student is really not that different. Students dash from room to room, building to building, receiving bite-sized portions of "intellectual exposure." Information does not travel this way in the modern world. What students need is a method of collecting data across multiple subjects and synthesizing that data for cross-comparison.

Rethinking the Norms: Tools for the Fourth Paradigm Classroom

Understanding Environmental Scanning

Environmental scanning could help unite diverse curricula and aid students in the process of sorting data. Environmental scanning is a rather simple process as described by Mark Champion (2008). A researcher, in this case the student, constructs a data stream by pulling from multiple resources. In Champion's approach, he used the internet to combine finance, technology, and demographic data to identify scenarios and patterns for the future. This approach to the digestion of data would be infinitely more useful for our students based on its interdisciplinary nature, yet we still seem to cling to the traditional, compartmentalized education of tradition.

Environmental scanning is basically the attempt to understand complex trends and patterns and how they influence the world. The environmental scanning concept owes a great deal to economics, for those in business regularly practice data collection. Any time spent watching a financial channel like CNBC will overwhelm those not accustomed to raw data streams, and making some stock picks typically requires many hours of research and strategy formation. In *The Strategic Management Journal*, Detelin S. Elenkov (1997) explains that the hybrid nature of environmental scanning is what makes it useful: "[e]nvironmental scanning is the means through which managers perceive external events and trends (Hambrick 1982; Culnan 1983). It has the task of reducing strategic uncertainty" (288). This quote shows a refined and carefully developed conception of scanning across the economic sector.

As the busyness of the typical CNBC screen illustrates (see Figure 11.1), a great deal of (mathematical) complexity exists within each environmental scan, making the concept and its project a bit intimidating. Perhaps due to its complex nature, environmental scanning hasn't been utilized in general educational contexts, despite the fact that the value of understanding patterns grows more important with each passing day. In fact, the lack of engagement with data streams is one of the many holes in secondary education as I see it currently constructed, and combating this problem will require dramatic rethinking of many educational norms.

Environmental Scanning in the Writing Classroom

My attempt at this rethinking is bringing environmental scanning into the writing classroom. Environmental scanning offers many of the insights and formulas to move past the traditional research paradigm and create an educational model that utilizes the skill sets NextGen students do not even know they have mastered. Environmental scanning provides students with the stimulation necessary to hold the attention span of the NextGen learner. The practice also has an uncanny ability to move across various fields and disciplines, combating the contained nature of traditional instruction which divides subjects into segregated blocks. Each experiment with this formula for research yields new insights and applications. It grows and evolves because students learn to modify and experiment with the technology

Figure 11.1   CNBC homepage

and apply it to various other functions. For example, my students have already incorporated Twitter posts into their research aggregates, formed separate websites to organize and present their data, and even used environmental scanning skills in other classes without any specific guidance from me. In short, this method moves our students from "exposure" to intellectual concepts to an immersion experience that can continue long after any assignment has concluded.

To create the immersion experience, I use an aggregate integration analysis assignment. The design of my assignment grew from the assessment field, and it relies on Champion's (2008) unique brand of environmental scanning: a mix of web crawling and close monitoring of RSS feeds. A teacher can use this specialized form of environmental scanning to harness the potential ability of the researcher to construct accurate scenarios of the future, allowing researchers to act on changes rather than react to them. Based upon the success of this format, I suggest other teachers consider implementing a similar combination of these ideas.

I designed the assignment where students gather together many different news sources and write evaluations of these sources very near the start of the semester. Using RSS feeds, bookmarking services like Delicious, and various social networking sites, students manage a portfolio of sources for topics like economics, fashion, technology, and medicine. Students also write out several predictions near the start of the semester in regard to the topics they plan to follow. We continually return to these sources throughout the semester for updates, discussing the ways events have unfolded. When the end of the class approaches, students do not just write about the information they find in quick bursts of power browsing. They discuss their research process and the myriad successes and failures within their predictions.

I harness this energy by requiring students to keep a detailed research journal summarizing weekly observations and bits of data. As the course moves along, we end up writing a fairly traditional research paper; the writing generated is not wholly fixated on raw data, but the reactions to data as they evolved over time. The writers begin to form opinions based upon their observations and the accuracy of their predictions. Students also begin to experience topic immersion, using more of the technical terms of their chosen fields as data begins to flood their own personalized portfolios. Students embrace this technology, and it shows within their work.

To highlight these points and effectively demonstrate environmental scanning in the writing classroom, it is necessary to demonstrate the technology. This can prove quite difficult in a written publication, as video and live presentations can walk viewers step by step through the process. For a quick tutorial and explanatory video to the nature and use of RSS feeds, an instructor can share a YouTube video by easy-computercoach (2008) titled "what is rss and what is an rss feed." What I do instead is present two images of my own research aggregates.

There are many RSS readers available for free on the open web, and various programs will offer different advantages or challenges. Figure

11.2 shows the RSS software suggested by Champion (2008). This is Yahoo!'s version of the RSS reader called My Yahoo!. It is a very basic system that allows one to organize data in a variety of ways.

This figure shows my business and economy page, the very same aggregate I built during the economic crisis of 2008. For a long time, this was the space I visited the most on the web. In the center is the widget I installed that tracks a customized stock and currency portfolio detailing the movements of the stock market each time I refresh the page. I have surrounded this widget with condensed RSS feeds from a variety of financial news organizations, including CNBC, Bloomberg, and even Jim Cramer's show "Mad Money." As stocks fluctuate, I can look around to the accompanying feeds and see various opinions concerning the market's direction. As articles interest me, I can follow the link to the original source and read the entire piece.

Figure 11.2   My Yahoo! (Reproduced with permission of Yahoo! Inc. ©2012 Yahoo! Inc. YAHOO! and MY YAHOO! are registered trademarks of Yahoo! Inc.)

My Yahoo! forms the foundation for my environmental scanning assignment. As one works with the software, various weaknesses become obvious. My Yahoo! is a service that only delivers data. As the feeds update, articles are lost and it becomes a burden to maintain a virtual log of pertinent data. There is, however, something about these pages that fosters collaboration. Students regularly post and share links on other social networking services, creating detailed bibliographies of sorts. The limitations of My Yahoo! make the aggregation project more social, as students construct virtual spaces to store data, a problem that encourages cooperation and social networking, skills with which most students are quite adept.

As I structure the environmental scanning assignment, I take advantage of this social behavior. I ask students to keep detailed logs with heavy journaling around the specific Yahoo! interface. Students eventually discover that various other systems and RSS readers exist on the web as they explore other virtual environments. I do not actively encourage them to experiment with other readers, but NextGen students are rarely satisfied with the tools that seem to have fixable problems. Several of my students quickly begin using Google's version of the software called Google Reader, and more and more students drift to Reader over time, a process of software discovery.

Google Reader eventually becomes the primary tool I use in the environmental scanning assignment, showing how NextGen students learn to adapt technology to their research needs. The one feature that makes Reader a superior product proves too useful to ignore: data archiving. Whereas the use of Yahoo! requires the construction and maintenance of a digital library, Google offers an advanced bookmarking service in Reader with its "starred items" folder. Using the starring system saves links and article summaries for later retrieval. The best part is that Google also offers a comment system so that a note can be saved with the links in the archive. Wedding data aggregation with customizable storage and cloud computing makes this process much more accessible and social and solves the need for a digital space to store and discuss articles.

Reader does many things that Yahoo! does not. The myriad features on the right-hand toolbar in Figure 11.3 have expanded quite a bit since my students first pushed to make Reader the central software for this process in our classroom.

Reader has in fact introduced a variety of new features, transforming the process in intriguing ways. The toolbar now highlights the starred items menu near the top, and it also has a "share" function in the same area. The box in the center of the toolbar displays various contacts the user has gathered. Google has also made a push into the social networking dimension that expands upon the archiving process. Instead of just storing articles in a private archive, users can actually share these items across a community built through personal contacts.

This social function has many uses. Students can store and share work this way, never saving items to independent hardware, which allows for group editing and project work to evolve in some pretty surprising ways. Students can create research journals similar to the

Figure 11.3 Google Reader

environmental scanning project, share sources and ideas, and actually write the document itself all in this convenient online space. One of the most common examples of this type of product is the online magazine. Students present their work in the form of a blog, but the material on the blog is created through shared texts edited in Google Documents, shared on Google+, and researched through Google Reader. This allows students to create and transform material in a rich social context rather than an isolated one. It is precisely this social dimension of environmental scanning that can make it a mainstream practice. It offers a source of engagement to NextGen learners as well as a manageable and beneficial application in both a professional and educational context. In short, it could take collaborative document creation to new heights.

When Tapscott (2009) discusses the ennui of the NextGen learner, it should be obvious that the social/cooperative layer of research provided by environmental scanning allows students to harness their unique abilities. Environmental scanning encourages students to actively pursue sources and data across a variety of possible subjects. I have seen students predict future economic conditions, project fashion trends in hopes of front-running new styles, and even suggest treatment innovations in the medical field. To be sure, their predictions are just that—educated guesses which may be wrong, but that is not the point of the environmental scanning assignment. Students benefit from this assignment by sharpening their critical thinking in profound new ways. Not only do they get to construct a scenario for the future and practice their argumentation, but students can also write a reflection analyzing what went wrong with their initial prediction, evaluating themselves and analyzing their own thought processes. The point is that students work with a variety of subjects in a very developed and elegant context.

Confronting the Naysayers: Justifying
Fourth Paradigm Structures

I sometimes wonder why environmental scanning has not captured a larger audience in higher education. Of course, some writers have considered the potential of environmental scanning, yet they either seem to downplay it or force it into an obscure context, thus negating its appeal. Bill Tancer (2008) discusses a practice similar to environmental scanning in his book *Click*. Tancer conducts heavy analysis into the various ways the web shows humanity's true colors. He gathers many data points, including Google searches, to gauge the commercial and social behavior of human beings over time. Tancer discusses everything from suicide rates based on Google searches for depression to predictions on winners of various reality talent shows. Yet when Tancer discusses prediction based upon his method called "arbitrage," exploring the difference between the moment when people do something en masse on the web and the moment it registers with financial indicators, he downplays the value of prediction as a whole:

> It seems like a simple distinction, but there's quite a difference between the art, often perceived as the voodoo, of prediction versus straightforward arbitrage. Predictions involve assumptions, calculations, and, above all, substantial room for error, depending on the precision of your underlying assumptions and calculations. Data arbitrage, on the other hand, is simply taking advantage of the time differential between when people do something on the internet (such as search for a home for sale, or place their residence up for sale) and when a financial indicator such as existing home sales would show that activity. The gap between the two can be a matter of days or weeks or even months. The greater the better. (156)

Tancer is correct about the value of arbitrage, and the greater the distance between data indicators and actual cultural shifts is extremely important, but I do wish he would leave the door open for more experimentation with arbitrage as a practice, rather than distancing the value of raw prediction associated with it.

Tancer (2008), though, reminds us of a key point to keep in mind as we move forward: The lingering distrust of both revolutionary forms of data and their evolving distribution may spur innovation by downplaying the potential value of these radical new practices. The "voodoo" behind prediction is due in large part to the once difficult nature of gathering and synthesizing data points. Now that our resources and access to information have changed, it has become much easier to explore and possibly strengthen our ability to accurately read and assess concerns across the cultural landscape. Environmental scanning in its fullest sense is available, equipping the new digital scholar with a research process unlike any other.

For students to function in a Fourth Paradigm–driven world, instructors across all disciplines must make it a priority to encode Fourth Paradigm research techniques into their classrooms. NextGen students have shown proficiency in some areas of the new research paradigm, but if instructors successfully hybridize the data-intensive research structure while also laying a solid foundation for analysis through writing instruction, students of the next generation will be capable of things far beyond our current ability to predict.

This procession to the Fourth Paradigm of Science can have a massive impact on the way we teach research and writing. As science moves to a focus on mass data and pattern recognition, it will become necessary to show our students communication technologies that allow them to conduct the research the modern world demands of them. Behavioral patterns of language and communication will be dictated not by educational institutions, but by the scientific and industrial processes that utilize these technologies the most quickly and efficiently. The new digital scholar will not conform to the old paradigms of the past, and any attempt to superimpose old pedagogical methods upon them will fail. It is imperative to adopt new student-centered practices that will encourage them to explore their world and create their own research process.

References

Champion, Mark. 2008. "Designing a Personal GIST-In-Time Futuring Webpage: Leveraging Technology to Create an Effective Futuring Tool." Paper presented at the second annual Conference on Best Practices in Institutional Effectiveness, Savannah, Georgia, July 13–16.

Culnan, Mary. 1983. "Environmental Scanning: The Effects of Task Complexity and Source Accessibility on Information Gathering Behavior." *Decision Sciences* 14 (2): 194–206.

Easycomputercoach. 2008. "What Is RSS and What Is an RSS Feed." YouTube. Accessed September 24, 2012. www.youtube.com/watch?v=I_ko-7PEDfA.

Elenkov, Detelin S. 1997. "Strategic Uncertainty and Environmental Scanning: The Case for Institutional Influences on Scanning Behavior." *Strategic Management Journal* 18 (4): 287–302.

Hambrick, Donald. 1982. "Environmental Scanning and Organizational Strategy." *Strategic Management Journal* 3 (2): 159–174.

Hey, Tony, Stewart Hansley, and Kristen Tolle (eds). 2009. *The Fourth Paradigm: Data-Intensive Scientific Discovery*. Redmond, WA: Microsoft Research.

Nicholas, David, Ian Rowlands, and Paul Huntington. 2008. "Information Behaviour of the Researcher of the Future." *EDUCAUSE*. Accessed September 24, 2012. www.jisc.ac.uk/whatwedo/programmes/resourcediscovery/googlegen.aspx.

Selfe, Cynthia L. 1999. *Technology and Literacy in the Twenty-First Century: The Importance of Paying Attention*. Carbondale, IL: Southern Illinois University Press.

Tancer, Bill. 2008. *Click: What Millions of People Are Doing Online and Why It Matters*. New York: Hyperion.

Tapscott, Don. 2009. *Grown Up Digital: How the Net Generation Is Changing Your World*. New York: McGraw-Hill.

Vidal, Gore. 1976. *The Selected Essays of Gore Vidal*. 1st ed. New York: Doubleday.

Yancey, Kathleen Blake. 2004. "Made Not Only in Words: Composition in a New Key." *College Composition and Communication* 56 (2): 297–328.

CHAPTER 12

NextGen Students and Undergraduate Ethnography: The Challenges of Studying Communities Born Digital

Neil P. Baird

For more than 30 years, undergraduate research as an educational reform movement has been conceptualizing students as scholars. As more in the humanities and social sciences take up the call to position undergraduate students as researchers, more needs to be known about the challenges undergraduate researchers face, especially when researching digital communities. Scholars in writing studies argue that digital communities pose new questions concerning identity and space, requiring traditional ethnographic methods to adapt in order to account for the complexity of experience: What identities are important to a digital community? How can these multiple subjectivities be used by the researcher to establish credibility as an insider? How can these identities be represented in order to capture their multiple and fluid nature? What new kinds of ethical dilemmas face the researcher who moves fluidly within hybrid spaces?

How undergraduate ethnographers understand identity has consequences for how they resolve these questions. Furthermore, how undergraduate ethnographers understand identity impacts not only how they conduct ethnographic research, but also how they view and approach research in digital spaces. When undergraduates begin to understand themselves as researchers through pedagogies that blur the boundaries between student and researcher, the digital spaces they inhabit become complex spaces rich for studying the kinds of knowledge needed to participate in such communities.

Drawing upon the work of a female student named Amber who studied the digital community formed by World of Warcraft and a male student named Seth who studied a female gaming clan called Pandora's Mighty Soldiers in Second Life,[1] this chapter will show how single and stable conceptions of identity, reinforced by traditional ethnographic methods, produce accounts that fail to present the complexity of experience found in communities born digital. For various reasons, undergraduates tend to conceive of identity as single and stable rather than multiple and fluid. In addition, ethnographic methods reinforce conceptions of identity and space as single and stable in digital environments. What is at stake in this chapter then is teaching undergraduate researchers how to listen to the lives of those born digital, which involves moving beyond an awareness of subjectivity to an interrogation of location. If undergraduate ethnographers do not learn what questions are appropriate to ask and interrogate their relationship with the digital, they will fail to account for the complexity of experience or, even worse, produce colonized accounts of those they study.

A Culture of Undergraduate Research

Despite the benefits of undergraduate students engaging in research, the humanities have been slow to participate in this educational reform movement (Dotterer 2002, 83); however, recent scholarship suggests faculty in the humanities are finding ways to engage students in undergraduate research (DeVries 2001; Grobman 2007; McDorman 2004;

Rogers 2003; Schilt and Gilbert 2008; Wilson 2003). The recently published *Undergraduate Research in English Studies* (Grobman and Kinkead 2010) offers essays that further conversations about faculty mentorship, ethics and representation, and opportunities for dissemination. Within writing studies, scholars are examining the effects of undergraduate research on students and faculty (Grobman 2009; Robillard 2006); the role undergraduate research might play in first-year writing (Downs and Wardle 2010; Kinkead 2007); the writing center as a fruitful space for undergraduate research (DelliCarpini and Crimmins 2010); and the ways instructors might foster undergraduate research when teaching genres commonly taught within writing studies, such as professional and technical writing (McNely 2010) and the memoir (Gray-Rosendale 2010). In addition, as researchers begin to raise questions about what the undergraduate writing major should be (Balzhiser and McLeod 2010; DelliCarpini 2007), scholars are taking a hard look at research methods courses and the relationship between undergraduate research and Institutional Review Boards (Rogers 2010; Traywick 2010). A "culture of undergraduate research" is thus being fostered (Merkel 2003, 42).

Kathleen Blake Yancey calls on scholars interested in furthering work on undergraduate research to consider such issues as how undergraduate research should differ from graduate research, where to begin emphasizing undergraduate research across the curriculum, what effective undergraduate research experiences should look like, and ways that faculty engagement in undergraduate research can be built into faculty retention and tenure models (2010, 250–252). Absent from Yancey's call to join such conversations about undergraduate research in English studies is an investigation into how undergraduate students engaged in qualitative studies of literacy adapt their methodologies given the nature of the digital environment. This chapter seeks to fill this gap by examining what it means to have students be ethnographic researchers in digital spaces they inhabit.

The Challenge of Studying Communities Born Digital

The publication of *Digital Writing Research: Technologies, Methodologies, and Ethical Issues* (McKee and DeVoss 2007) raises questions about the extent to which traditional research methods can account for digital literacy practices. Of importance to scholars with methodological commitments to ethnography are the contributions of Filipp Sapienza, Iswari Pandey, and Beatrice Smith, which explore the ways in which ethnographic methodologies have to adapt in order to conduct studies of digital communities.

Sapienza (2007) argues that ethos is marked differently in digital spaces: "Indeed, the most credible characters on MOOs and MUDs are usually not the ones who are stable over time but rather characters who are able to move around and transform their virtual identities rapidly in response to rhetorical exigencies. Although such transformations are often restricted to theatrical and ritualistic frames in real life, they form the fabric of socializing in online communities" (100). As a result, researchers must learn to enact multiple identities in order to foster fruitful relationships within the community under study. Pandey (2007, 109–113) argues that participants in digital communities enact postnational subjectivities, identities that can belong to multiple locations without having been an insider anywhere, enacting discourses of diaspora and migration that are doubly marked by more than one location.

For the ethnographer studying digital communities, the possibilities for miscommunication and misinterpretation are elevated because discourse is doubly marked and representing such fluid subjectivities in writing is challenging, if not impossible. Pandey (2007) argues, "No still representation that attempts to freeze a moment and preserve it as real can be real, for the nature of life in the postnational context is such that no moment will always remain fixed—at least for long" (121). Finally, Smith (2007) observes that traditional ethnographic principles rooted in studies of place-bound cultures "may not be as useful when we shift our focus to the hybrid environments created as a result of information technology" (138). More important, she

(2007) argues that we cannot bracket out virtual activities from their material settings, and because the virtual and material cannot be isolated from each other, traditional ethnographic methods, which are ill-equipped to study hybrid spaces, fail to account for the totality of experience (138).

Digital communities challenge the extent to which traditional ethnography can produce "thick descriptions" of online literacy practices, and as Sapienza, Pandey, and Smith argue, ethnographic methods must adapt to resolve new questions concerning researcher location, participant identity, and the field in which ethnographic work is done. How undergraduate ethnographers come to recognize and choose to resolve these questions will help faculty who value undergraduate research understand how to best mentor them.

Both Sapienza (2007) and Pandey (2007) present a postmodern understanding of identity that is challenging for many undergraduates. Sapienza's work is original in the notion that rapid role-play is valued over stability in establishing insider status within digital communities. That is, credibility in digital communities is signaled through the ability to perform multiple roles. However, undergraduates tend to conceive of identity as single and stable rather than multiple and fluid. Conceptions of identity as single and stable not only affect how undergraduate ethnographers enter digital communities, but also how they respond to and represent those they encounter. Pandey argues that members of digital communities enact postnational identities that are multiple and fluid, subjectivities that elude the common identity categories of race, gender, and class. For Pandey, boundary crossing forms the fabric of socialization in digital environments. The challenge for undergraduate ethnographers is resolving new questions about researcher location and participant identity. What identities are important to the digital community? How can these multiple subjectivities be performed to establish credibility as an insider? More important, how can these identities be represented in order to capture their multiple and fluid nature?

How undergraduate ethnographers understand identity thus has consequences for the thick descriptions they develop of the digital communities being studied. Smith (2007), however, suggests that how undergraduate ethnographers understand space also has consequences for the extent to which undergraduates gain insight into what it means to be a member of a digital community. Smith argues that the "work" of digital communities moves between embodied physical settings and the disembodied virtual environment, making it difficult to track (128). In other words, the virtual and material cannot be isolated from each other. The challenge Smith poses undergraduate ethnographers is resolving new questions about space. Where does the "work" of the online community being studied take place? Since our online lives disrupt our notions of bounded social spaces, how can the researcher participate in the online and offline lives of participants? How is access negotiated in multiple fields of study? Also, what new kinds of ethical dilemmas face the researcher who moves fluidly within hybrid spaces?

Studying Undergraduate Ethnographers

Both Amber and Seth were students in a second-semester writing course I taught at a midsized, research-intensive institution in the western U.S. Faculty who teach this course, which introduces students to scholarly research, are invited to organize the course around a theme. Rather than organize the course around a popular theme such as gender, race, or the environment, I organized this course around fieldwork as a research method because positioning students as primary researchers in digital spaces is, I believe, essential to helping them more critically engage these spaces. The primary text for the course was Elizabeth Chiseri-Strater and Bonnie Stone Sunstein's *Fieldworking: Reading and Writing Research* (2006), and students practiced ethnographic methods to study a community of their choice. Students struggled with issues of representation by composing an ethnographic essay of the community they studied. They also shared the behind-the-scenes story of their field experiences by submitting a research portfolio containing ethnographic exercises.

These exercises taught them how to do fieldwork through such activities as analyzing artifacts, mapping spaces, collecting verbal performances, reflecting on interviews, and seriously considering the biases they brought to their communities.

Sapienza's (2007), Pandey's (2007), and Smith's (2007) work allows me to ask two important questions about the undergraduate ethnographers I studied:

1. Since both researcher and participant subjectivities in digital environments are multiple and fluid, how did each student experience and respond to the slippages and overlaps in identity he or she encountered?

2. Since the space each student studied was an ever-shifting milieu, how did she or he experience and respond to the need to shift among multiple locations?

These two questions provide the frame for my analysis of Amber and Seth's ethnographic essays and their research portfolios.

"I Left His Online World": Amber's Boyfriend as Postnational Subject

Amber's interest in studying World of Warcraft emerged from a need to understand her relationship with her boyfriend more fully. She wanted to know why he devoted so much time to playing a video game and raiding[2] in particular. To answer this question, she spent the semester as a participant-observer in her boyfriend's guild.[3] Amber's experience highlights the ways in which subjectivity can affect how an undergraduate resolves issues concerning researcher location, participant identity, and the field in which ethnographic work is done. Amber clearly came to an awareness of her relationship to video games through the ethnographic exercises required by the course. Without an interrogation of her history with video games, however, this subjectivity prevented Amber from making an account of the complexity she encountered.

Amber's Subjectivity

As students began to compose their ethnographic accounts, I raised issues concerning representation and challenged them to experiment with unconventional forms that might represent their community more effectively than the standard research report. In her Preface, Amber explains the form she chose for her ethnographic essay:

> To truly represent my culture, I have written the paper in the form of a raid. ... I found the "raid" to be the most intriguing and complex part of the Warcraft culture ... The fantasy genre is a staple of this culture and the ground upon which this game was built, so I depicted the raid in the form of a fantasy story. I also included the dialogue in its original form to display the fast-paced communication within the game. I also wanted to show how unrefined (and raw) the language is while playing the game.

Her ethnographic essay tells the story of the destruction of two raid bosses, Nefarian and Ragnaros, in the form of a fantasy story in which the main characters are her undead rogue, her boyfriend, and members of his guild. Rather than dialogue, she uses material from synchronous chat transcripts of the two raids through which she shows the rampant sexism she experienced as a female gamer and the embarrassment her boyfriend has for her as a casual gamer.

In an ethnographic exercise asking her to reflect on her field notes, Amber writes about her attitude toward video games:

> Video games were not allowed in my household because my mother and father felt that literature and public broadcasting could bring more to our lives than a "mindless" video game. ... Gradually, video games infiltrated the family as my younger brother began to play more and more. Eventually, he became consumed. I, however, drifted away from the addiction ... When I would visit (my brother) in

the basement, we did not communicate; he merely answered with intermittent grunts. It saddened me. It was bearable, however, until I realized the boy I had been dating had the same addiction. That was the last straw; I needed to understand why the two most important boys in my life were addicted to screens.

Because of her history with video games, Amber is uncomfortable when she encounters and is forced to respond to the fluidity of identity and location in the community she studied.

Researcher Location

In an exercise asking her to analyze an artifact important to World of Warcraft, Amber chose to explore the importance of avatars, noting, "I feel [a player's avatar is the object] most important to this culture because it displays the *personality* of each player" (my emphasis). For Amber, an avatar is an extension of a singular personality. This understanding of an avatar does not acknowledge that identity online is multiple and fluid. In addition, the notion that avatars are "extensions" does not acknowledge the separation Sapienza argues exists between a person and the interacting character. This may be why Amber offers no analysis of the choices she made in creating her own avatar. That is, she may not be conscious that she is constructing an interacting character that can be separate from her and thus multiple and fluid.

Amber's understanding of identity as singular and stable causes her difficulties as she tries to foster credibility within her boyfriend's guild. Preceding the following exchange of words, Maeren (Amber's avatar) has made a critical mistake that leads to the death of the raid in a fight against Ragnaros:

> Shaman: Way to mess up, Maeren. ... You were supposed to be there!
>
> Maeren: I was trying, but I had so much homework. I just don't have this kind of time.

> Whisper from Boyfriend: I asked you earlier. I don't want people to make fun of you for not being serious. Can't you just blend in a little?

In this exchange, Amber performs a subjectivity that damages her credibility, positioning her as an Other outside this community. Rather than performing any number of identities that might allow her to save face, she performs the identity of a casual gamer, an extension of who she is offline, which invokes her boyfriend's ire.

Participant Identity

Amber is also clearly uncomfortable with the discovery of her boyfriend's postnational subjectivity. In an exercise asking her to reflect on how she established rapport with a community insider, she writes the following:

> [My boyfriend] and I have been dating for nearly three years, so it was not difficult to approach him when I began this project. I cannot say, however, that I did not get to know him better through my work. I was able to see him in an entirely different light and for the first time I saw his arrogance. [He] is generally a humble man. He does not boast, nor does he act in an arrogant manner, unless he is gaming. Warcraft is his world and he knows he is an excellent player and guild member. ... I learned one very important lesson, not to intrude on his interests, because this "world" gives him space. With me in his world he did not have the freedom he once had, so I left his online world.

When she encounters her boyfriend's fluid identity, her response is to retreat from it. The last part of this reflection highlights how difficult it is for her to move across multiple locations.

The Field

This difficulty moving across multiple locations is clearly seen in the way Amber represents herself visually in her research portfolio. Amber includes photographs of her boyfriend's dorm room in response to an ethnographic exercise asking her to map a space important to her community. Including these images suggests that she understands the virtual (the world of Warcraft) cannot be bracketed off from the physical (his dorm room); however, in the context of her research portfolio, I read these photographs as an inability to travel.

Many of these images are photographs of her boyfriend. Each of these images is shot from behind; thus, we see the back of his head and his monitor as he sits at his desk playing the game. These images juxtapose her boyfriend and his avatar as well as his dorm room and Azeroth.[4] These juxtapositions represent his ability to move across multiple locations, ultimately highlighting how the boundaries between the real and virtual become blurred for him. In images focused on Amber, we never see her screen or avatar. In one image, she is even looking up from her laptop into the camera. This photo is representative of her experience presented in her research portfolio. Her history with video games prevents her from valuing and understanding the fluidity of identity and space that often marks membership in an online community.

"A Game Within a Game! LOL": Seth and the Vertigo of Second Life

Seth, a student in the same course as Amber, discovered an all-female online gaming community called Pandora's Mighty Soldiers (PMS) while browsing internet sites devoted to Counterstrike, his favorite first-person shooter game. Knowing the sexism that female gamers often experience, Seth wanted to understand more fully what the PMS clan offered women who play video games. He began his project by trying to contact members of the PMS clan offline with little success. When he learned that the headquarters of the PMS clan was located in

Second Life, he created an avatar and tried contacting members there. Similar to Amber, Seth's subjectivity affects how he resolves issues concerning researcher location, participant identity, and the field in which ethnographic work is done. In contrast, Seth is an avid gamer and proceeds to impose the digital community he is most familiar with onto Second Life. As a result, Seth fails to move past the vertigo he feels and imposes an interpretation of Second Life which does not listen to the voices of insiders.

Seth's Subjectivity

Seth's ethnographic essay chronicles his conversations with several members of the PMS clan, including the community's co-founder Athena Twin, and his tour of their headquarters. Seth confesses that he does not know much about computers even though he defines himself as a gamer. Describing his first moments in Second Life, Seth writes, "I had been wandering around in this virtual world for ten minutes trying to figure out how to get in touch with the PMS girls. I'm not the most computer savvy person. This was all new to me. Although I've been a huge video game fan my entire life, I had never even communicated by instant messaging before and I had sent my first email just a couple of months earlier." In his research portfolio, he attributes this to his lower-class upbringing and worries about how this history might affect his relationship with members of the PMS clan. While he defines himself as a gamer, it is clear Seth does not consider himself a technologist or computer expert, and this history hinders his ability as an ethnographer to move from outsider to insider.

Researcher Location

Like Amber, Seth also includes images of himself and his research participants in his research portfolio; however, in contrast to Amber, his images are screenshots of Second Life rather than a physical/material space. Among these are several images of his avatar. His avatar is a white male with blue eyes and blond hair combed back. In most of the images, Seth's avatar wears a black blazer, gray T-shirt, blue jeans, and brown shoes. What strikes me is how much his avatar looks exactly like Seth and the absence of any discussion of the choices he made in creating his avatar. Similar to Amber, what this highlights is his uneasiness with assuming an identity other than his own.

Participant Identity

The way in which his ethnographic essay opens supports this reading of his experience. Seth opens with a description of what he saw after his avatar materialized at the Waterhead info hub.[5] He describes a woman sitting on a horse, a creature from the comic book *Spawn*, a man rocketing around on a pink phallus, a wizard traveling within a vortex, a UFO flying overhead, a 1940s airplane stalled in the sky, and a battle between robots modeled after those found in *Doctor Who*. Seth experiences a kind of vertigo fostered by the multiplicity of identities available in Second Life, which frustrates him. After describing the UFO and 1940s airplane, Seth writes, "Walking into the close encounter made me lose my last fiber of patience. My goal of reaching the PMS headquarters had been thwarted at every turn so far by bizarre and unexplainable events." What is telling is the way he gives presence to this multiplicity in the way he represents Second Life in his essay. Three out of 12 pages detail what he saw when he first logged into the game. In addition, almost every interview with members of the PMS clan chronicles how they were interrupted by other "bizarre and unexplainable events." The attention he gives is reflective of how uncomfortable he is with multiple subjectivities.

This sense of vertigo begins to explain his response to PMS avatars: "I can't overlook how clean and 'polished' the PMS avatars look. They obviously spend a good deal of time and effort improving their images. In business and marketing, good image is necessary for a strong business and profit." Here, Seth begins to make connections between the PMS clan and commercialism, and the attention he gives to understanding the appearance of their avatars is suggestive of his difficulty conceptualizing Second Life as a commercial space.

The Field

In fact, much of Second Life does not match up with what Seth defines as a video game. In reflecting on his field notes, he writes, "[Second Life] isn't what I would call a real game. Games are supposed to be fun and exciting." Reflecting on seeing a group of avatars dancing, he says, "It's a real spectacle. What do they get out of it? Seems pretty boring to me." When he logs out and reads that his avatar fell asleep, he wonders, "Why would an avatar need to sleep?" In addition, he references a game called "Greedy, greedy" throughout his research portfolio. This is a game that members of the PMS clan play in their headquarters. In every instance he mentions this game, he cannot believe what he is seeing. He exclaims, "They're playing games even when they're not playing games. LOL." His trouble conceptualizing Second Life as a commercial space and video game is reflective of his difficulty with the migrant nature of digital environments. Although he travels between Counterstrike and Second Life, he is unable to conceptualize Second Life except through the framework of Counterstrike.

Moving Beyond Representing "Mere Shadows of Struggling Lives"

The opening to Gloria Naylor's book *Mama Day* is often quoted in methods texts with commitments to ethnography. Reema's Boy, who comes back to Willow Springs after receiving a college education in order to put the island on the map by conducting an ethnographic study, is often presented as warning novice ethnographers about the possibilities of colonization and the power of representation. Reema's Boy begins his study by trying to figure out why members of the community say "18 and 23," and while most in the community were polite to him, the narrator voices her frustration concerning the way he conducted his study:

> If the boy wanted to know what 18 and 23 meant, why didn't he just ask? When he was running around sticking

that machine in everybody's face, we was sitting right here—every one of us—and him being one of Reema's, we woulda obliged him. He coulda asked Cloris about the curve in her spine that came from the planting season when their mule broke its leg, and she took up the reins and kept pulling the plow with her own back. Winky woulda told him about the hot tar that took out the corner of his right eye the summer we had only seven days to rebuild the bridge so the few crops we had left after the storm could be gotten over before the rot set in. ... Reema's boy coulda heard from them everything there was to tell about 18 and 23.

But on second thought, someone who didn't know how to ask wouldn't know how to listen. (Chiseri-Strater and Sunstein 2006, 123–125)

What is at stake in this chapter is teaching undergraduate researchers how to listen to the lives of those born digital, a feat made more difficult by the ways in which current ethnographic methods reinforce misconceptions about identity and space. Because they are place-bound, such methods emphasize dwelling over travel (Pandey 2007, 108) and produce the wrong answers to questions about digital environments. For example, Seth is clearly challenged by the question, "How do I gain access to the PMS clan?" Buying into a conception of identity that is single and stable, he answers this question by creating an avatar that is strikingly similar to his real-life appearance. Why did he choose a male avatar when the creation of a female avatar might have given him easier access to this community? Better yet, since a male and female avatar might offer different types of access and yield different kinds of data, why not create two (or possibly more) avatars and experience what it might be like to access the PMS clan as both? Pandey (2007) calls for a postnational ethics of location, an ethical position that can help undergraduates learn how to listen to those who live in digital communities; however, it is not enough to be aware of one's fixed and subjective position. According to Pandey (2007, 124), there needs to be an interrogation of location; otherwise, ethnographers produce "mere shadows of struggling lives."

As undergraduate research continues to grow, more students will be invited to take up qualitative research, and those who take up the challenge to study digital communities will have to be taught how to interrogate the ways their histories with computer technology position them. Because of their histories, Amber and Seth responded to the multiple and fluid identities they encountered and the need to shift among multiple locations in such a way that they created distance between themselves and those they studied. Amber ended her experience with the troubling conclusion that she does not belong. Seth asked good ethnographic questions: What do Second Lifers get out of dancing? Why do avatars need to sleep? Why play a game within a game? However, his history with Counterstrike did not allow him to move beyond the vertigo that produced these questions. Both undergraduates were clearly aware of their histories, but because they did not interrogate them, they produced author-saturated ethnographies (Chiseri-Strater 1996), ethnographic accounts that are so much about the author that they produce mere shadows of the communities studied.

Conclusion

How do we help undergraduates interrogate their location and the values associated with it? Such interrogation begins with the ways we situate studies of digital rhetoric in our curriculum. At my own institution, our curriculum sends the message that the virtual can be isolated from the material. In an effort to lay claim to digital rhetoric, we offer a lower-division course called Introduction to New Media Literature, an upper-division course called Computers and Writing, and a graduate course called New Media Studies. While our curriculum offers more courses devoted to the digital humanities than many other institutions, it also sends the message that the ways computers are transforming the ways we read, write, and research need only be taught in these three courses. If, as Beatrice Smith (2007, 138) argues, we cannot isolate the virtual from the material, we cannot bracket out the digital in the courses we teach.

For undergraduate researchers to truly interrogate their locations in order to offer more complex representations of digital communities, students need more exposure to the issues discussed in this chapter than one or two courses allow. We often assume that because students use computer technology more than we do that they are more knowledgeable about these issues. Amber, Seth, and the other students I have mentored on digital writing projects from studies of Madden NFL to file sharing communities suggest that students need to think more critically about their use and engagement with technology, which requires more exposure. We recently revised the descriptions of our core courses so that literature instructors include texts from around the world no matter what they teach. Perhaps we should revise them again to ensure a digital component.

In addition to more effectively situating studies of digital rhetoric within our curriculum, the qualitative research methods course needs to be reassessed. Our approaches to this course, especially the texts we choose to use, often bracket out the virtual. Because of this, undergraduates engaged in qualitative studies of digital communities often lack the guidance and mentoring necessary to produce original work that can be disseminated, which is at the heart of undergraduate research. Until methods textbooks begin to seriously consider the virtual, we will have to integrate the virtual into our research methods courses ourselves. One way to do so is to invite undergraduates, especially in courses with strong commitments to ethnography, to produce new media ethnographies.

Calls for positioning research participants as co-researchers and co-authors as well as for devising new ways of writing ethnographies that are polyvocal in nature are common within feminist research methods (Brueggemann 1996; Chiseri-Strater 1996; Kirsch 1992; Sullivan 1996). In *Rhetoric Online: Persuasion and Politics on the World Wide Web*, Barbara Warnick (2007, 26) argues that traditional assumptions concerning the rhetoric of speech and print do not hold for texts "born digital." Existing rhetorical theories need to be reshaped to analyze new media because of the ways these texts challenge traditional notions of authorship through interactivity and intertextuality. New media ethnographies offer ways of realizing calls for alternative representations since new media texts already embody several feminist values. In *The Making of Knowledge in Composition: Portrait of an Emerging Field*, Stephen North (1987) criticizes researchers in writing studies engaged in qualitative methods for not understanding the power of their methodologies. New media ethnographies may be one step closer to realizing the potential of qualitative methods, and undergraduate researchers who consume new media every day may be in the perfect position to offer such contributions. Asking undergraduate researchers to explore the potentials for such new media representations may provide a starting point for examining how students, teachers, and scholars can more fruitfully listen to and represent the lives of those in communities born digital.

Endnotes

1. Each student has been given a pseudonym to protect his or her identity.

2. Raiding is an activity designed for players whose characters have reached maximum level. In World of Warcraft, raiding requires the collaboration of 10 or more players to complete an event or defeat an important creature, often called a raid boss. Raiding requires players to have particular levels of skill, gear, and time (akin to a part-time job). At the time Amber raided, raids required the coordination of 40 people to be successful.

3. In World of Warcraft, a guild is a group of players that work together to explore the game's content. A guild's objectives can range from a combination of helping each other get achievements, role-playing, working through end-game content, and competing in player-versus-player tournaments. The guild Amber joined is devoted to raiding.

4. Azeroth is the name of the world where World of Warcraft takes place.

5. The Waterhead info hub is one of many "welcome areas" for new avatars in Second Life.

References

Balzhiser, Deborah, and Susan H. McLeod. 2010. "The Undergraduate Writing Major: What Is It? What Should It Be?" *College Composition and Communication* 61 (3): 415–433.

Brueggemann, Brenda Jo. 1996. "Still Life: Representations and Silences in the Participant-Observer Role." In *Ethics and Representation in Qualitative Studies of Literacy*, edited by Peter Mortensen and Gesa E. Kirsch, 17–39. Urbana, IL: NCTE.

Chiseri-Strater, Elizabeth. 1996. "Turning In Upon Ourselves: Positionality, Subjectivity, and Reflexivity in Case Study and Ethnographic Research." In *Ethics and Representation in Qualitative Studies of Literacy*, edited by Peter Mortensen and Gesa E. Kirsch, 115–133. Urbana, IL: NCTE.

Chiseri-Strater, Elizabeth, and Bonnie S. Sunstein, eds. 2006. *Fieldworking: Reading and Writing Research*. Boston: Bedford/St. Martin's.

DelliCarpini, Dominic. 2007. "Re-Writing the Humanities: The Writing Major's Effect Upon Undergraduate Studies in English Departments." *Composition Studies* 35 (1): 15–36.

DelliCarpini, Dominic, and Cynthia Crimmins. 2010. "The Writing Center as a Space for Undergraduate Research." In *Undergraduate Research in English Studies*, edited by Laurie Grobman and Joyce Kinkead, 191–211. Urbana, IL: NCTE.

DeVries, David N. 2001. "Undergraduate Research in the Humanities: An Oxymoron?" *CUR Quarterly* 21 (4): 153–155.

Dotterer, Ronald L. 2002. "Student-Faculty Collaborations, Undergraduate Research, and Collaboration as an Administrative Model." *New Directions for Teaching and Learning* 90: 81–89.

Downs, Douglas, and Elizabeth Wardle. 2010. "What Can a Novice Contribute? Undergraduate Researchers in First-Year Composition." In *Undergraduate Research in English Studies*, edited by Laurie Grobman and Joyce Kinkead, 173–190. Urbana, IL: NCTE.

Gray-Rosendale, Laura. 2010. "Rhetorics and Undergraduate Research: A Journey into the Genre of Memoir." In *Undergraduate Research in English Studies*, edited by Laurie Grobman and Joyce Kinkead, 212–228. Urbana, IL: NCTE.

Grobman, Laurie. 2007. "Affirming the Independent Researcher Model: Undergraduate Research in the Humanities." *CUR Quarterly* 28 (1): 23–28.

———. 2009. "The Student Scholar: (Re)negotiating Authorship and Authority." *College Composition and Communication* 61 (1): W175–W196.

Grobman, Laurie, and Joyce Kinkead. 2010. "Illuminating Undergraduate Research in English." In *Undergraduate Research in English Studies*, edited by Laurie Grobman and Joyce Kinkead, ix–xxxii. Urbana, IL: NCTE.

Kinkead, Joyce. 2007. "How Writing Programs Support Undergraduate Research." In *Developing and Sustaining a Research-Supportive Curriculum: A Compendium of Successful Practices*, edited by Kerry K. Karukstis and Timothy E. Elgrens, 195–208. Washington, DC: Council on Undergraduate Research.

Kirsch, Gesa. 1992. "Methodological Pluralism: Epistemological Issues." In *Methods and Methodology in Composition Research*, edited by Gesa Kirsch and Patricia A. Sullivan, 247–269. Carbondale: Southern Illinois University Press.

McDorman, Todd. 2004. "Promoting Undergraduate Research in the Humanities: Three Collaborative Approaches." *CUR Quarterly* 25 (1): 39–42.

McKee, Heidi A., and Dànielle Nicole DeVoss. 2007. *Digital Writing Research: Technologies, Methodologies, and Ethical Issues*. New York: Hampton Press.

McNely, Brian J. 2010. "Cultivating Rhetorical Dispositions through Curricular Change in Technical and Professional Communication." In *Undergraduate Research in English Studies*, edited by Laurie Grobman and Joyce Kinkead, 229–244. Urbana, IL: NCTE.

Merkel, Carolyn A. 2003. "Undergraduate Research at the Research Universities." In *Valuing and Supporting Undergraduate Research: New Directions in Teaching and Learning*, edited by Joyce Kinkead, 39–53. San Francisco: Jossey-Bass.

North, Stephen. 1987. *The Making of Knowledge in Composition: Portrait of an Emerging Field*. Portsmouth, NH: Boynton/Cook Publishers.

Pandey, Iswari. 2007. "Researching (with) the Postnational 'Other.'" In *Digital Writing Research: Technologies, Methodologies and Ethical Issues*, edited by Heidi A. McKee and Dànielle N. DeVoss, 107–125. Cresskill, NJ: Hampton Press.

Robillard, Amy E. 2006. "Young Scholars Affecting Composition: A Challenge to Disciplinary Citation Practices." *College English* 68 (3): 253–270.

Rogers, Jacqueline M. 2010. "An Undergraduate Research Methods Course in Rhetoric and Composition: A Model." In *Undergraduate Research in English Studies*, edited by Laurie Grobman and Joyce Kinkead, 74–92. Urbana, IL: NCTE.

Rogers, V. Daniel. 2003. "Surviving the 'Culture Shock' of Undergraduate Research in the Humanities." *CUR Quarterly* 23 (3): 132–135.

Sapienza, Filipp. 2007. "Ethos and Researcher Positionality in Studies of Virtual Communities." In *Digital Writing Research: Technologies, Methodologies and Ethical Issues*, edited by Heidi A. McKee and Dànielle N. DeVoss, 89–106. Cresskill, NJ: Hampton Press.

Schilt, Paige, and Lucia A. Gilbert. 2008. "Undergraduate Research in the Humanities: Transforming Expectations at a Research University." *CUR Quarterly* 28 (4): 51–55.

Smith, Beatrice. 2007. "Researching Hybrid Literacies: Methodological Explorations of Ethnography and the Practices of the Cybertariat." In *Digital Writing Research:*

Technologies, Methodologies and Ethical Issues, edited by Heidi A. McKee and Dànielle N. DeVoss, 127–149. Cresskill, NJ: Hampton Press.

Sullivan, Patricia A. 1996. "Ethnography and the Problem of the 'Other.'" In *Ethics and Representation in Qualitative Studies of Literacy*, edited by Peter Mortensen and Gesa E. Kirsch, 97–114. Urbana, IL: NCTE.

Traywick, Deaver. 2010. "Preaching What We Practice: RCR Instruction for Undergraduate Researchers in Writing Studies." In *Undergraduate Research in English Studies*, edited by Laurie Grobman and Joyce Kinkead, 51–73. Urbana, IL: NCTE.

Warnick, Barbara. 2007. *Rhetoric Online: Persuasion and Politics on the World Wide Web*. New York: Peter Lang.

Wilson, Reed. 2003. "Researching 'Undergraduate Research' in the Humanities." *Modern Languages Studies* 33: 74–79.

Yancey, Kathleen Blake. 2010. "Afterword." In *Undergraduate Research in English Studies*, edited by Laurie Grobman and Joyce Kinkead, 245–253. Urbana, IL: NCTE.

Programmatic Solutions to Enrich the Research and Writing Practices of NextGen Students

Teaching Researching in the Digital Age: An Information Literacy Perspective on the New Digital Scholar

Barry M. Maid and Barbara J. D'Angelo

Research Becomes Information Literacy: Creating the Context

Research is the ultimate gold standard for what academics do. Yet application of the word "research" has become so broad as to be almost meaningless. Think about it like this. Should we describe the process that scientists use to find vaccines for life-threatening diseases or the process that others use to find a cost-efficient and carbon-neutral bio-fuel with the same word as the process people use when they read Zagat reviews to decide where they're going for dinner? Today, all of these processes, and so much in between, are called "research." It's no wonder more and more people are finding the phrase information literacy (IL) to be more meaningful.

As is true of the word "research," IL can have multiple meanings. IL, as many readers of this work may know, is defined by the American Library Association (ALA) as the ability to recognize the need for as well as the ability to find, evaluate, and use information. In 2000, in the publication "Information Literacy Competency Standards for Higher Education," the Association of College and Research Libraries (ACRL) detailed five standards and accompanying performance measures and objectives as a framework to define and assess IL specifically for higher education. Although the IL standards may be seen as reductionist in the level of detail used to outline skills and abilities, the document ultimately delineates research and information skills as a process. Further, the IL standards extend beyond research to include other information-related skills that are relevant to the disciplines of writing studies, including those related to the organization, management, and presentation of information and knowledge. Since IL and writing are so intertwined, regardless of whether a project is academic or applied, we feel that it is crucial for a college writing curriculum to include teaching IL skills just as much as teaching writing skills. After a brief survey of IL, we will suggest just such a curriculum.

Expanding Views of Information Literacy

IL emerged as a concept in library and information science out of the bibliographic instruction tradition and became associated with the rise of the internet and communication technologies. External to librarianship, differing views about the definitions of information, knowledge, and literacy within disciplinary discourses compound difficulties to define the scope of IL. Barbara Fister (1993), for example, notes that one of the reasons for disagreement over the role of IL within writing programs is that librarians emphasize *finding* knowledge whereas writing instructors emphasize how to *construct* it. This distinction lends itself to faculty views of IL as a continuation of or new name for traditional bibliographic or library instruction.

However, as bibliographic instruction evolved into IL at the end of the 20th century, librarians began to focus on more than simply directing students in the use of the library databases and sources, moving toward more full-fledged attempts to teach students to deal with the changing nature of access to information and to think critically about information and its use (for example, see Bodi 1988, 1990; Kautzman

1996). In addition, some librarians began to focus on teaching IL rhetorically so that students would learn to search for and use information within the context of the rhetorical situation. Fister (1993), in particular, emphasizes that teaching research as information retrieval in the bibliographic instruction tradition valorizes retrieval as the purpose of research so that information becomes decontextualized and research is solely about finding information, any information, related to the topic whether it is relevant or not. For her, when IL is taught rhetorically, however, retrieval and evaluation of information are placed within the context of the audience, the argument to be made, and the evidence presented in support of the argument.

Views of IL as related to critical thinking and research as a process continue to ground it within the practice of library or secondary research instruction, albeit with the added context of finding and evaluating sources of information within the rhetorical context. These views reflect a notion of IL as a practice in librarianship related to information products rather than processes and confound attempts to broaden the scope of IL beyond information search and retrieval.

Historically, librarians have been viewed as the maintainers and gatekeepers of information products; that is, as primarily concerned with quality control. The gatekeeper role is often manifested in assignments in which instructors require the use of sources found in the library with the implication that such sources are of higher quality than those found elsewhere (typically the internet). In this conception of library as gatekeeper of information quality, IL instruction treats individuals as passive consumers of information instead of active knowledge makers, placing it at odds with constructivist paradigms of making meaning.

Cushla Kapitzke (2003) shares this view. She states that IL emphasizes the consumption of information but neglects sociocultural, historical, and ideological processes of knowledge construction. Instead, she proposes a hyperliteracy approach which acknowledges social, technological, and epistemological developments and approaches to the development of pedagogical frameworks in order to help students focus and reflect critically on the process of finding solutions to problems. Rebecca Moore Howard (2006), the co-author of Chapter 5 in this book, argues that IL must reach beyond the use of a format hierarchy to evaluate data. She ponders the emergence of rhizomatic processes in which information seeking in new media may go in multiple unplanned directions to connect disparate threads. Given this rhizomatic approach to information seeking, she argues, teaching research as a linear or recursive process at both the undergraduate and the graduate levels is useless.

Other research and scholarship further urge us to expand our understanding of the nature and scope of IL. Christine Bruce (1997) delineates seven different conceptions or definitions of IL based on user experience and ties IL to learning. Bill Johnston and Sheila Webber (2003) review the state of IL education and critique views of IL as prescriptive and tool-based thus leading to superficial learning approaches. Mandy Lupton (2004) advocates for a shift from a training paradigm (such as library or bibliographic instruction in source use) to an education paradigm in which learning is contextualized. Similar to Johnston and Webber, she critiques current views of IL as skills-based and as a decontextualized concept resulting from library practice rather than student experience. Lupton argues for a view of IL connected to learning that is defined not as a characteristic of the learner but as a response to context and situated within the topic, the course, and the discipline. Agneta Lantz and Christina Brage (2006) describe "applied IL" in order to place instruction practices and assignments within real world contexts, and Annemaree Lloyd and Margaret Somerville (2006) further advocate for understanding IL as situated within context, in their case the context of the workplace. These researchers have attempted to move IL research away from a library-centric focus to that of the user as situated within a task or social context.

Seeing Research as a Process

Conceptions of research as a process, which emerged approximately at the same time as the process movement in the field of writing studies, have likely been the impetus which encouraged library and information science professionals to identify with their writing colleagues and establish pedagogical partnerships and collaborations.[1] Since the idea of research as a process is more established in the field of library and information science, we wish to briefly review that literature for those, especially in the field of writing studies, who may not be familiar with it.

The research of Carol Kuhlthau (2004) delineates research as a process that is remarkably reminiscent of the writing process, from topic selection to search closure to the communication of information. Kuhlthau's stages emphasize finding, using, and communicating information to seek meaning. Originally conducted with middle school students, her longitudinal research was later repeated with a variety of information-intensive professionals to confirm findings in other settings. Kuhlthau's delineation of stages in the search process influenced the library and information science field's view of instruction and reference services as well as prompted continued research related to information-seeking and use behaviors. Grounded in library and information science, Kuhlthau's research is reminiscent of Fister's (1993) distinction between the library science perspective on finding knowledge and most disciplinary perspectives as constructing knowledge.

For our purposes, then, we define IL as the ability to find, discriminate, analyze, manage, organize, and present information as a process in which research is placed in the context of constructing knowledge for a specific purpose and audience—whatever the purpose might be and whoever the audience might be—and we suggest that writing classrooms similarly adopt such a definition. If this is the case, then how do we go about designing an effective IL strategy to embed in our writing curricula? How do we move beyond assigning the IL version of the traditional "research paper"? We seek to answer these questions in the following sections.

Intertwined Processes

If we are to be serious about establishing an effective IL pedagogy for a writing curriculum, then we must stop separating the two inherently intertwined processes of information gathering and reporting. It makes little difference whether the project is academic or applied in nature; gathering information without disseminating that information in some form is pointless. Still, we can break down the steps in the process, as we do here, in order to help students as they move through this complex process.

Information Discovery

One of the real changes that the digital revolution has facilitated is the simple ability to find information. When anyone—student, instructor, or member of the general public—now wants information, he or she is most likely to use Google or some other search engine to retrieve it (see Chapters 6 and 7 in this book). Despite what many instructors tell their students, students are also likely to look at Wikipedia, if for no other reason than it is often the first resource suggested in most search engine returns. Realistically, searching for background information using an encyclopedia is a solid research strategy (how many instructors would quibble if students first consulted *Encyclopædia Britannica* or a subject-specific encyclopedia as part of their information gathering?). Pedagogically, rather than banning tools of information discovery for background information, instructors should encourage students to use them as tools to refine and focus their topics.

This early stage of the process is critical for students to learn more about their topic in order to refine and focus it into a manageable question. The key is to help students understand and differentiate information discovery during topic formulation from the more specific and focused type of discovery needed to answer a focused research question. Without a clearly focused purpose and audience for the research (question, hypothesis, statement), then there is no context within which to analyze information and no meaning. That creates a situation where all information is equal. As Project Information Literacy (2009,

2010) research has shown, students find topic formulation and refinement to be the most difficult part of the research process. Students typically look to their instructors for guidance at this stage in the process but too often receive little help. In fact, in videos produced as part of Project Information Literacy's research, students discuss the frustrations students feel about conducting research, including the belief that their instructors aren't giving them sufficient guidance on the research process. Without this guidance, student research questions remain overly broad (or too focused), resulting in haphazard searches. The results of ill-defined searches produce information that might be helpful but rarely has a clear focus.

A curricular strategy to facilitate research question formulation is to incorporate more processing assignments related to invention. For example, an instructor might ask students to summarize a Wikipedia entry (or other background reading) on the topic and then formulate two or three more focused research questions based on their newfound understanding.

The almost universal access to and use of search engines means that finding information is now rarely a problem. What is a problem now, however, is that it is too easy to find too much information. Simply typing a word or a phrase into a search engine usually gives an individual more potential information than anyone can realistically process (see Chapter 4 of this book, where Brian Ballentine discusses how this plethora of information is influencing the brain). One step in helping students reasonably limit their searches is to make sure they use Boolean operators. Understanding how to use Boolean operators when doing web searches can significantly eliminate irrelevant results, though even with the use of Boolean operators the amount of information that is generated can be overwhelming. As a result, instructors need to help students learn how to use their background research to formulate appropriate keywords or phrases and to make useful discriminations about the quality of information their searches reveal (see Chapter 8 of this book, where Ruth Mirtz discusses students' use of keywords). That way, students will be able to narrow and wade through the glut of information their search produces more effectively, rather than simply using the first five or 10 results.

However, even more important than assigning information-gathering exercises to NextGen students is modeling these behaviors in ways that will engage them. If instructors are teaching face-to-face classes, they might do some searches in class to model formulating and revising of keywords, using subject headings or index terms to select relevant keywords for narrowing searches, and using Boolean operators. Depending on the available classroom technology, everyone can watch while the instructor or one student is doing one search and brainstorm along with the searcher, or else students can engage in multiple searches. The search results can be compared, analyzed, and discussed. If the class is online, the instructor can suggest students do defined searches and then report on findings on the class discussion board where a similar comparison, analysis, and discussion can take place. Forming small social media networks for the class or groups within the class is another way of having students engage in information-gathering activities in both face-to-face and online classes. They can use the various information-sharing functions of the particular social media platform.

Information Discrimination

Once instructors have guided their students to find information, probably more information than the students can possibly use, they need to help students learn how to make meaningful discriminations about the value of that information. This process of discrimination needs to occur on multiple levels. Instructors need to have their students learn how to ask questions of the information they find so that students can learn the rhetorical nature of research. Questions may include the following:

- Is this information relevant to the research question, and is it tied to the purpose of the research? Asking this question points to the necessity of first ensuring that students have a focused research question in order to determine whether or not the information is relevant. This way, students can come to understand that the information they select must meet a purpose and be based on their audience's needs. Sometimes "good" information is irrelevant to a particular research question.

- Is this information from a reliable source? We tend to tie the issue of source reliability to the rhetorical appeal of ethos. However, to do so means that we must necessarily ground our students in what ethos is and how it works in framing arguments. With the explosion of information available online, ethos becomes more difficult to determine. No longer can students rely on the source or academic credentials to certify reliability or authority. After all, a blog post by Robert Reich (www.robertreich.org) on the impact of the economy in a presidential race may be more authoritative than an article in *Forbes* that has been compiled or reprinted from a news wire. To determine that, though, students need to dig deeply to understand the qualifications of an experienced and credible authority.

- How does one piece of information relate to the other pieces I have found? This is an important and, often, difficult question for students to answer. Not all information is equal. Some information is only relevant in the context of other information. Librarians and faculty push students to find sources that articulate different perspectives, to analyze them, and to integrate and synthesize them so that they come to a fuller and more complete understanding of the topic or issue.

Having students understand the relevance, reliability, and relationship of information is crucial as they move from gathering information to putting that information to use.

Exceptionally important when finding information in digital environments is the ability to postpone snap judgments. We need to help our students understand that, unless they already have some familiarity with the area they are researching, they will need to learn which sources are more likely to produce the quality of information they need to discover. Commonplace assumptions such as "websites with .edu and .gov domains are always more reliable than websites with .com domains" may be generally true, but they are dependent on the context and purpose of the research question or hypothesis. In the context of business research, for example, white papers and corporate documents available online, even company and executive blogs, for that matter, may be more appropriate and relevant than traditional print documents.

However, we need to remember that, when working in digital environments, students may understand some concepts even better than instructors. For example, anyone (in a developed area) can now have easy access to huge amounts of information that may have significant value outside of an academic context. Indeed, when working with applied writing situations, some of these nonacademic contexts may be primary. For example, students in an advanced applied writing class might be assigned to create the script for an instructional video. A group of students might decide to write the script for a video on safe procedures for mountain biking. In a project of this nature, traditional academic sources are likely nonexistent. The students would first need to define their rhetorical situation in a way that would enable them to know where to research. The students would then need to do the research that would give them the right information to script the video. For example, they would need to keep in mind who their particular audience might be and where their audience might intend to mountain bike. Mountain biking is very different in the mid-Atlantic states than it is in the national parks of southern Utah, for instance. Assignments of this nature can fit seamlessly into the curriculum of applied writing classes. However, in order to take advantage of students' existing digital skills and to develop those skills even further, crafting similar assignments in all writing classes, except those whose sole purpose is traditional academic writing, seems to be prudent.

Information Analysis: Recursive Research Process

Once students find and sift through information that appears to be most valuable for their particular research question, they need to understand that they may need to revise their research question. Then, they may need to go back to redo their search for more information that is specific to their refined question and to check on some of the information they initially culled out to analyze that information in the new context. Students need to learn to understand that this is a recursive process: Find the information, analyze that information in light of the research question, see if the research question needs to be revised, analyze the information again, and so on. What is most important for students to understand is that they need to analyze their information in the context of their research question and that research questions are not static, but go from broad to narrow as more information is gathered and new information helps to refine and focus the question. Information can be interesting, useful, or valuable, but unless it helps researchers find answers to their specific research questions, that information is best used in a different situation.

Instructors and programs have multiple options to help students take more effective control over classroom research assignments. Some of these might include the development of instructional materials like videos, writing tasks that students are invested in, and courses with a theme in order to make research "content" more focused to students. No matter what methods a program might choose, "research" must be clearly defined in them.

From our perspective, there appears to be a clear gap between what students and instructors see as research. In order to bridge that gap, instructors can begin the research assignment by acknowledging that there are different kinds of research and then articulating a statement that lets students know what constitutes research "in this class" or "in this discipline" as well as helping students to "read" the assignment to understand expectations. Next, instructors need to help students understand that research is not simply one stage in the writing process, which is somehow separated from the rest of the process. One strategy to accomplish this goal is to break projects down into multiple tasks and assignments so that students are strategically stepped through research and writing as a process. (For example, a first step would be to have students develop the research topic or question.)

Students could also keep a research log in which they articulate their research strategies: databases used, keywords used, revision of keywords or phrases, number of results, and number of sources selected from those results. During this work, instructors can explain the value of primary and secondary sources, the expectations of source variety, and the possibilities of specific disciplinary databases and resources. After composing a research log, an annotated bibliography (or other synthesis tool) can be used to have students describe and analyze each source prior to using it in their final document (Rachel Milloy offers a new spin on such an assignment in Chapter 10). This step can be particularly key in helping students to think through not only whether a source is credible and reliable, but also whether the source is relevant for the text they are writing.

Thinking programmatically, by making sure course and program outcomes reflect the entire research process and then assessing courses to make sure these program outcomes are being met, is an effective way of accomplishing this goal. For example, entry level or orientation courses may introduce the research process and help students to learn search techniques, with more advanced courses helping students to learn disciplinary sources and research methods aligned with particular disciplines. In addition, by thinking programmatically, we can more effectively decide which courses should introduce students to topics such as the ethics of using human participants, the difference between applied and academic research-writing, and other advanced topics. Instructors should help students learn that just as presenting information (whether in writing, speech, video, or some combination of these) is rhetorical in nature, research itself is rhetorical and should be conducted with attention to context, audience, and purpose. For example, students writing funding proposals need to conduct research on the funding agency's values, mission, and priorities. They need as much as they can possibly find on how the organization operates in order to compose an appropriately persuasive proposal. None of this information is likely to be found in scholarly academic sources. Instead, students need to research and analyze the funders' own documents as well as websites and news accounts. While not "scholarly" in nature, these sources fit the purpose of the research and genre of writing that the student is learning to compose.

Information Management/Organization

Before the digital age, people who taught research often talked of organization in terms of formal outlines. Likewise, instructors taught students to use 3 x 5 note cards to jot down citations in order to facilitate the creation of an accurate reference list. Instructors also taught students to use note cards to take notes that could then be sorted and rearranged to help with the process of organizing the structure of a paper. Though no one used the term at the time, clearly, the manipulation of note cards is a kind of "information management."

In the age of word processors and citation management software such as EndNote and Zotero, some instructors seem to assume that information management does not need to be taught. Since these processes are now mechanized and digitized, some instructors think that students learn all on their own to engage in the underlying cognitive functions of taking notes, sorting, and arranging those notes in order to facilitate an organizational structure for a document or presentation. In addition, instructors may assume that somehow students will figure out how to use these resources to generate a reference list.

Instead, teachers should embed in their courses instruction on how to manage these processes: from reading and analyzing sources, to note taking, to sorting and organizing, and finally to citation management. Teaching students how to use citation management software such as Zotero, for example, can help alleviate problems associated with the convention of constructing in-text citations and reference lists and, by doing so, allow for more concentration on how to integrate sources into texts (or other forms of presentation of information). However, it is important to help students understand that information management is much more than managing citations. Citations are information: chunks of data that are arranged and organized based on the use of a disciplinary style manual. One way to help students realize this, though admittedly time-consuming, is to teach students some basic database skills, such as creating and naming fields. That way, students can understand how to break information down into chunks that are labeled and stored to facilitate effective retrieval and then presented based on the organizational or arrangement needs of the genre or style requirements.

We must also formulate curricula that help students realize that both the genre and the medium of presentation can have a significant impact on its organization. Carolyn Rude (1995) comments on how a lack of understanding of the nature of what she calls "the report for decision making" impacts the form of those reports (170). While some applied genres have a firm organizational pattern that helps define the genre (e.g., memos and IMRAD reports), other organizational patterns are more determined by context. A decision-making report in a technical communication course for engineering students, for example, may require a different report structure than a decision-making report for business communication students. One strategy to help students understand how to organize and manage information is to have them present it in different genres targeted to different audiences. For example, the results of a research question related to nutrition may be presented in an abstract for an undergraduate research conference proposal, in a funding proposal for a community nonprofit organization, in a scholarly article, and in a newspaper or magazine article intended for the general public. All of these genres have different conventions of formatting and different audience needs and, therefore, different organizational patterns.

As these organizational patterns are based on audience expectations, IL curricula must explicitly acknowledge disciplinary differences. Scientists, for example, expect background and historical context to precede results and discussion. In contrast, when communicating with the general public, presenting the bottom-line or "so what" point of the message is preferable (American Association for the Advancement of Science 2012). Genres, then, reflect the organizational patterns expected of their audiences. However, the content itself emerges from the same research question, and the information from the research is the same. What changes is the way it is rhetoricized and organized for presentation to the specific audience.

Information Presentation

The final stage in the IL process that we suggest should be taught in writing courses is presenting information. The presentation can take multiple forms. It can be a traditional written presentation; an oral presentation; or a digital production rich with written, oral, video, and even animated components. For teachers of writing, the presentation has often been the most important part of the process. As we stress the inherently rhetorical nature of information gathering, analysis, and management, it is just as important that we stress the rhetorical nature of the choice of genre and medium. Yet, in a world where narrative text is sometimes the last choice for presentation, we need to be preparing our students to write about the information they've discovered by incorporating multiple media options. Our students are as likely to need to know how to write a narrative text proposal as they are to need to know how to write a proposal that essentially comprises filling in the chunks in a template to be stored in a content management system database. Likewise, they will need to know not only how to create a slideshow using presentation software, but also how to script the narrative for that slideshow so it can be recorded and presented online.

The kind of writing that is expected in many academic disciplines still privileges traditional thesis-support narrative prose. As a result, our students need to know how to produce that genre. However, most of the writing our students will do involves genres beyond the prose narrative and media beyond printed text. While in many situations both academic and workplace genre and medium are predetermined, understanding genre conventions and constraints along with media strengths and weaknesses can help the writer create the best possible presentation.

Selecting and using the appropriate genre and medium, though, is an often-overlooked IL standard.

We can look at manuals for consumer products as prime examples of the evolution in information presentation. Historically, the manuals simply gave instructions, usually step-by-step, in how to operate the product. The manuals were printed. Over time, warnings and precautions driven by liability concerns appeared before anything else in the manual. As printing costs for graphics dropped, there was a greater reliance on graphics over text—especially when the target audience for the product might be people who have trouble understanding written English. Now, most of those manuals are also available online, usually in PDF format.

Yet, we expect that as more and more consumers get used to accessing this material online, we will see a movement away from the PDF and into information that is presented in multiple formats and placed in content management systems so that needed sections can be accessed via an app on a mobile device, such as a tablet or a smartphone. We can already see the beginning of this in the websites www.HowStuffWorks.com and TLC Guides (tlc.howstuffworks.com/home), as well as some of the examples on the website for a corporate entity such as Williams-Sonoma (www.williams-sonoma.com). In addition, there is an iPhone/iPod app for HowStuffWorks, and one of the cookbooks created as an iPad app by Williams-Sonoma features videos.

As this discussion illustrates, our students will need to be able to use digital means to find the best, most current, and most appropriate information to answer their research question and then be able to make determinations about the best way to present their results to their intended audience. The "best way" will involve some kind of digital media.

Conclusion: Developing an Information-Literacy-Based Curriculum for the Digital Age

What we've attempted to accomplish here is to begin to have instructors think about which pedagogical strategies all of us need to employ in order to develop an IL-based curriculum that is relevant in the digital age. That means understanding that students must learn not only how to find information, but also how to manage and present it. It also means that students need to understand that for most of their lives they will be working with information and writing in nonacademic settings where they will need to provide texts that are delivered and accessed in multiple media. As technologies change and evolve in the digital age, understanding and teaching research and writing as one single process becomes critical. We have presented suggestions for improving pedagogy and curricula to help students learn that research is not an isolated step in the process of communication and to help them understand that the information they find and use is critical to success—whatever "success" may be in the rhetorical context of the communicative act. The more we can break away from old, print-based, curricular patterns, the better we will be serving our students.

Endnote

1. Research as process has been discussed since at least the mid-1980s (Maid 1985); however, it has not been embraced with as much enthusiasm as writing as a process.

References

American Association for the Advancement of Science. 2012. "Communicating Science: Tools for Scientists and Engineers." Accessed September 28, 2012. communicatingscience.aaas.org/comm101/3point.shtml.

Association of College and Research Libraries. 2000. "Information Literacy Competency Standards for Higher Education." Accessed September 28, 2012. www.ala.org/acrl/standards/informationliteracycompetency.

Bodi, Sonia. 1988. "Critical Thinking and Bibliographic Instruction: The Relationship." *Journal of Academic Librarianship* 14 (3): 150–153.

———. 1990. "Through a Glass Darkly: Critical Thinking and Bibliographic Instruction." *Catholic Library World* 61: 252–256.

Bruce, Christine. 1997. *The Seven Faces of Information Literacy*. Adelaide, Australia: Auslib Press.

Fister, Barbara. 1993. "Teaching the Rhetorical Dimensions of Research." *Research Strategies* 11 (4): 211–219.

Howard, Rebecca Moore. 2006. "Insufficient Information Anxiety: Rebuilding Pedagogy for Researched Arguments." Paper presented at the annual meeting of the Conference on College Composition and Communication, Chicago, IL, March 22–25.

Johnston, Bill, and Sheila Webber. 2003. "Information Literacy in Higher Education: A Review and Case Study." *Studies in Higher Education* 28 (3): 335–352.

Kapitzke, Cushla. 2003. "Information Literacy: A Positivist Epistemology and a Politics of Outformation." *Educational Theory* 53 (1): 37–53.

Kautzman, Amy M. 1996. "Teaching Critical Thinking: The Alliance of Composition Studies and Research Instruction." *Reference Services Review* 24 (3): 61–65.

Kuhlthau, Carol. 2004. *Seeking Meaning: A Process Approach to Library and Information Services*. 2nd ed. Westport, CT: Libraries Unlimited.

Lantz, Agneta, and Christina Brage. 2006. "Towards a Learning Society—Exploring the Challenge of Applied Information Literacy through Reality-Based Scenarios." *ITALICS* 5 (1). Accessed September 28, 2012. www.ics.heacademy.ac.uk/italics/vol5-1/pdf/lantz-brage-final.pdf.

Lloyd, Annemaree, and Margaret Somerville. 2006. "Working Information." *Journal of Workplace Learning* 18 (3): 186–198.

Lupton, Mandy. 2004. *The Learning Connection: Information Literacy and the Student Experience*. Adelaide, Australia: Auslib Press.

Maid, Barry. 1985. "Hunting and Gathering: A New Model for Research Writing." Paper presented at the annual meeting of the Conference of College Composition and Communication, Minneapolis, MN, March 21–23.

Project Information Literacy. 2009. "PIL Dialog, No. 3: Frustrations." Accessed September 28, 2012. youtu.be/rmEzo51e_SQ.

———. 2010. "PIL Dialog No. 5: Finding Context." Accessed September 28, 2012. youtu.be/0adM-YpThHs.

Rude, Carolyn. 1995. "Report for Decision Making: Genre and Inquiry." *JBTC* 9 (2): 170–205.

CHAPTER 14

Teaching and Assessing Research Strategies in the Digital Age: Collaboration Is the Key

Thomas Peele, Melissa Keith, and Sara Seely

At the turn of the century, as the conversion from print to digital media gained speed, writing faculty at our institution (Boise State University) became bewildered by the variety of research strategies available to students and frustrated by the research that students were actually doing. Every week, it seemed, the library added databases to the virtual library, and writing faculty couldn't keep up with the additions. We didn't necessarily know which databases were new, what they contained, or how to search them. Further, features of the databases kept changing; search methods changed from one visit to the next. Students, in the meantime, weren't making use of the databases very much if at all. In fact, the writing program's assessment of student writing portfolios showed that students were taking the path of least resistance: general Google searches and Wikipedia citations. With so many library resources available to us faculty and so much information available to students, where to begin? More to the point, how could we help our NextGen students navigate information that *we ourselves* found overwhelming?

Our first-year writing program's solution to these problems was twofold. First, we collaborated with our institution's librarians, who eagerly pointed out the databases that would be most useful to our students, showed us how to use them, and kept us aware of changes in access and search interfaces. They also collaborated with us to teach library research as a part of English 102, a course titled Introduction to College Writing and Research. Second, this collaborative group began to develop a series of web-based, information literacy (IL) video tutorials to introduce students to the databases in our virtual library. This collaboration is the focus of our chapter.

In this chapter, we first offer a brief review of the history of library–writing partnerships. We next introduce readers to what we now call the Project Writing and Research, or PoWeR, program, which pairs librarians and writing instructors to develop an IL curriculum, including shared assignments and course schedules. In the process of discussing the evolution of the program, we not only discuss how the collaboration between writing instructors and librarians developed, including the creation of video tutorials and an etextbook designed to help strengthen the research skills of our NextGen students, but also provide one model for library and writing program collaboration that other institutions might adapt.

The Value of Library–Writing Program Partnerships

Collaboration between librarians and writing faculty has been key to the success of the PoWeR Program (which we describe in detail in the next section). As the Association of College and Research Libraries (2000) notes in its "Information Literacy Competency Standards for Higher Education," achieving "competency in information literacy requires an understanding that this cluster of abilities is not extraneous to the curriculum but is woven into the curriculum's content, structure, and sequence" (5). In our collaboration, writing faculty and librarians have worked together to create assignments that serve the needs of both areas of instruction.

Other collaborations between discipline faculty and librarians have shown positive results over time. Heidi Jacobs (a librarian) and Dale Jacobs (a professor of writing) note that their initial conversations about research instruction led them to the observation that "effective research does not happen in just one sitting but involves iterative processes such as revision, reworking, rethinking, and above all, reflection" (2009, 72). Teaching research as a recursive practice rather than a one-time event and embedding IL instruction in assignments are in stark contrast to the traditional one-shot introduction to IL instruction. While the one-shot introduction effectively introduces students to the library itself and, usually, to a reference librarian, it often does not aim to do much more. In Chapter 3 of this book, John Eliason and Kelly O'Brien Jenks similarly note the need for long-term collaborations, such as their own, and review literature documenting other successful partnerships.

Our model follows Joan Lippincott's "learning community" model as described by Jacobs and Jacobs (2009). This model is characterized as "opportunistic, lasting for the duration of the course, and focused on the information environment. Here the librarian is a faculty partner who both learns and teaches." The learning community model of instruction relies on much more than just conversation between the writing instructor and the librarian, but instead includes "the IL librarians, the English subject librarian, the librarians teaching in the writing program, the writing graduate instructors, and the writing students" in the discussion (Jacobs and Jacobs 2009, 75). We have, then, been collaborating in a broad sense.

As such, IL instruction is no longer the responsibility of either the writing instructor or the librarian, but rather a responsibility shared by all stakeholders. In our model, librarians and writing faculty team together to develop assignments, course schedules, and research activities that are designed to reach the goals of the first-year writing program and the library's research instruction courses. As Jacobs and

Jacobs (2009) note, such collaborative efforts, in addition to being fruitful for our students, are enormously beneficial to the large group of writing faculty in working together to understand each other's expectations, vocabularies, and pedagogies for research instruction.

Librarians Debbie Malone and Carol Videon (2007) conducted a survey of 252 college libraries in which they determined that "successful IL programs usually fall into three basic categories: (a) those in which the goals and objectives of the program are integrated into the general education curriculum for first-year students, (b) those in which IL plays a pervasive role in first-year seminars, and (c) those in which stand-alone courses provide broad coverage of skills related to IL." Malone and Videon emphasize, however, that in "all of these models, extensive collaboration between librarians and classroom faculty members plays a crucial role in the development of the program" (2007, 51). Malone and Videon report that, as in our program, the large-scale support of writing classes was initiated and continues to be supported by the librarians. As a result, librarians "have developed productive relationships with many classroom faculty members that allow them to tailor IL instruction to specific class assignments and research needs, making the value of IL skills more apparent to students" (2007, 53).

Writing of their work at the University of California–Berkeley, Elizabeth Dupuis, et al. describe a grant from the Andrew W. Mellon Foundation that allowed the faculty to work toward the IL goals outlined by the Boyer Commission in 1998 to engage "undergraduate students through inquiry-based learning" (Dupuis, et al. 2007, 5). Dupuis, et al. write:

> Transformation of undergraduate education demanded that more attention be directed toward developing students' ability to thrive in a research-based learning environment. The institutional support needed to position and develop these skills in meaningful ways within the curriculum required a shared commitment from faculty, librarians,

educational technologists, and other pedagogical experts. (2007, 5)

Jacobs and Jacobs (2009), Malone and Videon (2007), and Dupuis, et al. (2007) all describe collaborative endeavors where IL assignments are not afterthoughts or tasks that students must complete on top of the writing projects. Instead, the IL assignments inform the students' writing process, making them central to the students' learning and writing experiences.

Turning On the PoWeR: The Project Writing and Research Program

The collaboration between our writing and library faculty along with the development of the video tutorials are both based on the results of the first-year-writing program's annual assessment of student writing portfolios. Since 1999, faculty at Boise State have collected between 10–15 percent of the writing portfolios created by students during the academic year in three classes, including English 102, our course designed to introduce students to college writing and research. Ongoing assessment of student research practices in these portfolios revealed a need for improved instruction on how to locate, evaluate, and incorporate information from sources within academic writing projects. The 2007 and 2008 Assessment Reports note that students demonstrated little understanding of digital research practices (Estrem 2008). In order to address this issue, the first-year writing program offered instructors opportunities to learn more about teaching IL and researched writing.

As a part of our effort to address this need of improved research instruction, Tom Peele, as one of the first-year writing program administrators, received a State Board of Education Technology Incentive Grant to support the development of IL video tutorials that would address the specific needs of students at our institution. The grant brought together English 102 instructors, including Melissa Keith, with one of our campus's instructional librarians, Sara Seely, to create web-based IL tutorials and consider other redesigns of our approach to research instruction suggested in the student learning outcomes for English 102. For the tutorials, the writing instructors and their librarian colleagues identified the most salient and recursive research instruction topics and prioritized those topics appropriate for web-based instruction. The tutorials were developed in 2007 and served as the foundation for a joint curriculum that both library and English faculty could make use of while enhancing research instruction in English 102.

Beginning in 2008, the same writing instructors and librarians who collaborated on the tutorials came together to enhance the PoWeR Program's effectiveness and linked the three-credit, English 102: College Writing and Research course with the one-credit University 106: Library Research course. Until this point, librarians had been teaching University 106 as a stand-alone course for first-year students with instruction primarily on the basics of library research, though Sara and her librarian colleagues were looking for opportunities to teach research strategies in the context of a real academic research project. Because English 102 instructors needed help with research instruction, the pairing of these courses met the needs of both parties, and, perhaps more importantly, responded to the need for more intensive research instruction identified during the portfolio assessment process. In the fall of 2008, we piloted the program by linking four sections of English 102 and University 106; in the spring of 2009, we linked an additional seven. In the spring of 2010, we linked 20 sections of these two courses (about one-third of the total sections of English 102).

We have done a variety of assessments throughout this pilot program, including portfolio assessment of students' research-based writing projects, surveys of student perceptions of themselves as researchers, and a task-based assessment of student research skills. We explain these assessments in more detail in the next section.

Assessing PoWeR

Beginning in the spring of 2009, library and writing faculty met to assess writing portfolios for evidence of research proficiency. In order to assess students' research abilities, the PoWeR team developed a rubric that is in accord with the IL VALUE Rubric (Association of American Colleges and Universities 2008) and the IL criteria developed by the Association of College and Research Libraries (ACRL):

- Determine the extent of the information needed.

- Access the needed information effectively and efficiently.

- Evaluate information and its sources critically.

- Incorporate selected information into one's knowledge base.

- Use information effectively to accomplish a specific purpose.

- Understand the economic, legal, and social issues surrounding the use of information, and access and use information legally. (Association of College and Research Libraries 2000, 2–3)

While we would not expect students to have mastered research at the level implied by this list, the criteria described in our course outcomes and in our assessment rubric reflect most of the expectations listed by the ACRL (8–14). The rubric evolved over time (see Appendixes A, B, and C) to reflect our current expectations of students' research abilities, and the creation and evolution of the rubric was fundamental to our assessments.

Spring 2009 PoWeR Portfolio Assessment

In the spring of 2009, the PoWeR team conducted an assessment of student writing portfolios from both PoWeR and stand-alone sections of English 102. Library and writing faculty developed the first iteration of the rubric (Appendix A) to aid in the assessment process, which includes four areas of evaluation that were derived from our combined (English 102 and University 106) research-related student learning outcomes, focusing on students' ability to

- Define a research topic or question.

- Determine source appropriateness.

- Incorporate a variety of sources.

- Understand and use the conventions of citation.

Proficiency was defined as meeting the learning outcomes in each of these key evaluation areas. As the Spring 2009 Assessment Report notes, faculty evaluated all portfolios from each of the four PoWeR sections and another 18 from stand-alone English 102 classes with a normed rubric (Albertsons Library 2009). This small sampling gave the Portfolio Assessment Team an opportunity to work through the process of conducting a focused, comparative assessment.

The team found that 100 percent of the PoWeR student portfolios reviewed achieved "proficiency" in source appropriateness (quality of information sources), and almost all PoWeR portfolios demonstrated "proficiency" in source variety (types of sources cited). This preliminary review of student work comparing PoWeR and stand-alone sections indicated that "Students in PoWeR sections appeared slightly more likely to gain 'proficiency' across all of the evaluation areas: research question, source appropriateness, source variety and citation practices" (Albertsons Library 2009, 7). The team realized, however, that it needed to add a "Research Strategies" section to its rubric in order to capture a fuller picture of students' research activities. We learned some things about student proficiency with specific research strategies from our Spring 2009 assessment, but we had not yet developed a means for assessing how well students were able to write about and reflect on these research practices.

Fall 2009 PoWeR Portfolio Assessment

In January 2010, faculty gathered to assess 80 student writing portfolios produced in the four pilot sections of linked English 102 and University 106 during the Fall 2009 term, and we used the revised rubric (Appendix B) that now allowed us to account for the strategies students were using to locate their sources. The portfolio assessment revealed that 81 percent of the portfolios were either "proficient" or "highly proficient" in nearly all areas assessed, and the portfolios were strongest in their demonstration of source appropriateness. The portfolios were weakest in the demonstration of research strategies, with less than 40 percent of students being "proficient." The weakness in this area was particularly troubling because, to us, it is the most important strategy that students can take away from these courses.

As we further developed our research instruction, we wanted to be sure that we cultivated students' awareness of their own research practices so that as they moved forward in their academic and professional careers they would continue to hone them. For years, writing scholars have endorsed the need for reflective activities in writing classes that push students to develop an awareness of their writing process (Hillocks 1995; Yancey 1998; Swartzendruber-Putnam 2000), and like Jacobs and Jacobs (2009, 72), we believe students should also develop a level of meta-awareness regarding their research process. Having students articulate their research strategies would be one way to achieve that awareness.

Spring 2010 PoWeR Portfolio Assessment

Hoping to gain a richer understanding of the research-writing practices of students across our first-year writing program, we significantly expanded the scope and sample of the research focus in the portfolio assessment for the Spring 2010 term. Since students performed so poorly in demonstrating research strategies on the previous assessment, we first considered ways to revise the rubric (Appendix C). We refined our focus to consider students' "Description of Research Strategies," which more closely reflected our belief that NextGen students need to be able to articulate their writing *and* research processes if they are going to be savvy digital scholars. While our ongoing assessment of specific research strategies enabled us to focus our attention on the area of research strategies, our initial assessment showed us that we were not doing enough to promote students' meta-awareness of them.[1] We also expanded the sample size to randomly select three student portfolios

from every section of English 102 (including PoWeR sections), resulting in a review of approximately 210, or 12 percent, of all student
portfolios. As shown in Figure 14.1, the portfolios demonstrate that

- English 102 PoWeR portfolios were between 8 percent and
  19 percent more likely than their mainstream counterparts to
  be ranked as proficient in the areas of research listed.

- PoWeR English 102 portfolios are particularly strong in the
  writers' abilities to describe their research strategies.

Spring 2010 Student Self-Assessment

In addition to portfolio assessment, we administered a student self-
assessment survey in both PoWeR and stand-alone sections of English
102 near the end of the Spring 2010 term. PoWeR students' responses
to the question "How would you classify yourself as a researcher?"
show that these students are significantly more likely to classify themselves as "advanced researchers" at the end of the semester than students in the stand-alone sections. PoWeR students are 17 percent more
likely than mainstream students to think of themselves as having
advanced research proficiency. While 5 percent of PoWeR students
considered themselves to be "expert researchers," none of the

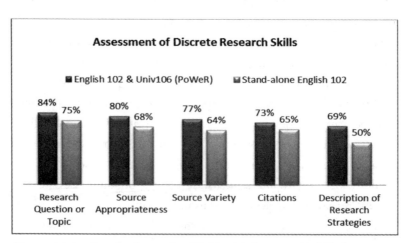

**Figure 14.1   Comparison of proficiency of research skills between
PoWeR and stand-alone English 102 portfolios**

mainstream students placed themselves in this category. Even though these students are likely to be overconfident about their research abilities (after all, they are still first-year writers and researchers), the self-assessment demonstrates to us that PoWeR students describe themselves in more confident terms than mainstream students, and this survey provides us with another way to measure students' perceptions of themselves as researchers.

Spring 2010 English 102 Task-Based Assessment

We also piloted during the Spring 2010 term a task-based instrument in which students were asked to complete specific research tasks, such as finding a particular article in a database. The test was distributed to all English 102 students late in the semester, and 247 students responded. While members of the assessment team rejected most of the results of this test because of a design flaw (the only requirement for credit was *completion* of the test, but one could "complete" the test without actually doing any of the tasks, as many students quickly understood), we were able to make use of the results of the question that asked them to describe their research strategies.

When students were asked to name at least three research strategies, students in the linked PoWeR sections of English 102 identified specific resources and research strategies, while students in nonlinked sections used far more general terminology. We provide tag cloud examples of word frequencies from the PoWeR sections of English 102 (see Figure 14.2) and from the stand-alone sections (see Figure 14.3). In these tag clouds, the larger the word, the more frequently it appears in students' descriptions of their research strategies.

Students in PoWeR sections on the text-based assessment appear to use the word "library" more than their stand-alone counterparts, who opt for the word "sources." We mark this use of "library" as a success, as we want students to be aware of the library in both its material and virtual forms. The words "articles" and "books" are also significantly more prominent in the cloud formed from PoWeR students' comments, while the term "Google" is more prominent in the cloud formed

Figure 14.2 Tag cloud for PoWeR sections of English 102

Figure 14.3 Tag cloud for stand-alone sections of English 102

from stand-alone students' comments. Based on these visual representations of students' descriptions of their own research strategies, PoWeR students seem to have access to more specific language to describe those strategies.[2] Students in the stand-alone sections of English 102 describe the same strategies, but appear to do so less frequently.

The multiple forms of assessment demonstrate to us that students in mainstream sections of English 102 are receiving adequate research instruction, yet students in the PoWeR sections are performing significantly better in terms of their own awareness of research strategies in general and of themselves as researchers. With the success of the program holding steady, the PoWeR team was next faced with a new dilemma: How could this kind of intensive research instruction be scaled for *all* sections of English 102? Since manpower in the library could not accommodate such high instructional demand, we explored the idea of a research-focused etextbook.

The Next Phase of PoWeR

After several iterations of the assessment process, faculty in the PoWeR program and throughout our first-year writing program now recognize the magnitude of the challenges facing us in educating the new digital scholar. Therefore, the next phase of the PoWeR program was the creation of the *Project Writing and Research E-Textbook*, a resource collaboratively developed by library and writing faculty.[3] In 2011, this etextbook was added to the prestigious collection of teaching resources, Peer-Reviewed Instructional Materials Online (PRIMO). This etextbook (in both student and instructor versions) packages instructional videos, research activities, and assessment tools (some of which can be directly imported to Blackboard) for multiple research practices and strategies.

The etextbook is being hosted on Boise State University's Albertsons Library (2010) website and is currently being further developed by librarians. Every instructor teaching English 102 at our institution has now been exposed to the PoWeR program and the etextbook, and our librarian colleagues received an Idaho State Board of Education Technology Incentive Grant that funded a series of institutes, which allowed librarians and writing faculty time to collaborate on how to incorporate the etextbook in their classes.

Conclusion

As accomplished as writing faculty are, the challenge of keeping up with the rapid changes in IL is greater than many expect or understand. In dedicating themselves to the PoWeR program, our writing and librarian colleagues have helped to facilitate the move from a face-to-face, one-shot library session to a web-based, comprehensive, integrated instructional approach. Students and faculty now have access to a modern and regularly updated database of instructional materials developed specifically for our students, and the students' improved research abilities are the result of this work. Our assessment measures over the years clearly show that students benefit from the PoWeR program; the portfolios they produce are more likely to be rated "proficient" or "highly proficient" than the portfolios written in stand-alone English 102 classes.

As the web plays an increasingly important role in the production and distribution of information, we hope that even more faculty across our campus (and others) might be inspired by instructional materials in our etextbook and decide to collaborate with librarian colleagues in creating web-based materials specific to their own disciplines. Since our goal in IL instruction is to have students not only demonstrate competency in research at the first-year level, but also apply their skills to research-writing projects in their other courses, we look forward to working with our colleagues across campus in strengthening our undergraduate research-writing program. To this end, the next step of our investigation will be to have the PoWeR team explore to what extent students are transferring their research skills to their other courses. In this way, we hope to continue to contribute to the ongoing analysis and discussion of how NextGen students are making the transition into digital scholars.

Endnotes

1. With this information we have been able to modify our curriculum to better inform students' awareness of their own work. One change was to standardize the reflection prompts for students' portfolio cover letters across English 102 courses so that all students were asked to name at least three research strategies they used to locate sources for their research-writing projects.

2. We plan to use the tag clouds generated from our Spring 2010 assessment in our future research to see how students describe their research strategies as they move through their college careers.

3. The *PoWeR E-Textbook* was developed with significant contributions from Ellie Dworak and Kim Leeder, Boise State University librarians.

References

Albertsons Library. 2009. "Instruction Program Assessment Report, 2008–2009." Accessed September 28, 2012. library.boisestate.edu/assessment/Instruction%20 Program%20Assessment%20Report%202009.pdf.

———. 2010. "Project Writing and Research E-Textbook." Accessed September 28, 2012. guides.boisestate.edu/power.

Association of American Colleges and Universities. 2008. "Information Literacy VALUE Rubric." Accessed September 28, 2012. www.aacu.org/value/rubrics/index.cfm.

Association of College and Research Libraries. 2000. "Information Literacy Competency Standards for Higher Education." Accessed September 28, 2012. www.ala.org/ala/mgrps/divs/acrl/standards/standards.pdf.

Dupuis, Elizabeth A., Christina Maslach, Cynthia D. Schrager, and Sarah McDaniel. 2007. "Information Literacy and Undergraduate Research: Meeting the Challenge at a Large Research University." In *Information Literacy Collaborations that Work*, edited by Trudi E. Jacobson and Thomas P. Mackey, 5–18. New York: Neal-Schuman.

Estrem, Heidi. 2008. "First-Year Writing Program Portfolio Assessment Report 2008." Boise, ID: Boise State University.

Hillocks, George. 1995. *Teaching Writing as Reflective Practice*. New York: Teachers College.

Jacobs, Heidi L. M., and Dale Jacobs. 2009. "Transforming the Library One-Shot into Pedagogical Collaboration." *Reference & Users Quarterly* 49: 72–82.

Malone, Debbie, and Carol Videon. 2007. "Models of Library Instruction for First-Year Students." In *The Role of the Library in the First College Year*, edited by Larry L. Hardesty, 51–68. Columbia: National Resource Center for The First-Year Experience and Students in Transition, University of South Carolina.

Swartzendruber-Putnam, Dawn. 2000. "Written Reflection: Creating Better Thinkers, Better Writers." *English Journal* 90: 88–93.

Yancey, Kathleen Blake. 1998. *Reflection in the Writing Classroom*. Logan: Utah State University Press.

Appendix A: Spring 2009 Portfolio Assessment Rubric of Students' Research Abilities

Criteria	Highly Proficient - 4	Proficient - 3	Not Proficient - 2	Needs Work - 1
Research Question or Topic	The writer is able to craft a research question/topic that is focused and innovative.	The writer is able to craft a research question/topic that is appropriate to the scope of the project at hand.	The writer includes a research question/topic that is not appropriate in some way: It is unclear, overly ambitious, and/or not taken up throughout the project.	The writer has not articulated a clear research question/topic. Or, the question is unclear or significantly underdeveloped.
Source Appropriateness	The writer cites advanced or complex sources such as obscure or primary documents.	The writer cites appropriate sources consistently.	The writer cites sources that are not consistently appropriate.	The writer cites inappropriate sources throughout the work.
Source Variety	The writer cites a wide variety of sources that reflect a deep and balanced level of research.	The writer cites three or more types of sources consistently.	The writer cites one to two types of sources.	The writer only cites websites both in text and in the reference or works cited list.
Citations	The writer uses an academic documentation style consistently and appropriately, with no errors.	The writer uses an academic documentation style consistently and appropriately, with few errors.	While a documentation style is used, the citations have many errors that are distracting for the reader.	The writer does not use an identifiable academic documentation style in their work.

Appendix B: Fall 2009 Portfolio Assessment Rubric of Students' Research Abilities

Criteria	Highly Proficient - 4	Proficient - 3	Not Proficient - 2	Needs Work - 1
Research Question or Topic	The writer is able to craft a research question/topic that is focused and innovative.	The writer is able to craft a research question/topic that is appropriate to the scope of the project at hand.	The writer includes a research question/topic that is not appropriate in some way: It is unclear, overly ambitious, and/or not taken up throughout the project.	The writer has not articulated a clear research question/topic. Or, the question is unclear or significantly underdeveloped.
Source Appropriateness	The writer cites advanced or complex sources such as obscure or primary documents.	The writer cites appropriate sources consistently.	The writer cites sources that are not consistently appropriate.	The writer cites inappropriate sources throughout the work.
Source Variety	The writer cites a wide variety of sources that reflect a deep and balanced level of research.	The writer cites three or more types of sources consistently.	The writer cites one to two types of sources.	The writer only cites websites both in text and in the reference or works cited list.
Citations	The writer uses an academic documentation style consistently and appropriately, with no errors.	The writer uses an academic documentation style consistently and appropriately, with few errors.	While a documentation style is used, the citations have many errors that are distracting for the reader.	The writer does not use an identifiable academic documentation style in their work.
Research Strategies	The writer is able to clearly articulate their research process in a way that reflects the use of a variety of research strategies. The writer's work reflects that s/he has been able to use at least three research strategies.	The writer explains her/his research process and both discusses and includes evidence for at least two research strategies.	The writer explains a research process. The process is underdeveloped or limited in scope.	The writer is not able to articulate her/his research process. Or, her/his work does not include evidence of more than one research strategy.

Appendix C: Spring 2010 Portfolio Assessment Rubric of Students' Research Abilities

Criteria	Highly Proficient - 4	Proficient - 3	Not Proficient - 2	Needs Work - 1
Research Question or Topic	The writer is able to craft a research question/topic that is focused and innovative.	The writer is able to craft a research question/topic that is appropriate to the scope of the project at hand.	The writer includes a research question/topic that is not appropriate in some way: It is unclear, overly ambitious, and/or not taken up throughout the project.	The writer has not articulated a clear research question/topic. Or, the question is unclear or significantly underdeveloped.
Source Appropriateness	The writer cites advanced or complex sources such as obscure or primary documents.	The writer cites appropriate sources consistently.	The writer cites sources that are not consistently appropriate.	The writer cites inappropriate sources throughout the work.
Source Variety	The writer cites a wide variety of sources that reflect a deep and balanced level of research.	The writer cites three or more types of sources consistently.	The writer cites one to two types of sources.	The writer only cites websites both in text and in the reference or works cited list.
Citations	The writer uses an academic documentation style consistently and appropriately, with no errors.	The writer uses an academic documentation style consistently and appropriately, with few errors.	While a documentation style is used, the citations have many errors that are distracting for the reader.	The writer does not use an identifiable academic documentation style in their work.
Description of Research Strategies	The writer clearly describes a comprehensive research process that incorporates a variety of research strategies.	The writer explains her/his research process and both discusses and includes evidence for at least two research strategies.	The writer explains a research process. The explanation of the process is underdeveloped or limited in scope.	The writer does not articulate his/her research process. Or, his/her work does not include evidence of more than one research strategy.

Understanding NextGen Students' Information Search Habits: A Usability Perspective

Patrick Corbett, Yetu Yachim, Andrea Ascuena,
and Andrew Karem

In her study of 2,877 first-year students at New Mexico State University, Kate Manuel (2005) finds that although students are sophisticated seekers of information in their daily lives, they hold deep misconceptions about locating and using sources in most academic settings. Manuel cites dozens of research studies that characterize students' existing information literacy (IL) practices in terms of deficit, failure, or defiance and provocatively questions whether pedagogy guided by this portrayal of students can successfully address the root causes of their struggles.[1] Manuel criticizes the body of IL research for not addressing failures in IL pedagogy from a student-centered perspective.

This troubling dynamic represents only part of the deep systemic challenges that pressure NextGen students and educators (writing instructors *and* librarians) alike. This chapter argues that students avoid researching from the digital library in large part because of the design of digital library tools. To illustrate, we offer our own experience pursuing a usability perspective to better understand students' responses to digital library interfaces. The series of usability tests we describe in this chapter demonstrates how our NextGen student participants perceived the functionality and use of the digital academic library through the lens of their interaction with Google, which they perceived to be a well-designed digital tool. We found that they failed to analytically study the utility of either Google or the digital library card catalog for academic research.

Our participants interacted with the digital library in ways that puzzled us as writing studies specialists (Patrick and Andrea) and computer engineers (Yetu and Andrew). Further discussions with our writing studies and librarian colleagues led us to conclude that not only did our NextGen participants misperceive key differences between consumer and academic information-seeking tools, but the design of both directly contributed to this problem. This conclusion forms the basis of this chapter's thesis: Usability testing is one way to better understand the information-seeking habits of NextGen students. Implemented at the programmatic level, usability testing stands to inform strategic questions about the information architecture and use of research interfaces.

Our usability studies were part of a cross-disciplinary PhD seminar at the University of Louisville (U of L) between the Department of English and the Department of Computer Engineering and Computer Science. The U of L is a metropolitan research university with three campuses and six libraries holding collections of more than 2.2 million items. The University Libraries are U of L's principal information repository and provide information services to more than 15,000 undergraduate students, including a large nontraditional and commuter population. The Libraries' holdings are located using the Libraries' Online Public Access Catalog (OPAC), also known as Minerva. As part of the Libraries' integrated management system known as Voyager, Minerva is a prepackaged digital catalog sold by a global vendor, the Ex Libris Group.[2]

The academic professionals for whom Minerva is designed understand that it gives easy access to a valuable collection of information not realistically accessible otherwise. We have observed that our colleagues believe that while Minerva is not an elegant interface, it *is* functional and downright revolutionary compared to the paper card catalog it replaced. The NextGen students who helped us test Minerva, however, treated it with fundamentally different logic. Even though they could use the basic features of Minerva proficiently to find sources, nearly all said they prefer to use Google to complete their research-writing projects. Our usability tests revealed the near ubiquitous influence of Google on our participants' search habits and behaviors. We began to refer to this influence as the "Google Effect" and came to realize that regardless of our original intention to study the design of Minerva, what we were really studying was the direct influence of Google, and the information-seeking habits and behaviors it fosters, on our participants' use of Minerva.

Literature Review

We approached our study armed with anecdotal observations that NextGen students had problems using Minerva to find sources for research-writing coursework. This resistance both intrigued and frustrated us (and our colleagues), as we were invested in the value of Minerva and used it productively in our own academic work. Though we had general usability research to guide us at the time of our studies, existing usability studies were far afield of research-writing pedagogy and higher education contexts. In early 2007, when we conducted our usability studies, the closest thing to a usability perspective on research-writing and IL was a prescient article written in 1994 by Cynthia L. Selfe and Richard J. Selfe Jr., which predicted that the meteoric rise of digital interfaces would have a transformative effect on classroom practice and educators who ignored this influence did so at their own risk. In 2009, Susan Miller-Cochran and Rochelle L. Rodrigo edited a collection that assessed the progress of usability research during the intervening 15 years since Selfe and Selfe's 1994 study. The collection shows that the usability literature in writing studies focuses almost entirely on professional writing environments, not the writing classroom or digital information-seeking tools. Given the central role of usability research in developing and improving user-centered designs (Kuniavsky 2003; Norman 2002), we need to do more to study how NextGen students are using research interfaces for academic work.

In Miller-Cochran and Rodrigo's collection (2009), Douglas Eyman argues that writing and IL educators must rearticulate usability as a way of looking at writing tools used for specific purposes and conduct usability tests under actual, local conditions of use, not just in experiments (see Chapter 7 by Mary Lourdes Silva and Chapter 8 by Ruth Mirtz for studies that begin to do this work). The ethnomethodological approach Eyman advocates would produce a wealth of narratives that show how students navigate research-writing interfaces. In the same collection, Selfe and Selfe (2009) return to their 1994 argument to add that usability could serve as a discourse and approach for writing teachers to connect pedagogy and practice to the evolving research and writing tools used by students and other writers. Though we did not have the benefit of this instructive collection for our own usability studies, we share its argument that usability testing strengthens the strategic position of educators, writing teachers and librarians particularly, with respect to information technology because of the nearly complete migration of the shared work of these disciplines to digital tools, all of which are mediated by interfaces. Beyond strategic technology considerations, educators who improve their understanding of NextGen students' information-seeking habits and behaviors can rethink their own assumptions about how students use these tools to complete research-writing work.

Educators who ignore NextGen students' technical and ideological assumptions fail to understand why NextGen students seek information in ways that are not optimal for academic research-writing tasks. Selfe and Selfe write, "English teachers cannot be content to understand the maps of computer interfaces as simple, uncomplicated spaces" (1994, 500). Usability testing reveals that digital interfaces are not only complicated spaces, but also *contested* spaces. Interfaces are ideological contact zones that influence teaching and learning possibilities because they shape the perception and behavior of the people who use them. Our own design and usability testing process, which we explain in the next section, attempts to reveal the ideological dimensions of our participants' use of Minerva. Following the description of our design and testing process, we discuss how Google played an unavoidable role in participants' search behaviors. Finally, we return to the idea of constructing a usability effort at the programmatic level, where interface-related issues with NextGen students can be addressed more effectively through regularly committed resources and multidisciplinary expertise.

Usability Test Methodology and Design Prototypes

Our usability study consisted of a series of three sets of usability tests over the course of 6 weeks with three groups of NextGen students who were completing a research-writing assignment in U of L's required first-year writing course. For the first study, Andrew and Andrea observed students' digital library browsing experience and found an unexpected issue related to Minerva's design. They found that participants were surprisingly familiar with the basic functions of Minerva, but they used these functions with noticeable reluctance. Yetu and Patrick then tested Minerva's Robotic Retrieval System (RRS) interface and confirmed that participants showed few problems using Minerva for basic search tasks, but retrieving books from the RRS archive so confounded students that they gave up before completing their process. We found four sources of their confusion:

1. The RRS sub-interface from a Minerva record was placed outside of students' visual scanning pattern.[3]

2. RRS features had low "information scent," or predictive cues about content that was not immediately available (Pirolli 2007).

3. Participants needed more guiding information earlier in the requesting process.

4. Participants easily triggered Minerva's generic error message, which they found to be discouraging and ambiguous in meaning.

To address our shared interest in studying NextGen students' understanding and use of Minerva, we combined our two similar research efforts and created three multimodal tutorial designs for a potential Minerva help system. Given the trend of using multimodal tutorials for digital library tools, we wished to test whether this type of learning support could help students successfully use Minerva while outside of the classroom. Because our research showed that U of L students already had a basic command of Minerva, we created tutorials that gave step-by-step advice for using the Boolean AND operator in Minerva's advanced search interface.

Recruiting Student Participants

For our theoretical sample set in the third series of tests, we recruited eight NextGen students (Matty, Nicholas, Ashlie, Brittany, Mort, Samantha, James, and Raquel), all of whom had some previous exposure to Minerva through coursework, as shown in Figure 15.1. These participants mostly described themselves as experienced seekers of online information, but they lacked confidence searching and using information in an academic setting, particularly when forced to use Minerva to find sources. Six participants routinely avoided using the U of L Libraries, two occasionally used the main campus library, and one student used the public library whenever possible. One student, Raquel, had not used Minerva in 3 years to locate a source, despite several classroom introductions to it.

Designing Multimodal Minerva Tutorials

While conducting our first two series of usability tests, we consulted with U of L librarians and library staff, both on- and off-the-record, about our findings. We met with and took advice from the Libraries'

Test Type & Order	Participant	Gender & Age	Computer Experience	Minerva Experience
Video Help				
1	Matty	M/20	High	Low
2	Nicholas	M/19	Medium	Low
Text-and-Image Help				
3	Ashlie	F/18	Medium	Medium
4	Brittany	F/18	High	Medium
5	Mort	M/20	High	Low
Interactive Help				
6	Samantha	F/19	Medium	Medium
7	James	M/19	Medium	Low
8	Raquel	F/22	High	Very Low

Figure 15.1   Test order and participant data

assessment team, the circulation supervisor, and the Minerva adminis-trator. Consulting with our campus librarians gave us two additional design parameters for our tutorials based on the Libraries' own con-straints and concerns:

- The visual design and functionality of Minerva could not change. The design of Minerva is static with respect to individual institutions' needs. The Libraries purchase products from Ex Libris with few options for customization, and any changes to Minerva would involve a major capital planning and approval process.

- The Libraries did not have the resources at that time (due to a developing state budget crisis) to implement any additional student services. If an eventual tutorial system were to be implemented, it would have to be departmentally housed and maintained. Our design decisions needed to be made accordingly.

Though critical perspectives exist on the usability of online help sys-tems and video instruction (see Choi and Johnson 2006; Grayling

1998), we had no firm expectations about how writing students would respond to the introduction of different modalities in Minerva. Because we had no directly relevant usability research to draw from, we tested two initial tutorial designs and then created a third design based on the lessons of the first two. We used the Firefox web browser scripting extension Greasemonkey (available at www.greasespot.net) to skin our designs over a working Minerva session and embed our tutorials into Minerva's webpage interface. Greasemonkey allowed us to create a near-seamless visual integration and design continuity between individual tutorials and Minerva.

For each design, Yetu scripted pages and Patrick created the textual and visual elements of the tutorials. We retested and tweaked tutorials while Andrew managed the administrative aspects of the project. Matty and Nicholas tested the first design—a 3-minute annotated screencast with voiceover narration explaining Boolean search with a step-by-step visual example. Ashlie, Brittany, and Mort tested the second design—a step-by-step text example with annotated screenshots demonstrating a Boolean AND search. Samantha, James, and Raquel tested the third design, which combined the improved elements of the first two designs—better text formatting, image borders, and three highly modified 10-second videos—with the functional Boolean interface (see Figure 15.2). As participants searched using the tutorial interface, their results opened in a new window that cascaded to the right of the original page.

Usability Test Procedure and Activities

As shown in Figure 15.3, we segmented the usability test procedure for the tutorials into five activities. Our test moderator (Andrea) used semi-structured interview techniques to guide participants through each activity, reminding them frequently that it was the interface being tested, not their search skills, and that they should experiment frequently. She spoke from a prepared script, asking participants to think aloud and share their experience verbally with the team.[4] When participants appeared frustrated, intrigued, or did something unusual

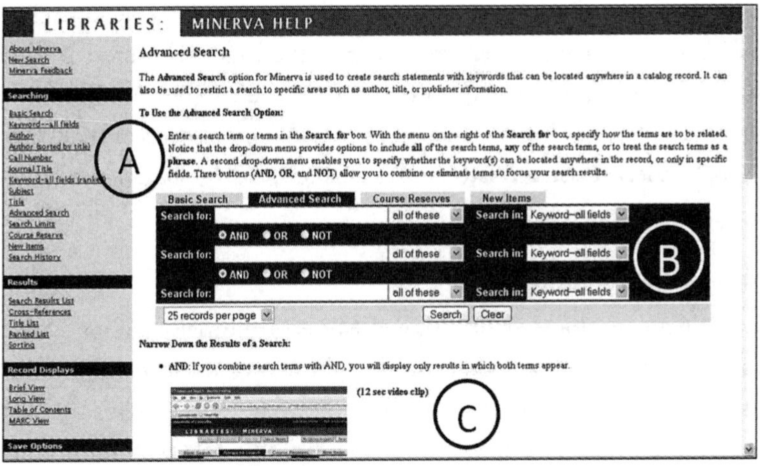

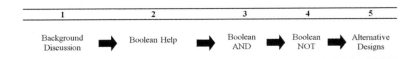

Figure 15.2 Interactive help page for Minerva (This test page consisted of [A] static text to explain the search features, [B] a fully functional clone of the actual search tool to facilitate experimentation, and [C] annotated screencasts with voiceover narration to demonstrate features.)

with Minerva, Andrea asked simple but specific questions to elicit more nuanced information. The rest of the team observed silently while taking notes and recording participants' interactions with the tutorials and Minerva.

Background Discussion (Activity 1)

Each usability test began with a background discussion where participants described their prior experiences with digital technology, computers,

1	2	3	4	5
Background Discussion	Boolean Help	Boolean AND	Boolean NOT	Alternative Designs

Figure 15.3 Usability test activities

online research, the digital library, and Minerva. This information helped us frame participants' interactions within the larger IL context of their lives. The data from these questions were valuable to our interpretations of students' actions because they revealed additional aspects of IL, like the Google Effect (discussed later in this chapter), that we began to consider as our study progressed.

Minerva Help (Activity 2)

Participants explored their assigned Minerva tutorial page for as long as they wished. When they finished browsing the tutorial, Andrea asked them to verbally review the tutorials' features in order to help us determine which aspects of it they focused on while browsing. When necessary, she elicited more information with questions about their actions, intentions, and personal opinions concerning design features.

Boolean AND Search (Activity 3)

Participants used the Boolean AND search function to locate sources on Queen Elizabeth II that also featured her marriage. When participants sought assistance, Andrea guided them with conceptual advice about Boolean searching and possible options (e.g., trying a different Boolean feature), but she avoided discussing actual solutions to the usability test activities.

Boolean NOT Search (Activity 4)

Participants then used the Boolean NOT search function to find sources about Martin Luther, the 16th-century theologian. We designed this test to oblige students to use the NOT function to exclude sources from the much larger Reverend Dr. Martin Luther King Jr. collection, which an ambiguous "Martin Luther" search would produce first in the search results.

Design Discussion (Activity 5)

Each usability test concluded with a design discussion between participants and the entire team. These discussions typically ran 25 minutes as the participants explored the tutorial designs they did not officially test. They offered their opinions on the tutorials, Minerva, and (inevitably) Google. We encouraged participants to be candid, and they were as eager to discuss their distaste for our tutorials as they were to offer their bleak assessment of the usefulness of Minerva.

Study Results: The Influence of the "Google Effect"

Our NextGen student participants were puzzled about why we would take the time to design and test tutorials for an interface like Minerva, which by their standards lacked the visual sophistication, elegant design, and responsiveness of Google. Google was their "design model," the tool that had shaped their understanding of information seeking and which they preferred in their own everyday information-seeking lives. Participants' reliance on Google directly contributed to their perception of Minerva as a "LastGen" interface, even as they acknowledged that it must hold some utility for multiple instructors to expect them to use it for their research-writing. They revealed to us that they only used Minerva to the minimum extent they felt would suffice, or simply not at all. Participants did not see Minerva as a personally useful resource because they have a radically different design sense, aesthetic, and set of expectations for functionality that Minerva does not provide. It feels counterintuitive and counterproductive to them, while Google provides immediate content that can be incorporated into a research-writing project. Minerva returns a catalog record that must be taken to the largest library in the metropolitan region (where they can seek assistance or, if they don't ask for help, wander alone through the maze-like stacks). In short, the research process that Minerva supports is far more complicated than what participants had come to expect through their experience of instant results from Google. The instruction our participants received from writing teachers and librarians did not engage this difference between the research processes; thus, it did not present the participants with compelling reasons why they should include Minerva in their research strategy.

Immediacy and "Information Scent"

Participants' avoidance behavior can be better understood by considering Peter Pirolli's idea of information scent theory (2007). Pirolli, of Xerox's Palo Alto Research Center, explains how information scent theory works: "[It] refers to the detection and use of cues ... that provide users with concise information about content that is not immediately available ... guiding users to the information they seek" (68). Pirolli argues that information scent plays a vital role in a person's decision about how long he or she will use an interface before making a decision to move on. Participants' primary complaint about Minerva was the lack of immediacy of information, and their frustration was visible as they searched. James summed up his experience best when he said that he was "looking for something right now," as he combed through record after record. All other participants had difficulties with information scent in Minerva records as well. They mistook existing links for content and looked for contextual clues that Minerva did not provide (e.g., content previews, page ranking by algorithm, and search suggestions). Information scent theory suggests that participants simply gave up on Minerva because they did not feel the value of the information it provided (i.e., OPAC records) warranted the frustrations of using it.

Simplicity and User Optimization

Participants showed a strong desire to optimize their search activity and believed that Google's simple, intuitive interface helped them accomplish this goal. In contrast, they saw Minerva as a complex system, which contributed to their perception that it was difficult to use. Minerva's design relies on drop-down menus, radio buttons, and submenus to select important search options. If a participant fumbled their search syntax, they received an opaque error message, which did not tell them what they did wrong or how to correct their mistake. Google, on the other hand, required no understanding of syntax to retrieve results and never produced an error message. In fact, when they misspelled search terms (as two participants did), Google provided suggestions to correct the mistake.

Participants' experiences with Google's minimalist interface and algorithmic presentation of records that are rich in information scent led them to make incorrect assumptions about the relative differences between Google and Minerva. Most participants believed that Google and Minerva provided equivalent access to secondary sources, when, in fact, they provided access to two different corpuses. Participants also believed that Google provided superior access to these same information sources because of its modern design and its ability to deliver content directly. These two assumptions led to surprising exchanges, like Matty's somewhat indignant confusion over why we would even bother testing a LastGen artifact that was still a text-only interface. He cut Activity 4 short to demonstrate how Google worked, inviting us to usability test it if we wanted to see (in his opinion) what really works for research. Nicholas, Brittany, James, and Raquel also talked about their desire to use Google rather than Minerva because they were convinced that it provided a significantly lower opportunity cost for them to use compared to Minerva. With Google, participants could decide which content to select with a few mouse clicks, but the "cost" of using Minerva involved making a trip to the campus library and locating and browsing each source or using Minerva to link to other academic information-seeking tools for online journal content. Of all eight participants, only Mort said that he would use Minerva to access print library sources (though he hadn't yet), and only Samantha said that she regularly used Minerva's digital databases to access journals for her research-writing.

Based on our study, we concluded that while our participants were sophisticated seekers of information for nonacademic projects, their everyday information-seeking habits severely interfered with their use of library tools for academic research-writing. Matty, Samantha, and Raquel, the most sophisticated information seekers of the participants, could easily have completed the exercises using Google, but they would have done so without making an informed choice about how the

Libraries' holdings could help them. For example, they did not know that U of L Libraries provide students with a (prepaid) collection of academic information resources that far exceeds what they could access through Google. Our participants did not yet possess the particular IL skills or perspectives necessary to function with the degree of research autonomy expected of them within their first-year writing classes. They demonstrated a strong need for direct instructional support that did not address *how* to use Minerva, but, instead, *why* doing so would ultimately improve their research experience and the intellectual product of their efforts (for an example of student-centered scholarship in service of these goals, see McClure 2011).

The Struggle of NextGen Students Using LastGen Interfaces

U of L considers the ability to sustain an extended and critical inquiry involving secondary sources to be a fundamental general education skill.[5] Presumably, no one expects NextGen students to acquire this skill through Googling information, but the Google Effect looms large in the research-writing classroom. Our conclusion from three series of Minerva usability tests was that what our NextGen student participants needed most was not additional technical information-seeking skills, but critical perspective to help them contextualize their own information-seeking behaviors and develop a reflective information-seeking practice. For instance, when Ashlie discovered that she could not click through entries in the Minerva records, she said, "Now what I really want to do is go to Google to type it in and see what I get." Students like Ashlie need guidance through their usability concerns and problems. Understanding these moments as breakdowns in interface usability can prepare educators to demonstrate how and when to use popular tools (like Google) and ensure that students are comfortable using academic tools (like digital library card catalogs) when they need to do so to meet course objectives (Corbett 2010). Even Raquel, who successfully completed the search tasks, said, "Instead of just giving me the facts—the author, the title—I don't know—Some kind of description would help. I'm not going to want to go to the library and find every one of these books to see what it has." Despite 3 years as a part-time student, Raquel had never used the U of L Libraries to find a source. What our study reveals is that usability issues in Minerva directly contributed to her not doing so.

Even if the case can be made for insisting students learn to use a digital tool like Minerva, the case for why the design of these types of tools should remain static cannot. The influence of these technologies on student information-seeking habits will start the first time their hand touches the device. Mike Kuniavsky writes that "usability is good design" (2003, 20). Good usability promotes engagement, but in the case of Minerva, an inflexible interface, which was not designed with pedagogy in mind, has failed to keep pace with the development of intuitive interfaces found on the devices of NextGen students' everyday lives. Despite the success NextGen students might have with Google, the challenge of helping NextGen students adapt to the institutional realities of poorly aging tools is unlikely to abate soon because the outcomes of general education are unlikely to forsake the campus library. Furthermore, open access to academic information remains elusive, and few incentives exist for vendors like Ex Libris to address student usability issues to improve student access to the collections mediated by the OPAC it sells. As one librarian said off-the-record about Minerva, "We don't like it either, but it's what we have to work with—and that's not going to change."

Usability Studies as a Programmatic Solution

Best practices and professional support are needed for studying the relationship between student research-writing and the interfaces that mediate these activities. As Selfe and Selfe first wrote in 1994, understanding the interfaces of academic life is a necessary part of teaching the new digital scholar. The need for a disciplinary usability perspective and local programmatic solutions increases with each new academic information product handed to educators with the expectation that they will somehow make it work. Usability advocates in the writing studies and IL fields can push for student-centered design, pedagogy that is informed by systematic study of digital tools, and collaborative projects that draw diverse perspectives to usability issues. Without the support of writing programs and libraries, however, this work will continue to occur slowly and in ad hoc fashion. While usability testing can be done quickly as a way of defining usability problems for further study, designing actual solutions with programmatic impact requires planning and a commitment of time, expertise, and technological resources.

The studying of human–computer interaction is, by nature, a multidisciplinary activity. Usability studies can be used to gather and share evidence that addresses usability concerns around common concerns, like the impact of certain digital tools on student learning. For future usability studies of research-writing tools, we believe librarians should not only be consulted, but also directly involved with the testing of any digital library tool. First, librarians often provide NextGen students' introduction to library tools, and their insight into student behavior is complementary to that of writing teachers. Second, having librarians on board would help to shape the collective response to usability testing inquiries.

Usability studies designed with this level of support can be used by educators across disciplines faced with similar issues and similarly intransigent tools. These common concerns are a natural opportunity to pool the skills, perspectives, and resources of multiple stakeholders. Bringing attention across academic disciplines to how students actually *do* use interfaces could shift our understanding of how to better connect new students to the information architecture of their academic lives.

Endnotes

1. Reviews of relevant literature from writing studies are found in this volume: Randall McClure (Chapter 1), and Barry M. Maid and Barbara J. D'Angelo (Chapter 13).

2. Ex Libris Group's Voyager solution is one of the primary digital information infrastructure providers for libraries across the United States, Europe, and Asia.

3. For more information on the visual scanning patterns most often employed by consumers of web content, particularly research using eye-tracking "heatmaps" to indicate spots of prolonged focus, see Jakob Nielsen (2006).

4. The ability of a think-aloud protocol to faithfully relay inner speech or correlative cognitive development is unlikely to regain traction in writing studies literature (see Long and Flower 1996; Flower and Hayes 1981; for a response, see Bartholomae 1985; Bizzell 1982). Though the discipline is wary of researchers using think-aloud protocols to cognitively map or theorize writing through *etic* data (i.e., data gathered for generalization), these methods are widely used in the field of human–computer interaction as one method of gathering *emic* data (i.e., data locally meaningful). For more on an adaptation and application of the think-aloud protocol for studying NextGen students' research behaviors, see Janice R. Walker and Kami Cox's Chapter 16 in this book.

5. Like many other universities, U of L places a strong emphasis on finding and using secondary sources in its outcomes for the entire general education program (see University of Louisville 2012 for specific language).

References

Bartholomae, David. 1985. "Inventing the University." In *When a Writer Can't Write: Studies in Writer's Block and Other Composing-Process Problems*, edited by Mike Rose, 134–165. New York: Guilford.

Bizzell, Patricia. 1982. "Cognition, Convention, and Certainty: What We Need to Know About Writing." *PRE/TEXT* 3: 213–243.

Choi, Hee Jun, and Scott D. Johnson. 2006. "The Effect of Problem-Based Video Instruction on Learner Satisfaction, Comprehension and Retention in College Courses." *British Journal of Education Technology* 38 (5): 885–895.

Corbett, Patrick. 2010. "What About the 'Google Effect?' Improving the Library Research Habits of First-Year Composition Students." *Teaching English in the Two-Year College* 37 (3): 267–277.

Ex Libris. 2012. "Voyager Integrated Library System: Bringing Your Library Information Foundation into the 21st Century." Accessed October 1, 2012. www.exlibrisgroup.com/category/Voyager.

Eyman, Douglas. 2009. "Usability: Methodology and Design Practice for Writing Processes and Pedagogies. In *Rhetorically Rethinking Usability: Theories, Practices, and Methodologies*, edited by Susan K. Miller-Cochran and Rochelle L. Rodrigo, 213–228. Cresskill, NJ: Hampton.

Flower, Linda, and John R. Hayes. 1981. "A Cognitive Process Theory of Writing." *College Composition and Communication* 32 (4): 365–387.

Grayling, Trevor. 1998. "Fear and Loathing of the Help Menu: A Usability Test of Online Help." *Technical Communication* 45 (2): 168–179.

Kuniavsky, Mike. 2003. *Observing the User Experience: A Practitioner's Guide to User Research.* San Francisco: Elsevier.

Long, Elenore, and Linda Flower. 1996. "Cognitive Rhetoric." In *Encyclopedia of Rhetoric and Composition: Communication from Ancient Times to the Information Age*, edited by Theresa Enos, 108–109. New York: Routledge.

Manuel, Kate. 2005. "National History Day: An Opportunity for K-16 Collaboration." *Reference Services Review* 33 (4): 459–486.

McClure, Randall. 2011. "The Digital Information Divide." In *Adaptation, Resistance, and Access to Instructional Technologies: Assessing Future Trends in Education*, edited by Steven D'Agustino, 1–18. Hershey, PA: IGI Global.

Miller-Cochran, Susan K., and Rochelle L. Rodrigo. 2009. "Introduction." In *Rhetorically Rethinking Usability: Theories, Practices, and Methodologies*, edited by Susan Miller-Cochran and Rochelle Rodrigo. Cresskill, NJ: Hampton.

Nielsen, Jakob. 2006. "F-Shaped Pattern for Reading Web Content." Accessed October 1, 2012. www.useit.com/alertbox/reading_pattern.html.

Norman, Donald A. 2002. *The Design of Everyday Things.* New York: Basic.

Pirolli, Peter. 2007. *Information Foraging Theory: Adaptive Interaction with Information.* New York: Oxford University Press.

Selfe, Cynthia L., and Richard J. Selfe Jr. 1994. "The Politics of the Interface: Power and Its Exercise in Electronic Contact Zones." *College Composition and Communication* 45 (4): 480–504.

———. 2009. "Reflections on 'The Politics of the Interface: Power and Its Exercise in Electronic Contact Zones.'" In *Rhetorically Rethinking Usability: Theories, Practices, and Methodologies*, edited by Susan K. Miller-Cochran and Rochelle L. Rodrigo, 35–38. Cresskill, NJ: Hampton.

University of Louisville. 2012. "University-Wide General Education: Competencies, Content Areas and Learning Outcomes." Accessed October 1, 2012. www.louisville. edu/provost/GER/GER-Preface.pdf.

University of Louisville Libraries. 2012. "Library Catalog." Accessed October 1, 2012. www.minerva.louisville.edu/vwebv/searchBasic.

CHAPTER 16

Remixing Instruction in Information Literacy

Janice R. Walker and Kami Cox

In the past few years, research into and testing of students' skills in information literacy (IL), usually defined as the ability to locate, evaluate, and use information from outside sources, has proliferated. The results of most of these tests and studies, however, is to tell us what we, as educators, already know: Whatever we are doing now to teach essential IL skills to our students is just not working. That is, even though teachers and librarians have tried a wide variety of ways to teach these skills, students continue to fare poorly in assessments of them. There are problems with many of these assessment instruments, to be sure; nonetheless, I[1] believe we are right to be concerned, as the two student videos I discuss in this chapter will show. The problem is not a lack of instruction or a lack of instructional materials dealing with IL. Of these, we have an embarrassment of riches. Instead, we may need to reconsider how, when, and where we provide students with this instruction.

Much of our current instruction in IL begins by attempting to steer students away from Google and other internet searches, instead of beginning where our students are—and where most of us probably begin our own searches as well. Further, many of our library and database search sites remain complicated and forbidding, requiring some knowledge of the wide variety of types of source materials and varying search methodologies, often confusing students rather than facilitating the research process. Moreover, we may be asking too much of students when we encourage them to use library databases to locate peer-reviewed scholarly journal articles or books that are written for an audience of scholars, not at a level accessible to most. Finally, we offer a dizzying array of lessons and tutorials about research, almost all of which require students to step outside of the research and writing process in order to review them. Seldom does our instruction begin with the most basic questions of all: How do I know when I need information? How do I know what kind of information I need? Ultimately, we need to be comfortable with the realization that sometimes Google *is* the right place to begin.

In this chapter, I first look at some of the research that has already been conducted in response to these basic questions of IL. Next, I discuss how a just-in-time learning model might help integrate the teaching (and learning) of research skills that are more useful, more readily transferable, and more appropriate for training the new digital scholar. Finally, with the help of Kami Cox, a former undergraduate student who lends her voice to this conversation, I discuss plans for a pilot project looking at students' information-seeking behavior, the LILAC Project. Information being gathered for this project can help us see where the gaps may be between what we (faculty, librarians, curricular designers, and others involved in providing instruction in IL) are teaching and what our students are learning, so that, ultimately, we can determine what curricular and/or programmatic changes we may need to take. I am not naïve enough, of course, to believe there is a one-size-fits-all solution; nonetheless, I am confident in my belief that NextGen students need to learn different skill sets than we are used to teaching and that we may need to learn different skills in order to teach them.

Who Says There's a Problem?

Tom Peele and Glenda Phipps (2007), in "Research Instruction at the Point of Need," discuss how they require students to keep a "research log," a written, step-by-step record of their research process, "as a last resort." Most tutorials, they argue, are "either too general to be effective … or simply not used at the point of need." Peele and Phipps are not alone in their recognition that the instruction we are providing our students may not be enough. Indeed, preliminary findings from the Educational Testing Service's (ETS's) 2006 Information and Communication Technology (ICT) Literacy Assessment testing of almost 4,000 college and high school students accused an appalling 87 percent of students of being information illiterate (Foster 2006). ETS (2006) notes that these "bleak" results "show us that institutions need to consider how to better integrate ICT literacy skills into and across the curricula." Betsy Barefoot (2007), co-director for the Policy Center on the First Year of College and associate professor of Education Leadership at Brevard College, agrees; she argues that we need to make library instruction "an integral part of courses across the curriculum" through "continuing and creative collaboration between librarians and professors" (B16).

Many librarians and faculty are already collaborating, of course. For example, Peele (a writing teacher and administrator) and Phipps (a librarian) formed a virtual partnership for an online, research-based advanced writing class, developing instructional media specifically for their students. Peele, Melissa Keith, and Sara Seely discuss a similar project in Chapter 14 of this book. At Georgia Southern University, Lisa Smith, a reference librarian, and Mildred Pate, a teacher of first-year writing, formed a partnership in which Smith taught one of Pate's 50-minute class sessions each week throughout the semester. Of course, most institutions do not have enough librarians available to work one-on-one with every faculty member. And, even if there were enough librarians to go around, the success of these initiatives may be limited. That is, as Barefoot (2007) also notes, these skills may not transfer into other courses, whether those courses are within a given discipline or cross disciplinary boundaries.

The ETS test results, however, are not necessarily reflective of the true picture. That is, the ETS limits its definition of IL to "the ability to use technology to solve information problems" (Thacker 2006). Now dubbed "iSkills," the ETS assessment consists of "a simulation-based test designed to measure … a student's ability to navigate, critically evaluate and communicate information using digital technology, communication tools and networks" (Educational Testing Service 2007). The net effect of this assessment is to "trivialize the notion of information literacy while assuring various stakeholders that this important skill is being addressed" (Perelman 2008, 137). The test, that is, seems to omit all information and communication that is not digital, or at least that is not accessed through digital means, so that many would argue that ETS is confusing *information* literacy with *technological* literacy.

It is precisely this kind of confusion that may be what leads to assertions such as Stanley Wilder's (2005) that IL is "harmful because it encourages librarians to teach ways to deal with the complexity of information retrieval, rather than to try to reduce that complexity." He argues that librarians should teach writing instead, an idea with which, as a writing teacher, I obviously take umbrage. Of course, Wilder's understanding of IL also seems, in my opinion, a bit off the mark, as perhaps evidenced by his assertion that

> Information literacy remains the wrong solution to the wrong problem facing librarianship. It mistakes the nature of the internet threat, and it offers a response at odds with higher education's traditional mission. Information literacy does nothing to help libraries compete with the internet, and it should be discarded. (B13)

In addition to the conflation of IL with technological literacy, this "either/or" fallacy—*either* the library *or* the internet—is the source of much confusion both in our testing and our approach to teaching. Many of the instructional materials we offer students suffer from this same kind of binary approach, often to the extent that students are guided to specific databases or publications for use in their course papers, rather than being taught how to determine where they need to look—and why—for themselves.

At any rate, as Steven Bell (2006) argues in his response to Paul D. Thacker's (2006) rather inflammatorily titled article "Are College Students Techno Idiots?", "If institutions think the answer to the problem is to just have librarians demonstrate databases and preach about information literacy in freshman english [*sic*] seminars, we're likely to continue seeing poor results on information fluency tests—and in the papers they write." And yet we continue to subject students to demonstrations and lectures about information skills, we author more tutorials, we assign readings in handbooks and style guides, and we require students to attend library and university orientations. Then, all too often, we set them loose to find information on their own and, of course, many of them turn to Google. Why is it that, even though we have provided them with all of this instruction and, at most institutions, reference librarians are standing at the ready to provide one-on-one help, our students still turn to the "tried and true" internet search engine—often with disastrous results?

Just in Time

While many institutions do have successful models of writing-across-the-curriculum (WAC) or writing-in-the-disciplines (WID) curricula that help to extend the important work of instruction in IL skills common to college-level writing assignments, others still find themselves in the uncomfortable position of limiting such instruction to first-year courses and then assuming (or at least hoping) that students have "gotten it." However, as the Foreword contributors to this book Alison J. Head and Michael B. Eisenberg (2009) note, almost half of the students in their study had "nagging uncertainties with concluding and assessing the quality of their own research efforts" (3).

Most research nowadays is conducted online. Not only do students search via Google, Wikipedia, or other such internet-based information gateways, but they also search library catalogs and databases accessed via the internet, usually through online portals, and many students, as well as some scholars, specifically target information sources that are available in full text online, eschewing the walk to the library itself. The vast amount of information available online makes this a viable choice for many. However, students are then tasked with remembering what they have been taught previously about finding and evaluating sources. Johndan Johnson-Eilola (2005), in talking about how people learn skills related to software and computer interfaces, argues that people are "increasingly unlikely to look outside their immediate interface for assistance" (51). Michael Twidale (n.d.) agrees: "It is almost a truism in interface design that many users rarely read manuals or use online help."

Instead, Twidale (n.d.) argues for a model of "over-the-shoulder learning," or OTSL, noting that "[p]eople are likely to ask for help when they have a particular real-world task and need help." Of course, even if we had sufficient numbers of faculty or librarians to peer over the shoulders of each student—and even if we were willing to join them in their midnight forays to the library the night before a paper is due—many of our students are working from home or dormitory computers so that this approach might not be feasible. Moreover, ultimately, we would, of course, like our students to learn to perform these tasks without our help.

Just-in-time (JIT) learning, or the provision of knowledge as it is needed, might be one way of moving our educational efforts in this direction. We are, of course, already providing such information through online tutorials, and many libraries even offer real-time "Ask a Librarian" chat services. However, as I will discuss later in this chapter, we are not providing the information in a manner that reaches students at the point of need (over their shoulders, as it were). JIT learning is not about technology, even though technology is what allows it (Brandenburg and Ellinger 2003, 310). Rather it is an "evolutionary response to the demands of a knowledge-driven and speed-oriented marketplace" (311). While JIT learning and teaching will not replace more traditional learning and teaching, nonetheless they require "some fundamental rethinking of the ways in which we have historically designed, developed, and delivered learning and performance solutions" (316).

The LILAC Project

The Learning Information Literacy Across the Curriculum (LILAC) Project consists of a group of faculty and librarians dedicated to finding a way to assist students (and others) with learning how to locate, evaluate, and synthesize information, whether that information is online or in print or in some other medium, by helping them to know

- When information is needed
- What kind of information is needed
- Where to go to locate that information
- How to evaluate what they find
- How to integrate the information they discover with their own ideas
- How to adequately cite information, ideas, words, pictures, and other borrowings

These skills are based on those suggested by the Association of College and Research Libraries (ACRL). The ACRL (2000) also offers a detailed list of Standards, Performance Indicators, and Outcomes for students and a "practical guide" for "instruction librarians and coordinators" tasked with teaching these skills.

The first phase of the LILAC Project seeks to determine what kind of help students actually need and then to consider where and when students need this help along with the best ways to provide it. We hope to discover answers to the following questions:

1. What (and how) are students being taught regarding IL skills?

2. How well are students understanding, learning, and using these important skills?

3. How well do these skills and this instruction transfer to other courses or "real-world" work?

4. Where might we need or be able to intervene more effectively to help students?

5. What is the best way to provide such intervention?

Using a "research aloud protocol" (RAP), along with interviews and surveys, we attempt to determine what students are taking away from current classroom and library-based IL instruction so that we can determine what needs to be done to better equip students with research skills that will transfer beyond the first-year writing classroom.

The RAP methodology is borrowed in part from *The Composing Processes of Twelfth Graders*, in which Janet Emig (1971) asks students to "compose aloud" in the presence of a tape recorder and an investigator in order to examine the processes these writers use (40). According to Marsha E. Fonteyn, Benjamin Kuipers, and Susan J. Grobe (1993), such "Think Aloud (TA) studies provide rich verbal data about reasoning during a problem solving task. Using TA and protocol analysis, investigators can identify the information that is concentrated on during problem solving and how that information is used to facilitate problem resolution" (430).

While there has been discussion about the effectiveness of such think aloud protocols, we believe asking students to talk about what they are doing and why they are making the choices they make in the process of conducting research can be an effective tool for our purposes. For this study, using Camtasia Studio software, we capture screen activity along with the students' RAP about their activity. We then code the students' activities so that we can tabulate the results and use the information to draw conclusions about what students are actually doing when they conduct research. At this juncture, we have captured only a limited number of videos, allowing us to tweak our methods before we begin a full study. Two students have given me permission to discuss their RAPs in this chapter.[2]

Let's RAP!

Student volunteers are asked to spend approximately 10 minutes online, conducting research for a writing project. Using Camtasia Studio, the videos capture what the students are doing on the computer screen as well as the students' voices detailing what they are doing and why. At the time the videos discussed in this chapter were captured, one student was a senior, a double major in political science and in writing and linguistics; the other was a sophomore psychology major. Both students had completed the university's first-year experience course, which introduces students to "academic research," and the two-semester first-year writing sequence, which also includes instruction in research skills. Both had been successful in writing college papers for their first-year writing courses as well as for courses in their majors. Both students also believed their research skills were at least above average when compared with their peers.

In the first sample video,[3] the student begins with a Google search. She proceeds to quickly scan the results, noting "a few news articles that might be worth looking at," a Wikipedia definition ("It's always there for you," she says), and a university department webpage which, she says, is the only site she might actually use since the others appear to her to be "sponsored sites" and "opinions"; in other words, "nothing you could really use to support a research paper."

She then searches Google Scholar, which she says contains "mainly books." She's more interested in finding articles, however, not books, so she then tries searching library databases online. She finds the library site a bit confusing to navigate, but she manages to find the general purpose database search page. She again quickly scans the results. "[I] find a lot of things that are absolutely not relevant, and I'm not sure how they got in that search, but there's a few things that pop up that you might be able to use," she says. She selects one listing to view the information for an article from a scholarly journal available for download, which she believes might be worth reading. She notes that, once she has found two or three articles through the library database, she would then return to Google to find another one or two sites or articles and then begin drafting her paper.

The second student[4] begins her research for a paper on Elton John by immediately going to the musician's website. She finds information in his Bio page that she is interested in using. She also goes to the website of his lyricist, but finds it "under construction." She comments, "There are no books on Elton John [or his lyricist] at my college's library," so she uses Google to find "actual good sites." She finds information on the Songwriter's Hall of Fame and the Rock and Roll Hall of Fame websites, which she asserts are credible because they are "an actual website, not a blog or a fan site." She also finds an article in "an actual web magazine, or webzine," dated 1996, which she says "is not that old." She is "definitely gonna use" an archived web magazine article she believes is a "very reliable source." She also locates an article in an online newspaper, *The Guardian*, as well, noting that "since it is a newspaper it is a reliable source."

As these two videos show, our students have indeed learned that they need to evaluate the sources they find, and they have learned that, for academic projects, they need to at least make an attempt to look for sources through the university library. However, upon viewing these videos, I would suggest that we need to continue to reinforce and build upon our students' information-seeking behaviors and IL skills throughout their college careers.

Student Response

After writing a draft of this chapter, I invited one of the students in the videos, Kami Cox, to respond. Here is what she said:

> As a former student and a major in Writing and Linguistics, I can share some perspective about what students are taking away from IL instruction and why Google will forever be a staple for internet research. As a whole, I would like to believe that students today realize going to Google and Wikipedia are not, and never will be, "acceptable" forms of

research. However, because of the ease of access and count-less repetition, students will almost always try this path first to see what they can get quickly.

Most students do realize that, alone, such searches will not cut it, and so they try their luck with scholarly searches and library databases such as GALILEO (the web portal for the state of Georgia to its collection of databases). But this is where many lose focus and tend to give up. We are very much an "instantaneous" generation, and if, after two or three tries, [our searches] are still fruitless, well, then it is time to give up, and there must not have been anything rel-evant there to begin with. This is the mindset that students need to overcome when using library searches; to do so, many are going to have to learn how to use these searches properly to achieve maximum results.

Of course, this is asking for the student to contribute something to the process in order to be successful, but if they are taught the correct ways to go about performing academic searches and integrate those into their already-formed Google habits, then perhaps they will feel more comfortable going to these types of sites for information to begin with. Students also need to be made more aware of professional periodicals and publications, for example, online publications such as SAGE. Granted, you can find many articles from these publications through GALILEO, but often going straight to the site will offer a plethora of information that GALILEO may not point you to.

Getting to see and actually go back and hear yourself explain your thought processes and why you are choosing to go where you do (by participating in this video project) really provides clarity for the student, as I can testify first-hand. This is a tremendous learning tool for both the stu-dent and the teacher. For the teacher, it provides information about the student's choices and where teachers should focus their instruction in the future to enable those students to make better choices and form wiser habits when it comes to IL. Once we can break the ease-of-access mindset, not only will IL begin to actually take root with students, but [also] I believe we will see improvement across the board.

Programs such as LILAC are so useful because they are not just teaching one repetitive skill set that the student may or may not use. Instead, these programs are infusing the student with a knowledge base they can draw from and build upon throughout their academic career. That is, students are not only being taught IL, but they learn to evaluate information, to take from it what they need, to synthesize the information for themselves instead of merely regurgitating something back onto a page.

Peele and Phipps (2007) agree with Kami that ease of access and students' comfort with internet search engines such as Google and Yahoo!, are, at least in part, primary reasons why students continue to use these tools. However, as I'm sure Peele and Phipps would agree, the answer is not to try to steer our students away from internet search engines, as so many "research" tutorials attempt. That is, I believe a large part of the problem with students' research skills begins with us, teachers and librarians, intent on fostering a restrictive approach to academic IL, an approach poorly suited for the new digital scholar. Our intent is certainly commendable; our methods need reconsideration.

Information Literacy Instruction Now and for the Future

Ultimately, I believe that the model of JIT learning provides one way for programs and perhaps whole institutions to approach training the new digital scholar. That is, if we can intervene in the research process itself, perhaps by integrating some of the information we already have in ways that new smart technologies already allow, then we can provide over-the-shoulder JIT learning opportunities when and where students need them most. For example, when Kami goes to Google to conduct a search, a pop-up window could open that suggests, "You might also want to search for information in ..." or, perhaps a window could open offering a video tutorial or worksheet on recognizing the kind(s) of information the researcher might need and where and how to most effectively search for that type of information. Even a simple "Would you like help with this?" prompt could link students to librarian chat services, online tutorials, or other OTSL sites.

Many of the components to inaugurate such a JIT process are, in fact, already in place. Tutorials are available in a dizzying array of formats, and many libraries even include instant messaging or email "ask a librarian" services, allowing students to initiate email or chat sessions with reference librarians for one-on-one help. Of course, many of these services are only available during limited hours, so that real-time help is not always available for students, and, of course, students must step outside of the research process itself in order to search for the information they need to learn in order to be more effective researchers. That is, right now, students must search for the information we are providing them about how to search for information. It is as strange as it sounds.

Georgia Southern University's Zach S. Henderson Library's homepage, like most university websites these days, offers links to search the library catalog, GALILEO, and other information. After students (somehow) decide what information is needed and where to search for it, help is available (if students look for it) on how to search the library catalog, how to search in GALILEO, and "How to Use the Library" linked from the main library webpage. It is only from the "How to Use the Library" page that we finally find a reference to the web. This help page, however, reflects a distinct bias against the web, totally ignoring the fact that it, too, is on the web (see Figure 16.1).

Other universities are trying to find ways to make it easier for students to access library sources as well. For example, Stanford University's Jackson Library has developed a model of a toolbar designed for use by students and faculty in their Graduate School of

INFORMATION SERVICES • ZACH S. HENDERSON LIBRARY • GEORGIA SOUTHERN UNIVERSITY

The Web: Can It be Trusted?
Evaluating Sites on the World Wide Web

Anyone with Web access and a little bit of computer know-how can put **anything** on the World Wide Web. No one checks to see that information is reliable or worthwhile before it is permitted to appear on the Internet. In this way, Web publishing differs from most publishing in print form, where editors intervene to select what things will be published and these undergo review and revision before they become available to the public. There is a lot of valuable information on the World Wide Web, but there is also a lot that is absolute junk! You need to be able to tell the difference. You must use your critical judgment to decide which Web sites are reliable sources of information. This guide gives you some pointers for evaluating Web sites and also lists some ways to find Web sites that have already been evaluated and judged to be worthwhile.

Figure 16.1 Zach S. Henderson Library's information for students on evaluating websites (library.georgiasouthern.edu/libref/webeval.pdf)

Business (GSB) (Chang and Keil 2006). Named "FastJack," the toolbar was created using the Dynamic IE Toolbar Builder (Chang 2007) for Internet Explorer or Firefox browsers. It enables users to use drop-down boxes to access a customizable set of popular library resources, such as catalogs, databases, electronic journals, research papers and guides, ask-a-librarian services, and frequently accessed Stanford GSB pages, such as the student intranet, faculty seminars, and more (Chang and Keil 2006).

Daphne Chang and Helen Keil (2006), the two-person team who started the project, report that "The month after the official release of the toolbar … , website usage [for the GSB library] … showed a jump of about 50 percent for total site visits compared to the previous month and to the same month in the previous year. High site traffic continues to date." However, they also note problems not yet addressed, such as the need for users to re-enter all of their customization choices when the toolbar is updated, and they suggest that future developments might include such features as

> Highlighting search terms on a web page; storing search histories; receiving RSS feeds; displaying real-time stock quotes … ; protecting users against phishing scams and downloading unwanted files, spam, and viruses … ; [and] managing and storing passwords to enable seamless access to restricted sources. (42)

They also suggest that smaller or corporate libraries could include additional add-ons, from enabling database searches directly from the toolbar to live one-on-one chats with librarians.

Zotero is another tool that operates as an extension of the Firefox browser, allowing researchers to capture websites, database articles, PDF files, and more; tag them; annotate them; and cite them (see Figure 16.2). More features are promised for the future. Indeed, the popular open source browser, Firefox, now comes preloaded with Zotero. And, in addition to Microsoft Word, Zotero also supports the Open Office suite, includes drag-and-drop integration with desktop files, and runs on both Windows and Linux systems. Because it is open source, however, Zotero will "probably never be available for Internet Explorer" or other proprietary browsers, according to Kari Kraus (2007), one of its developers (Poster Presentation). Zotero promises to continue development in response to the needs of researchers and developers in the open source community, and it goes a long way toward providing a JIT means of collecting, managing, and citing online sources.

Another attempt to provide the kind of JIT instruction I argue for is the GALILEO toolbar (see Figure 16.3) developed by the University System of Georgia (USG). This is "a browser plugin for the Firefox and Internet Explorer web browsers from LibX that provides direct access to your library's resources" (University System of Georgia 2010). The link to this free, downloadable toolbar is hard to locate from the library homepage at my institution, but once downloaded and installed, it is extremely easy to use. USG students must be proactive in locating the toolbar, downloading and installing it on their computer, and learning

Figure 16.2 Zotero homepage (www.zotero.org)

how (and when) to use it. My institution's library still has not made this toolbar available on most of the computers on campus—including its own computers—and no instruction for students is currently offered through the library.

All of these tools are attempts to allow easy searching of both library and web sources from within the browser itself. That is, recognizing that most research begins by opening an internet browser and then deciding where to search, the developers of these tools are working to find ways to make the process mirror the kinds of tools students are already familiar with on the web.

Researchers in the writing program at the University of California Santa Barbara (UCSB) have also been testing options for incorporating IL into the SAKAI open source course management system (CMS). The first option they considered—and rejected—was a separate library website tailored to the specific needs of the course but located outside of the CMS. While many of these sites already exist at UCSB (as elsewhere), they require students to step outside of the

Figure 16.3 The GALILEO LibX toolbar for easy searching of library resources (www.galileo.usg.edu/scholar/ databases/libx)

learning environment. Instead, therefore, they are considering the following options:

- A library site within the SAKAI system

- A "Resources" folder dedicated to library materials (also within the SAKAI system)

- A new SAKAI "role" called "Librarian"

- A link to library resources embedded in the standard tool list

- A set of 2-minute videos that explain different library resources (Lunsford and Faulkner 2007)

All of these offerings are, of course, a move in what I believe is the right direction, recognizing where students *are* when they are conducting research, and recognizing, too, that our students, even with the best instruction in essential IL skills, need more than what we are currently offering them.

That is, we need something that combines the functionality of FastJack and/or the GALILEO Toolbar with that of Zotero, something that is available to students working inside a CMS, or outside of it, so that students can still use it when they need to conduct research for other courses throughout their tenure at the university and beyond it. We need a tool that recognizes when users are searching for information in the first place, for instance, something that automatically recognizes when users access a site such as Google or the library homepage, and that offers to help by providing useful—and timely—information. In other words, we need to determine how we can provide point-of-need instruction and help with IL skills—not just access to yet another tutorial or to pre-vetted library sources and websites.

To provide students with the foundation they need, we do not need to reinvent the wheel, as it were; we can use components already in place—internet toolbars, text or voice messaging, blogs, pop-ups, mashups, podcasts, etc.—or we can develop new ones, if needed, in a layered or scaffolded structure that offers "in your face" access to learning IL, providing students and other researchers with instruction *at the point of need* rather than decontextualized from the actual process of research. Our challenge is to quit worrying about outmoded teaching and assessment measures (even ETS acknowledges this as they develop a new generation of tests[5]). That is, right now, while the instruction students need to be effective researchers *is* available, it usually requires that students step outside the research and writing process to access it.

Even when information is customized and available to students as part of their research process, it is usually designed specifically for a discrete course or purpose. Thus, students may not readily be able to generalize from the learning process. At any rate, they may not be able to carry what they have learned away with them beyond the confines of a specific assignment or classroom, as the LILAC videos clearly illustrate, and certainly not beyond the bounds of the university itself. Instead, LILAC and other similar projects must consider how to make this essential information an integral part of the research-writing process itself, by making its wheels turn together, using the tools already in place in a way that reaches students where they are now and, with any luck, in a way that can accompany them to wherever they might be going next.[6]

Endnotes

1. Unless otherwise noted, "I" refers to Janice R. Walker. Comments by Kami Cox are specifically noted in the text. Kami has given permission to include her video and her name in this project. She has also contributed her own words in response to the discussion of her video and is listed as a co-author of this chapter.

2. Both students have given permission to use these videos in this chapter. I have also shared preliminary copies of this chapter with the students.

3. The video for this student is available online at www.youtube.com/watch?v=7E-K2u9Dy30.

4. The video for this student is available online at www.youtube.com/watch?v=TKv83lczA7Q.

5. In "Reinventing Assessment," Randy Elliot Bennett (1998) predicted that the future of testing would require students to demonstrate the ability to "pose the right questions and find, analyze, and organize relevant knowledge" (14). Unfortunately, the iSkills assessment product, as noted earlier in this chapter, seems to measure students' proficiency with digital finding tools (e.g., information technology skills) rather than their IL skills.

6. I would like to thank the editors of this volume and the anonymous reviewers for their thoughtful comments.

References

Association of College and Research Libraries. 2000. "Information Literacy Competency Standards for Higher Education." Accessed October 5, 2012. www.ala.org/acrl/standards/informationliteracycompetency.

Barefoot, Betsy. 2007. "Bridging the Chasm: First-Year Students and the Library." *The Chronicle Review* 52 (20): B16.

Bell, Steven. 2006. "Not Crazy about the Headline for This Story." Response to "Are College Students Techno Idiots?" by Paul D. Thacker. *Inside Higher Ed*, November 15. Accessed October 5, 2012. www.insidehighered.com/news/2006/11/15/infolit.

Bennett, Randy Elliot. 1998. "Reinventing Assessment: Speculating on the Future of Large-Scale Educational Testing." *Policy Information Report.* Accessed October 5, 2012. www.ets.org/Media/Research/pdf/PICREINVENT.pdf.

Brandenburg, Dale C., and Andrea D. Ellinger. 2003. "The Future: Just-In-Time Learning Expectations and Potential Implications for Human Resource Development." *Advances in Developing Human Resources* 5 (3): 308–320.

Chang, Daphne. 2007. Personal communication, April 10.

Chang, Daphne, and Helen Keil. 2006. "Need Another Toolbar for Your Toolbox?" *Searcher* 14 (9): 39–43.

Educational Testing Service. 2006. *College Students Fall Short in Demonstrating the ICT Literacy Skills Necessary for Success in College and the Workplace.* Accessed October 5, 2012. www.marketwire.com/press-release/College-Students-Fall-Short-Demonstrating-ICT-Literacy-Skills-Necessary-Success-College-698327.htm.

———. 2007. *ETS Renames Its ICT Literacy Assessment and Introduces New Institutional Score Reports.* Accessed October 5, 2012. www.marketwire.com/press-release/ets-renames-its-ict-literacy-assessment-introduces-new-institutional-score-reports-728661.htm.

Emig, Janet. 1971. *The Composing Processes of Twelfth Graders*. Urbana, IL: NCTE.

Fonteyn, Marsha E., Benjamin Kuipers, and Susan J. Grobe. 1993. "A Description of Think Aloud Method and Protocol Analysis." *Qualitative Health Research* 3 (4): 430–441.

Foster, Andrea L. 2006. "Students Fall Short on 'Information Literacy,' Education Testing Service's Study Finds." *Chronicle of Higher Education*, October 27: A36.

Head, Alison J., and Michael B. Eisenberg. 2009. "Lessons Learned: How College Students Seek Information in the Digital Age." *Project Information Literacy Progress Report*. Accessed October 5, 2012. www.projectinfolit.org/pdfs/PIL_Fall2009_Year1Report_12_2009.pdf.

Johnson-Eilola, Johndan. 2005. *Datacloud: Toward a New Theory of Online Work*. Cresskill, NJ: Hampton Press.

Kraus, Kari. 2007. "Zotero Poster Session: An Open-Source Research Tool for the Firefox Web Browser." Poster presented at the annual Computers and Writing Conference. Wayne State University, Detroit, Michigan, May 17–19.

Lunsford, Karen J., and Jane Faulkner. 2007. "SAKAI Materials for Library Orientations: A Collaboration between the UCSB Libraries and the Writing Program." *Kairos: A Journal of Rhetoric, Technology, and Pedagogy* 11 (2). Accessed October 5, 2012. praxis.technorhetoric.net/index.php/Webcoursetools/lunsford_faulkner.

Peele, Tom, and Glenda Phipps. 2007. "Research Instruction at the Point of Need: Information Literacy and Online Tutorials." *Computers and Composition Online* Fall. Accessed October 5, 2012. www.bgsu.edu/cconline/PeeleandPhipps.

Perelman, Les. 2008. "Information Illiteracy and Mass Market Writing Assessments." *College Composition and Communication* 60 (1): 128–141.

Thacker, Paul D. 2006. "Are College Students Techno Idiots?" *Inside Higher Ed*, November 15. Accessed October 5, 2012. www.insidehighered.com/news/2006/11/15/infolit.

Twidale, Michael. n.d. "Over-the-Shoulder Learning: Supporting Brief Informal Learning Embedded in the Work Context." Accessed October 5, 2012. people.lis.uiuc.edu/~twidale/pubs/otsl1.html.

University System of Georgia. 2010. "GALILEO Toolbar." Accessed October 5, 2012. www.galileo.usg.edu/scholar/databases/libx.

Wilder, Stanley. 2005. "Information Literacy Makes All the Wrong Assumptions." *Chronicle of Higher Education*, January 7: B13.

Zotero.org. n.d. "Zotero: The Next-Generation Research Tool." Accessed October 5, 2012. www.zotero.org/about.

The New Digital Scholar and the Production of New Knowledge

James P. Purdy and Randall McClure

I think if we do our job right … students will no longer think of research as "Write yet another paper on fate and Oedipus for an audience of one," but rather as "Let's add to the amount of knowledge in the world."
—Christopher Blackwell (Kolowich 2012)

In her Afterword to *Undergraduate Research in English Studies*, Kathleen Blake Yancey (2010, 246) affirms that undergraduate "students are [now] identified as scholars; they do conduct research." The chapters in this volume make the latter assertion clear and provide insight into the ways in which NextGen students use digital resources to conduct this research. They also gesture to what it means to see— really see—students as scholars, particularly within the context of first-year writing classes.

The contributors to Part One survey published literature that paints a picture ranging from enthusiasm to despair in the face of NextGen students' research and research-writing practices—not only because NextGen students research in ways that are often unfamiliar to us, but also because those practices change how they think. While much of this literature blames student laziness for a perceived lack of success in researching effectively, the contributors to Part Two show that this literature is only partly correct. Laziness is one of many influences on NextGen student research and research-writing behaviors—and likely not the most significant. NextGeners' familiarity and comfort with digital resources, their nonacademic research experiences, their sense of the purpose(s) of academic research-writing tasks, their perception of the role of the library and its resources, their understanding of methods of source integration, their alienation from the scholarly community, their time constraints, and their intrinsic and extrinsic motivations are all contributing factors.

Contributors to this volume employ a range of methods to study what NextGen students actually do for research-writing tasks, but, taken together, their studies yield six common insights:

- NextGen students' research and research-writing practices merit our attention. Dismissing students as dumb and/or corrupted by the digital resources they use is not productive and, frankly, misses the point. What students do with digital technologies matters.

- Writing teacher-scholars, librarians, and information literacy specialists have important perspectives to share with one another.

- The library does not—and cannot—function as a gatekeeper to knowledge. Popular search engines, particularly Google, are NextGen students' primary interface to the web. These students live, as one of us argues elsewhere (McClure 2011, 221ff), in a "Googlepedia" world.

- Intervention early in students' research-writing processes is key. The topics about which they write and the sources they consult significantly shape what they learn and what they produce.

- NextGen students, in many cases, are learning precisely what we (perhaps unintentionally) are teaching them: Research-writing entails demonstrating knowledge of what certain authorities have already written (rather than creating new knowledge), providing evidence of including appropriate (i.e., credible and authoritative) sources (rather than engaging with those sources), and adopting a new and foreign identity (rather than recognizing the multiplicity of identity).

- NextGen students know that research-writing asks them to be scholarly and work with scholarly sources, but they may not know how to, care to, or be able to enact what doing so requires.

These studies provide an important foundation for future research, locally, globally, and longitudinally, into students' digital research and writing activities.

The studies in this volume also support the idea that viewing NextGen students as potential scholars necessitates changes in how we frame and teach research-writing. Contributors to Parts Three and Four begin this hard work and offer a range of responses at classroom, curricular, and programmatic levels. While their particular approaches differ, all (explicitly or implicitly) share five common ideas:

- Research-writing should be more about creating new knowledge rather than demonstrating acquired knowledge. This volume is not the first to make this call (e.g., see Grobman and Kinkead 2010); however, it is among the first to connect evidence of what NextGen students actually do (and don't do) for research-writing tasks with responses that move beyond despair to plans of action for the writing classroom.

- Collaborative relationships—among NextGen students and writing teachers; among writing teachers, librarians, and information literacy specialists; among first-year writing programs and libraries—are essential. Notions of knowledge as isolated, protected, and owned (by particular disciplines or programs) do not serve the NextGen digital scholar well.

• Viewing research and writing as separate and separable processes is untenable. As one of us argues elsewhere (Purdy 2010) and this volume supports, digital technologies help make visible the inextricable connection between activities of research and writing. NextGen students have grown up immersed in technologies that allow them to research and write together, and the most productive pedagogies accept and exploit this fact.

• We do well to build on rather than quarantine NextGen students' existing digital skills and familiarity with Web 2.0 technologies. As being a good researcher means engaging with past conversations, being a good research-writing instructor means recognizing, valuing, and shaping students' existing practices.

• We may have something to learn from the (hard) sciences, particularly in their more explicit framing of students as researchers; their recognition of research as an inherently collaborative endeavor; and their realization that future research may shift from being about finding information to finding patterns in that information, as researchers now often have easy, sometimes instantaneous, access to volumes of data.

We don't pretend that these are easy "fixes." Academia, of course, has much invested in protecting the research enterprise as currently situated, and we are not advocating uncritical, unbridled enthusiasm for everything NextGen students do online. But we do see these responses as more productive than Carr's (2011) despair or Bauerlein's (2008) resistance.

We end with four suggestions for moving forward to enrich the research and writing practices of NextGen students. While some teacher-scholars and library professionals, such as those who contributed to this book, already embrace or enact some of these ideas, we offer them to the writing and library and information science communities writ large as ways to equip the new digital scholar for productive academic, professional, and civic careers:

1. *Reconceive the research project.* Contributors to this volume show that we need to move beyond seeing research projects primarily as means to assess content knowledge. Framing research-writing tasks as reports of what students already know yields results they and we find unfulfilling. Rather, research-writing tasks should ask students to contribute new knowledge to ongoing conversations—and to make the rhetorical moves necessary to gain a foothold in those conversations. Such an approach certainly does not mean that we should expect students in first-year writing classes to produce graduate-level or publishable scholarship; the scope should be appropriate for the level of the student. It means such projects should ask students to engage and share their work with discourse communities that matter (or should matter) to them.

   Research projects should situate research as a social process. This approach means rigor, rather than length, should be a defining criterion. Several shorter assignments that ask students to do more in-depth work with fewer source texts may yield more learning and engagement than one longer assignment that prescribes use of a large (and arbitrary) number of sources. Academic disciplines like English studies have begun to examine the role of the single, long-form, print-based, culminating text (i.e., the dissertation), considering graduate career capstone possibilities beyond the dissertation intended to become a print book (Smith 2010a, 2010b). We should likewise reconsider operating under such a model in first-year writing classes, where the culminating project has traditionally followed a similar model (i.e., the single, long-form, print-based, culminating text, usually the research paper). Research projects may certainly still take the form of papers or include essay components, but they should also allow for the possibility of other multimodal and multimedia forms, including the construction of research and research-writing resources that organize and make accessible the vast amount of textual information available on the internet. Such projects might include coding print texts for inclusion in digital archives, checking and correcting print texts scanned with optical character recognition, adding metadata to digital text collections, analyzing existing and designing new search tools, and writing summaries of and classifying unfiled text and artifact collections. Though such tasks take alternative forms, they are certainly research intensive and link research and writing activities in palpable ways.

2. *Share the work of professional researchers.* Much (if not most) of what professional researchers, such as academics and librarians, do is shrouded in mystery. By and large, we don't talk about it to the larger public or to our students. As a result, NextGen students often do not get the sense that what we ask them to do in the writing classroom connects to that work, that it serves a function beyond proving knowledge retention or is something that "real" professionals do. To remedy this situation, we need to be up front and honest about our own research and research-writing activities, why we engage in them, and the messiness of them. This is not a call to train all NextGen students to be academics (though some certainly might pursue that path). Instead, it is a call to stop taking a "Wizard of Oz" approach to our work. Make research and research-writing less intimidating by revealing what is behind the curtain—even if that means exposing the limits to our work.

3. *Exploit the potentials of digital technologies.* Whether students should use digital technologies for research and research-writing is beside the point. They are. Therefore, it is incumbent upon us to recognize with students what these technologies do well, to educate them about what these technologies do not, and to ask them to reflect critically on how these technologies work. This approach means using, demonstrating, analyzing, and comparing and contrasting blogs, wikis, folksonomies, social media, cloud computing, digital archives, databases, and so forth. We cannot—and should not be expected to—be experts in all of these digital technologies. As a collaborative community, however, we can draw on one another's expertise, as well as the proficiencies of our students, to discover what works in which contexts.

4. *Meet students where they are.* This suggestion is based on the notion that students are researchers and that they come to college as researchers. Their research skills, however, suit the fast-paced, interconnected, social, and public pursuits of their nonacademic lives. As a result, they can still learn much from academics and librarians about how to adapt these skills for the research that academic work entails. Pretending (or professing) that these skills and experiences do not exist or must be excised is both unrealistic and counterproductive (Purdy and Walker 2012). We need to see research and research-writing proficiencies on a spectrum, not as a binary.

This view of research and research-writing might help stem the credentialing approach to education that, at least according to studies such as Richard Arum and Josipa Roksa's (2011) *Academically Adrift* and Andrew Hacker and Claudia Dreifus's (2010) *Higher Education?*, is pervasive. It can, in other words, help us move past a view of higher education—and the required research-writing courses that frequently serve as a gateway to that education—as bitter pills to swallow or boxes to check off. Instead, this renewed view of research and research-writing can situate these courses as opportunities to produce knowledge, develop skills, and cultivate habits of mind that are applicable in the academic, civic, and professional worlds—both now and long after NextGen students are ThisGen.

References

Arum, Richard, and Josipa Roksa. 2011. *Academically Adrift: Limited Learning on College Campuses*. Chicago: University of Chicago Press.

Bauerlein, Mark. 2008. *The Dumbest Generation: How the Digital Age Stupefies Young Americans and Jeopardizes Our Future*. New York: Penguin.

Carr, Nicholas. 2011. *The Shallows: What the Internet Is Doing to Our Brains*. New York: W. W. Norton.

Hacker, Andrew, and Claudia Dreifus. 2010. *Higher Education?: How Colleges Are Wasting Our Money and Failing Our Kids—And What We Can Do about It*. New York: St. Martin's.

Grobman, Laurie, and Joyce Kinkead, eds. 2010. *Undergraduate Research in English Studies*. Urbana, IL: NCTE.

Kolowich, Steve. 2012. "Behind the Digital Curtain." *Inside Higher Ed*, January 27. Accessed October 5, 2012. www.insidehighered.com/news/2012/01/27/could-digital-humanities-undergraduates-could-boost-information-literacy.

McClure, Randall. 2011. "Googlepedia: Turning Information Behavior into Research Skills." In Vol. 2 of *Writing Spaces: Readings on Writing*, edited by Charles Lowe and Pavel Zemliansky, 221–241. Fort Collins, CO and West Lafayette, IN: WAC Clearinghouse and Parlor Press.

Purdy, James P. 2010. "The Changing Space of Research: Web 2.0 and the Integration of Research and Writing Environments." *Computers and Composition* 27: 48–58.

Purdy, James P., and Joyce R. Walker. 2012. "Liminal Spaces and Research Identity: The Construction of Introductory Composition Students as Researchers." *Pedagogy: Critical Approaches to Teaching Language, Literature, Composition, and Culture* 13 (1): 9–41.

Smith, Sidonie. 2010a. "Beyond the Dissertation Monograph." *MLA Newsletter* 42 (1): 2–3.

———. 2010b. "An Agenda for the New Dissertation." *MLA Newsletter* 42 (2): 2–3.

Yancey, Kathleen Blake. 2010. "Afterword." In *Undergraduate Research in English Studies*, edited by Laurie Grobman and Joyce Kinkead, 245–253. Urbana, IL: NCTE.

About the Contributors

Andrea Ascuena is a faculty member in the English department at the College of Western Idaho, where her primary teaching assignment is first-year writing.

David Bailey grew up in Effingham County, Georgia, and attended Armstrong Atlantic State University. While earning his bachelor's degree in English literature, he worked in the Armstrong Writing Center first as a peer tutor and eventually earned the lead tutor position. There he encountered many of the theories that shaped his personal pedagogy. Bailey continued this work through graduate school at Georgia Southern University, serving the University Writing Center through various projects, including the shift from faculty consultants to a peer tutoring structure similar to the one at Armstrong. After graduating with his MA in English literature, he moved into the composition field after a brief stint as an institutional effectiveness assistant. He has taught writing courses at Georgia Southern University and presented at many conferences in both the literature and composition fields.

Neil P. Baird's current research examines how students learn to write in their majors. He is specifically interested in barriers to disciplinary enculturation. His ongoing ethnographic and case study research explores the role the body plays in the writing of collegiate football players, how perceptions of ownership influence thesis writing group discourse at the MA level, and barriers to transfer in 300-/400-level writing courses. Baird's research also investigates how advances in computer technology and social networking are transforming rhetorical theory and qualitative research methodologies. His most recent essay, "Virtual Vietnam Veterans Memorials as Image Events: Exorcising the Specter of Vietnam," was published in *Thirty Years After: New Essays in Vietnam War, Literature, and Film* and *Enculturation: A Journal of Rhetoric, Writing, and Culture* (enculturation.gmu.edu/6.2/baird). Baird continues this research at Western Illinois University, where he teaches writing studies courses at the undergraduate and graduate levels and directs the University Writing Center.

Brian Ballentine was a senior software engineer for Marconi Medical and then Philips Medical Systems prior to completing his PhD at Case Western Reserve University. This past work experience ties to his current research interests, which include open source software, technical communication, digital literacy, and intellectual property. Ballentine is currently an associate professor and coordinator for the professional writing and editing program at West Virginia University. Ballentine's recent publications have appeared in journals such as *Technical Communication, IEEE Transactions on Professional Communication, Computers and Composition Online*, the *Journal of Technical Writing and Communication*, and *Across the Disciplines*, as well as in several collected editions.

Patrick Corbett is a doctoral candidate in rhetoric and composition at the University of Louisville. His scholarship explores 21st-century literacies through qualitative research.

Kami Cox is a graduate of Georgia Southern University where she received a dual bachelor's degree in criminal justice and writing and linguistics. Cox has participated in conferences such as the Graduate Research Network, the Computers and Writing Conference, and the Savannah Literacy Conference. While at Georgia Southern, she was a member of the Gold Key International Honor Society and awarded Who's Who Among College Students.

Barbara J. D'Angelo is assistant clinical professor of technical communication at Arizona State University. She received her PhD in technical communication and rhetoric from Texas Tech University and her MSLIS from the University of Illinois at Urbana–Champaign. She teaches courses in technical communication, business communication, and health communication. Her research interests include writing assessment; the impact of assessment on curriculum development, outcomes, and pedagogy; electronic portfolios; and information literacy.

Michael B. Eisenberg is dean emeritus and a professor in the Information School at the University of Washington. He served as co-director and co-principal investigator of Project Information Literacy, the national research study, with Alison Head from 2008 through July 2012. He is co-author of the "Big6" approach to information problem-solving—the most widely used information literacy program in the world. Eisenberg is a prolific author (nine books and dozens of articles and papers) and has worked with thousands of students—pre-K through higher education—as well as with people in business, government, and communities to improve individual and organizational information and technology access and use.

John Eliason is an associate professor of English and the director of composition and the writing center at Gonzaga University. He teaches first-year writing and a variety of upper-division writing courses. His professional interests include writing pedagogy, writing and information literacy, writing across the curriculum, and writing centers. Eliason is co-chair of the High Mountain Affiliate of the Council of Writing Program Administrators and serves on the review boards of *The WAC Journal* and *Across the Disciplines*. He is also a member of Inland InfoLit, a regional consortium of librarians and teachers of writing dedicated to advancing students' information literacy. Some of Eliason's most rewarding professional experiences have involved partnerships with librarians at Philadelphia University (where he worked for 8 years as director of Writing Across the Curriculum) and with Kelly O'Brien Jenks and others in Gonzaga's Foley Center Library.

Alison J. Head is the founder and director of Project Information Literacy (PIL), a public benefit nonprofit dedicated to conducting ongoing, national research studies about college students and their research habits and strategies in the digital age. Since 2008, PIL has studied over 11,000 students on 60 U.S. campuses and conducted six large-scale studies. Head has been a fellow at Harvard University's Berkman Center for Internet and Society and a fellow at the Harvard Library Innovation Lab since 2011. She is an affiliate associate professor in the Information School at the University of Washington. From 2008 through July 2012, she co-directed PIL with Michael B. Eisenberg.

Rebecca Moore Howard is a graduate of West Virginia University who has taught at Colgate, Texas Christian, Cornell, and Binghamton Universities and is now professor of writing and rhetoric at Syracuse University. She has written and edited a number of scholarly and pedagogical books and essays, including *Standing in the Shadow of Giants: Plagiarists, Authors, Collaborators* (Greenwood Publishing Group, 1999) and *Writing Matters: A Handbook for Writing and Research* (McGraw-Hill, 2010). With Sandra Jamieson, she is a principal researcher for the Citation Project, a collaborative, multisite, data-based study of college students' use of research sources. To learn more about this research and related publications and presentations, consult the Citation Project website (www.citationproject.net).

Sandra Jamieson is professor of English and director of writing across the curriculum at Drew University. With Rebecca Moore Howard, she is a principal researcher for the Citation Project, a collaborative, multisite, data-based study of college students' use of research sources. To learn more about this research and related publications and presentations, consult the Citation Project website (www.citationproject.net).

Jamieson has published articles on the vertical writing curriculum, writing across the curriculum, the role of textbooks in writing, and multicultural education. With Howard, she has published *The Bedford Guide to Teaching Writing in the Disciplines: An Instructor's Desk Reference* (St. Martin's Press, 1993) and *Coming of Age: The Advanced Writing Curriculum* (also with Linda Shamoon and Bob Schwegler, Boynton/Cook Publishers, 2000).

Kelly O'Brien Jenks is the instruction coordinator librarian at Gonzaga University. She teaches graduate and undergraduate information literacy with her content specialist colleagues across the disciplines in Gonzaga's classrooms, online, and in distance settings. Lately she has been researching, writing about, and living with a variety of assessment projects including working on how students at Gonzaga are thinking about and conducting research. Her love is the frontier of learning, of investigation, of experience. New ideas, partnerships, practices, and technologies are her greatest professional passions, so it is natural that she serves on the Inland Northwest Council of Libraries, an organization dedicated to continuing education for those who work in libraries, and Inland InfoLit—where new relationships and ways of proceeding are forged between information literacy instructors and compositionists within and without their respective institutions.

Andrew Karem is a doctoral candidate in computer science and engineering at the University of Louisville. His areas of study include image processing and data mining.

Melissa Keith is the assistant director of the writing center and writing across the curriculum program at Boise State University. She is also a lecturer in the English department where she teaches first-year writing, nonfiction writing, and writing center theory classes. Keith's emphasis has been on providing grant-funded professional development opportunities for faculty in the areas of information literacy and online writing instruction.

Karen Kaiser Lee is an assistant professor of English at Youngstown State University where she teaches undergraduate and graduate courses in business, technical, and multimedia writing in the professional writing and editing program. Her current research interests include the rhetoric of science, new media, and participatory culture, particularly the ways that nonacademic experts publish their findings online.

Barry M. Maid is a professor, and for 10 years was program head, of technical communication at Arizona State University. Previously, he taught at the University of Arkansas at Little Rock where, among other things, he helped in the creation of the Department of Rhetoric and Writing. For more than 15 years, Maid has actively participated in online communities and used them as teaching/learning spaces. Along with numerous articles and chapters focusing on technology, outcomes assessment, information literacy, independent writing programs, and program administration, he is a co-author, with Duane Roen and Greg Glau, of *The McGraw-Hill Guide: Writing for College, Writing for Life* (McGraw-Hill, 2008).

Brian J. McNely is an assistant professor in the writing, rhetoric, and digital media program at the University of Kentucky. He researches professional communication in digital environments.

Rachel A. Milloy is a PhD student in the rhetoric and professional communication program at New Mexico State University where she also teaches first-year writing courses. She is the recipient of the graduate school's Outstanding Graduate Assistantship Award for her contributions to the research and teaching mission of New Mexico State University. Milloy serves as a writing program assistant and as a co-editor for the English department's textbook, *Paideia*, one of the main texts used in the university's first-year writing courses. Her research interests include online pedagogy, research methodologies, and writing technologies.

Ruth Mirtz is education librarian and assistant professor at the University of Mississippi. She also teaches in the first-year writing program for the Center for Writing and Rhetoric at the university. She received her PhD in English from the University of Nebraska–Lincoln and her MLIS from Wayne State University. As a professor in the Department of Languages and Literature at Ferris State University, Mirtz taught all levels of college writing and published articles about writing pedagogy, focusing on first-year college writing. Her most recent work in library science includes "From Information to Learning: Pedagogies of Space and the Notion of the Commons" published in *College and Undergraduate Libraries*.

Thomas Peele is an associate professor at Long Island University's Brooklyn campus, where he directs the first-year writing program. Since 2003, he has collaborated with librarians and English faculty to explore the opportunities that digital technology provides to teach research in the writing classroom. His emphasis has been on the collaborative creation of web-based, animated tutorials that could be used across multiple sections of first-year writing. He also works in queer cultural studies, basic writing, service-learning, and digital rhetoric.

Sara Seely is a librarian at Portland Community College where she provides reference and instruction services. She has a collaborative approach to teaching information literacy and was privileged to work closely with the first-year writing program at Boise State University. Seely's emphasis is on assessment of student learning and tailored video tutorials as an approach to embedding information literacy instruction in research-writing courses.

Mary Lourdes Silva is an assistant professor at Ithaca College. She received a doctoral degree in language, literacy, and composition studies from the Gevirtz School of Education at the University of California, Santa Barbara, and earned a master's of fine arts in creative writing at California State University, Fresno. Her current research examines the online navigational behaviors of college writing students throughout the research/revision process. Silva also researches the pedagogical use of multimodal and multimedia technologies in her classroom. Furthermore, she is currently designing multimodal and multimedia instructional materials for instructors and students.

Christa B. Teston is an assistant professor of technical communication at the University of Idaho. Teston researches rhetoric and writing in various environments. She studies public participation in pharmaceutical policymaking, the communication of climate change across expertise, and the ethics of electronic medical records.

Janice R. Walker is professor of writing and linguistics at Georgia Southern University. She has published books, journal articles, and book chapters about online research, documentation, and writing. Walker is founder and coordinator of the Graduate Research Network at the annual Computers and Writing conference and co-coordinator for the Georgia International Conference on Information Literacy, as well as chair of the Georgia Southern University Institutional Review Board.

Yetu Yachim is a software engineer in the automotive component supply industry. He is a graduate of the University of Louisville where he earned a master's degree in computer science and engineering.

About the Editors

Randall McClure has taught writing at several universities, including Georgia Southern University, Cleveland State University, and Minnesota State University, Mankato. He researches in the areas of information behavior and academic writing, teaching and learning online, and academic policy. He has published articles recently in *The Department Chair, Inside Higher Ed, portal: Libraries and the Academy, Computers and Composition Online, Academic Exchange Quarterly, Computers and Composition, Writing Spaces, WPA: Writing Program Administration, Writing & Pedagogy,* and the *Journal of Literacy and Technology.*

James P. Purdy is assistant professor of English and director of the University Writing Center at Duquesne University, where he teaches first-year writing, composition theory, and digital writing in the undergraduate and graduate programs. His research on digital writing and research practices and technologies has appeared in *College Composition and Communication, Computers and Composition, Computers and Composition Online, Journal of Literacy and Technology, Kairos, Pedagogy,* and *Profession,* as well as in several edited collections. With co-author Joyce R. Walker, he won the 2011 Ellen Nold Award for the Best Article in Computers and Composition Studies and the 2008 *Kairos* Best Webtext Award.

Index